TRADITIONAL, NATIONAL, AND INTERNATIONAL LAW AND INDIGENOUS COMMUNITIES

Indigenous Justice

MARIANNE O. NIELSEN AND KAREN JARRATT-SNIDER

Series Editors

EDITED BY
MARIANNE O. NIELSEN AND
KAREN JARRATT-SNIDER

TRADITIONAL, NATIONAL, AND INTERNATIONAL LAW AND INDIGENOUS COMMUNITIES

THE UNIVERSITY OF
ARIZONA PRESS
TUCSON

The University of Arizona Press
www.uapress.arizona.edu

ISBN-13: 978-0-8165-4041-9 (paper)

Cover design by Leigh McDonald
Cover art by Lomayumtewa K. Ishii

Library of Congress Cataloging-in-Publication Data
Names: Nielsen, Marianne O., editor. | Jarratt-Snider, Karen, editor.
Title: Traditional, national, and international law and indigenous communities / edited by
    Marianne O. Nielsen and Karen Jarratt-Snider.
Other titles: Indigenous justice.
Description: Tucson : University of Arizona Press, 2020. | Series: Indigenous justice | Includes
    bibliographical references and index.
Identifiers: LCCN 2019036841 | ISBN 9780816540419 (paperback)
Subjects: LCSH: Indians of North America—Legal status, laws, etc. | Indigenous peoples—
    Legal status, laws, etc.
Classification: LCC KF8205 .T73 2020 | DDC 342.7308/72—dc23
LC record available at https://lccn.loc.gov/2019036841

Printed in the United States of America
♾ This paper meets the requirements of ANSI/NISO Z39.48-1992 (Permanence of Paper).

This book is dedicated to our patient partners, Larry Gould and Gary Snider; to Dave, Debbie, and Kristin (from Karen); to Bob and JoAnn (from Marianne); and to the Indigenous scholars who are doing such necessary and innovative research for Indigenous communities.

CONTENTS

ACKNOWLEDGMENTS

We would like to express our gratitude to the authors and illustrator who contributed to this second book in the series. It took a while to get it into print, and we appreciate your willingness to stick with the project and continue to trust that we would get your work out there. We also thank the peer reviewers for their thought-provoking comments and useful suggestions that helped strengthen this book. To Delsey Benally, thank you for your support and assistance. We want to acknowledge Northern Arizona University for its commitment to Native American students and communities and for encouraging projects such as this. And finally, we want to say thank you to the good people at University of Arizona Press who believed in this project to the point of being willing to publish three (and maybe more) books in the series.

TRADITIONAL, NATIONAL, AND INTERNATIONAL LAW AND INDIGENOUS COMMUNITIES

INTRODUCTION

MARIANNE O. NIELSEN AND
KAREN JARRATT-SNIDER

THE RELATIONSHIP between law and ongoing criminal and social justice issues in Indigenous nations and communities is of paramount importance to Indigenous Peoples worldwide. Law has been used as a weapon against Indigenous Peoples since the early days of contact between Indigenous Peoples and the first explorers (Williams 2005). Sometimes this weapon was wielded with intention and sometimes with indifference, as in the case of *Lyng v. Northwest Indian Cemetery Protective Association* (1988), where it was acknowledged that a logging road that would have severe effects on the ability of Indigenous people to practice their religion was an "incidental effect" of a government program. Law has also been used to try to ameliorate some of the most tragic consequences of colonialism. In this book respected Indigenous and non-Indigenous scholars in the United States and Canada focus on the responses of Indigenous communities and nations to the impacts of law on Indigenous Peoples, including how Indigenous nations have used law as a strategic tool to attain better lives for their members.

The book focuses on current issues at the confluence of law and Indigenous Peoples, and the resilience, creativity, innovation, and ongoing capacity-building that Indigenous Peoples have shown in response. The context for this confluence is important for understanding the issues and responses described by the book's authors. One important context is that Indigenous Peoples have special legal status as the First Peoples of North

America and have a body of law that applies only to them. They have made important contributions to their countries' legal histories, as can be seen in several chapters in this book.

Another important context is that the United States, like many colonial countries, has multiple legal systems operating at the same time. It practices federalism, with federal, tribal, state, and municipal laws more or less nested together in terms of their jurisdictions (Calavita 2016). The United States also practices legal pluralism where military, British common law-based, French common law-based, and American Indian traditional law-based systems run in parallel. Unfortunately, in the case of Indigenous Peoples this overlap of systems can cause a "jurisdictional jungle," as in the case of criminal law (Cardani 2009). This jungle is the result of racism and continual change in federal Indian law and policy as the government tried to fix the "Indian Problem" throughout previous policy eras. As a result, American Indians living on tribal lands are subject to federal Indian and tribal laws, except in Public Law 280 states where they are subject to federal and state laws. If they live off reservations they are subject to municipal, state, and federal laws like every other citizen. Jurisdiction on Native lands depends on the race of the victim, the race of the offender, and the location of the crime, and too often justice falls between the cracks (see, generally, Getches, Wilkinson, and Williams 1998). Stereotypes and myths about Indigenous people are rampant and influence the decision-making of lawmakers and criminal justice personnel who administer those laws (Nielsen 2009). Federal Indian policy is discussed further in the introduction to part II, "National Law."

Adding to this complexity are the special international conventions that protect Indigenous rights such as the United Nations Declaration on the Rights of Indigenous Peoples (2007), but just because a colonial government signs such a declaration does not mean that it incorporates those principles into domestic law, as Indigenous Peoples worldwide are well aware (see Alvarado in this book). Further complicating the matter are the special government bodies, such as the Bureau of Indian Affairs in the United States and Indigenous Services Canada, with their layers of bureaucracy and shifting interpretations of federal law and policy. This legal jungle raises obstacles for communities as they try to achieve opportunity, justice, and fundamental legal and human rights protections, as several authors illustrate.

Another important context is that Indigenous people are a growing population in most colonized countries, many of whom live off Indigenous reservations or reserves. In the United States, for example, about 22 percent live on reservations, with the remainder living elsewhere (U.S. Department of Health 2018). In Canada, about 50 percent of registered Indians live off reserves, as do most of the Aboriginal people who are not registered Indians (Statistics Canada 2015). This means that the special laws in many countries that apply to Indigenous people on Indigenous lands do not affect the majority of Indigenous people, and the legal remedies sought by Indigenous nations do not apply to these individuals and communities (but see Marianne Nielsen in this book). This is a serious hole in the legal landscape that needs further research and future action.

Finally, Indigenous nations and communities are redeveloping their own laws and justice systems that are innovative while at the same time culturally based. Some of these initiatives have been adopted and modified by non-Indigenous society (see, for example, Nielsen and Zion 2005 about Navajo peacemaking). To provide more in-depth context for the issues and responses described by the contributing authors, this chapter briefly outlines the book's perspective on law, which is through an Indigenous lens that focuses on the resilience and capacity-building ongoing in Indigenous communities and nations. It then describes the identity of Indigenous Peoples and (because the past informs the present and the future) the historical, American colonial, and more recent American impacts of colonial laws. The chapter focuses mainly on the United States, but many of the general impacts of colonial law are applicable in Canada, Australia, and New Zealand, countries that were colonized primarily by Great Britain.

PERSPECTIVE ON LAW

This book is not about law in the abstract sense found in the legal professions, but about law as a social product of its time; it is about law as it has been and continues to be experienced every day by Indigenous people and how they respond to it. This is what Kitty Calavita (2016, 3) calls "real law" that affects every aspect of the lives of individuals, communities, and nations. The impacts of law are all-encompassing and sometimes nearly invisible in everyday life (Calavita 2016, 5). Long before colonization, Indigenous Peoples had law as an integral part of their social institutions. Law was usually not codified as such nor was it a separate institution. It was so closely woven into everyday life that children learned it as part of socialization; it was lived and breathed in every activity; it was rooted in relationships and spirituality (Williams 1997; Bluehouse and Zion 2009). These interconnected relationships were with everything and everyone, and law described those connections. Law in any society is about social control; it is enacted to provide rules to guide people, organizations, and individuals, but some groups, such as Indigenous Peoples after contact, were and are controlled more by law than others. In colonial times, the ideologies and mores were such that Indigenous Peoples were labeled inferior and exploitable, as were other nonwhite and some "lesser" white people. Their legal identity was based in the intersection of economics, racism, and law (Calavita 2016, 62), and for Indigenous Peoples—religion (Getches, Wilkinson, and Williams 1998; Williams 1990).

Race-based principles of inferiority and otherness were built into the "Indian" laws of the time so that the laws could be used to disempower Indigenous Peoples, disrupt their lifeways, and justify killing them and appropriating (or stealing) their lands and resources. The law also justified taking Indigenous children from their families to boarding schools to be brainwashed into losing their identities (Porter 2005), destroying Indigenous social and cultural institutions, and in general, violating the fundamental human rights (as we would term it today) of Indigenous Peoples. These principles still color many of today's laws relating to Indigenous Peoples (Porter 2005). As Calavita (2016, 5) writes, law "is marked by all the frailties and hubris of humankind."

Indigenous Peoples and communities have used law to challenge, with varying success, racist principles in colonial law and to protect and further their own rights. See, for example, legal cases and social activism cited throughout the book, such as the protection of sacred sites, as Chris Jocks describes in his chapter, and the efforts of Native American women in promoting protections for Indigenous women in the Violence Against Women Reauthorization Act (2013), as described by Mary Jo Tippeconnic Fox in hers.

Thus, law has the potential to both harm and help the efforts of Indigenous Peoples to recover from colonialism, but the pitfalls are many, and community responses play a critical role in determining outcomes.

WHO ARE INDIGENOUS PEOPLES?

In order to understand the complicated intersections of law, Indigenous nations, and Indigenous communities, it is necessary to understand just who Indigenous Peoples are. In the first book in this series (Nielsen and Jarratt-Snider 2018) we borrowed from Canadian lawyer Bradford W. Morse (1989, 1), who provides the definition used in this book: "all people who trace their ancestors in these lands to time immemorial." This simple but profound definition includes people of part-Indigenous ancestry and people who live away from ancestral lands. In the United States these Indigenous Peoples are referred to as American Indians, Native Americans, Alaska Natives, Native Hawaiians, Inuit, Aleuts, First Nations, or, most respectfully, by the name of their specific nation. In Canada they are First Nations, Aboriginal Peoples, Métis, or again, the people of their nation. In New Zealand, they are Māori; in Australia, they are Indigenous Australians.

There are Indigenous Peoples in any country that has been colonized—Brazil, Mexico, South Africa, China, Mongolia, Zambia, Norway, Greenland, Taiwan, and many others. They share many negative demographic characteristics, the majority of which were expedited by colonial law. Too many Indigenous Peoples are marginalized, lacking economic, social, and political power; are impoverished due to exploitation and loss of resources; are stereotyped and suffer from discrimination; have a history of coerced assimilation by the colonizing state; have little autonomy and self-determination; are recovering from serious social disorganization caused by the loss of population due to violence and disease, the loss of culture due to coerced assimilation, and the loss of social institutions due to imposed laws; and are overrepresented in the criminal justice systems of their country as offenders and victims (Coates 2004).[1] Colonial law set in motion and "justified" these conditions.

THE BEGINNING OF HISTORICAL LEGAL FICTIONS

It has been argued that colonialism is a crime perpetrated against Indigenous Peoples and justified by a long series of legal fictions (Nielsen and Robyn 2019). Early trade contacts turned into wholesale land and resource theft and attempted genocide by settler-colonists. Where there are economic interests in the exploitation of slave labor and the theft of Indigenous lands, "people could be counted on to develop theoretical justifications for doing so" (Calavita 2016, 63). European political leaders needed resources to continue their seemingly endless campaigns against each other and invested in "research and development," that is, they funded first explorers and then missionaries who could find and map out the "new worlds" and report back to them about the resources to be found (gold, gems, spices, foodstuffs, slaves, and so on) and the people who controlled them. They encouraged settler-colonization once it became apparent that resource exploitation would require a population in residence to buy furs, establish plantations, supervise mines, and collect slaves. Many settler-colonists came willingly to escape war, overpopulation, lack of opportunity, and religious persecution. Early settlers in North America were dependent on Indigenous Peoples in the unfamiliar environments; later they saw them as allies in military conflicts with other colonies, but this changed as settler-colonist numbers swelled, and diseases and disorganization reduced Indigenous populations (see Coates 2004; Dunbar-Ortiz 2014). The end result was similar in most colonized countries—Indigenous Peoples became marginalized and impoverished.

The trouble for the Europeans was that the lands they desired were already occupied and the resources were already under Indigenous control. European-based international law at the time gave colonial governments only two "legitimate" reasons for taking other peoples' resources—conquest and discovery. It is worth emphasizing that the Indigenous victims of these laws had no input into their formation. The Doctrine of Discovery required Europeans to imagine the lands as empty—terra nullius—even if they obviously were not. Legal theorists in England and France agreed that under the Doctrine of Discovery the two keys to taking Indigenous lands were current occupancy and actual possession. This legal fiction was based on agricultural use. Many Indigenous people practiced agriculture; however, it did not resemble European methods.

According to Pommersheim (2009, 95), "lands not put to the highest agricultural use (again, as defined by Europeans) were essentially 'vacant' or in a state of 'waste,' subject to European discovery and occupation." Monarchs like Henry VIII of England, who did not consider himself subject to the Catholic Church, and other royalty who relied on their supposed powers of divine right so that they "could proceed without the pope's blessing" used this doctrine (Nichols 2009, 146).

On the other hand, the Catholic pope had decreed that Indigenous lands were indeed inhabited. Spain and Portugal asked for papal decrees, or "bulls," focused on justifying war against infidels so that non-Christian lands could be acquired. The papal bull, "Inter caetera," issued by Pope Alexander VI, declared that only Christian rulers could legitimately claim ownership in the New World, giving most of it to the Spanish Crown (Vera 2012; Getches, Wilkinson, and Williams 1998; Williams 1990). These decrees were based in an ideology that inequality was a divinely willed natural condition for humans, and that "Christian government was the universal government that divine authority intended for all mankind" (Williams 1983, 21). This justification allowed the Church to "extend its influence and power over the uncharted lands and native civilizations of the entire Western Hemisphere" (Williams 1983, 21). Those who did not immediately accept rule of the colonizers and proselytizing of Christian priests were subject to "just war," meaning that the war was legally and morally justified and therefore that any mistreatment of colonized peoples at the hands of the colonizers would—legally—be their own fault (Getches, Wilkinson, and Williams 1998, 46–48). These papal-conferred rights gave the wealth of the New World as a reward for civilizing and Christianizing "the natives" on behalf of the pope (Williams 1983).

In response, Indigenous people showed remarkable resilience. They survived (barely) the epidemics brought by the Europeans and fought back to the best of their abilities against the unending inflow of settler-colonists. Colonial governments used violence in periodic massacres and especially in the "Indian Wars" in the United States. These proved to be extremely costly both politically and financially for the new colonies, so other tried-and-true strategies were used to justify and enable other forms of violence, including coerced assimilation in boarding or residential schools and isolation and economic degradation on reservations or reserves (see Dunbar-Ortiz 2014). The main tools to accomplish this in the United States continued to be the web of federal Indian law and policy as well as U.S. Supreme Court decisions. In other colonized countries, similar legal machinations occurred.

AMERICAN COLONIAL USE OF LAW

Law remained as an implement of Indigenous subjugation, exploitation, and disenfranchisement through the nineteenth and well into the twentieth century, despite early treaty-making. Early international law concepts such as "Discovery," in particular, were institutionalized into federal Indian law within the United States, as in, for example, the use of the term in *Johnson v. M'Intosh* (1823). Colonial governments signed treaties with the Indigenous inhabitants (as well as with the European competition in other colonies). At the time such treaties were signed, they were considered part of international law; they were (supposedly) "binding agreements between sovereigns" (Pommersheim 2009, 3). Wilkins and Lomawaima (2001, 251) define treaties then and now in this way: "Treaties are constitutionally privileged as the supreme law of the land and are legally binding statements of federal and tribal intent and responsibilities." Simply put, treaties are documents of agreement between sovereigns, and as such are evidence that from the beginning of the United States, American Indian tribes were legally viewed as politically distinct entities. Treaties were used to establish peace and to achieve military or trade alliances between the colonists and Indian nations; they were also used to gain access to natural resources of Native peoples, especially land.

According to Henry Knox, George Washington's secretary of war, westward expansion into Indian Country should be done by "purchase rather than by conquest" (Prucha 1984, 9).[2] Knox believed that the United States needed peace on all its frontiers in order to continue westward expansion. Concerns "over negative world opinion of the new republic, the probability of intense tribal resistance, and the costs of warfare in dollars and lives reinforced Secretary of War Henry Knox's views that the United States should operate its Indian policy from principles of humanity and honorable intentions—not conquest" (Wilkins and Lomawaima 2001, 40). The continued use of law through the treaties was the tool to accomplish this.

The Indigenous signatories to the treaties responded by signing, often reluctantly because of coercion, but in good faith. Not so the colonial signatories. Indian nations and the colonists had very different ideologies concerning treaties. According to DeJong (2015, 4), for the Indians they were "sacred moral pledges, [but] colonists considered them secular business transaction[s] that could be amended or discarded according to prevailing political considerations." (See also Williams 1997.)

Within short periods of time, the colonists and the colonial governments broke all the treaties (DeJong 2015)—actions that were clearly illegal by the laws of the time as well as today. The colonial governments and the colonial corporations (such as the railroads) worked hand in hand using the narrative of Manifest Destiny to legally justify their expansion westward and the double-dealings that ensued (Macdonald 2009). Based on the six hundred treaties signed between British and/or American colonial powers, the land held by Indians in the United States was reduced by 95 percent between 1800 and 1900 (Nies 1996, 223).

Another example is the Major Crimes Act (MCA) (1885) that is still in effect. It was enacted in response to the use of traditional justice methods in the case of a Lakota Sioux named Crow Dog who had killed another Sioux, Spotted Tail. The non-Native public was outraged that the "sentence" was the provision of restitution to Spotted Tail's family so that they did not suffer in his absence. In non-Native eyes, Crow Dog should have been hanged (Echo-Hawk 2010). It should be noted that at the time, Indian nations had jurisdiction over Indian crime and these reparations were quite legal. Through the MCA, the federal government took away their jurisdiction. Subsequent to the enactment of the MCA, American Indians lost a case (*U.S. v. Kagama* 1886) that challenged the constitutionality of that act. Here the court broadly interpreted a single constitutional phrase to create the plenary power doctrine, which would lead to the erosion of Indian sovereignty in criminal jurisdiction and much more.

The misuse of colonial law is too extensive to cover here. See Echo-Hawk (2010) for analyses of the most egregious colonial laws and legal cases that stripped American Indians of their land and resources and tried to remove their culture, language, and way of life.

RECENT USE OF LAW

Indigenous communities and nations continue to resist laws that justify the theft of Indian land and resources and that limit the authority of Indian nations over their lands, resources, and people. Many of these laws are based on continuing colonial attitudes of white superiority and supposed Indian inferiority. One such law that hinders justice in Indian Country is *Oliphant v. Suquamish* (1978), which denies Indian nations jurisdiction over non-Indians who commit crimes on Indian land. Considering that research has found that non-Indian men go "hunting" for Native women to sexually assault knowing that they can get away with it, such laws are discriminatory and even inhumane (Nielsen and Robyn 2019). Laws such as these left a void in Indian Country justice so that there was little to no protection or prosecution in Indian Country for serious crimes. Based on community activism and political lobbying, this situation has improved but not enough: for various reasons, U.S. attorneys declined to prosecute 37 percent of crimes in Indian Country in 2017 (U.S. Department of Justice 2018).

Legislation such as the Violence Against Women Reauthorization Act (VAWA) in 2013 (which as of May 2019 is no longer authorized) and the Tribal Law and Order Act (TLOA) of 2010 purported to increase the sovereign rights of American Indian nations and therefore provided hope that things were changing, but these laws are full of "strings." Under VAWA, for example, non-Indian men who come onto the reservation to find women to rape still cannot be prosecuted by tribal authorities; the law only applies to non-Indian men who have some sort of relationship with the victim or are employed on the reservation. Under TLOA, tribal courts must provide very expensive training and public defenders for the protection of the non-Indian accused. Only a few nations have been able to afford to do so, and some have simply refused because of the illegitimate light this casts on their current justice system (see also the chapter by Fox).

This greatly truncated overview of the history of the intersection of law and colonialism sheds light on the development of the specific issues and Indigenous responses discussed in this book. The major themes discussed in the chapters are outlined in the following paragraphs.

THEMES OF THE BOOK

The necessity of Indigenous Peoples responding to law cannot be understated, nor can the complexity of the relationship between the two. The underlying themes found in the chapters of this book are evidence of this. A thread running throughout all the chapters is the **persistence of community responses**. Indigenous Peoples are still here, despite the many obstacles encountered throughout centuries of challenges brought by discrimination in the law and the subsequent damage or outright dismantling of social, political, and religious institutions. The community responses in this book are all examples of **Indigenous community resilience** (Kirmayer et al. 2009). Resilience is a relatively new term in the literature of Indigenous/Native American studies. This model is in contrast to the deficit model used by many scholars who explore Indigenous issues (Kirmayer et al. 2009). The deficit model asks the question, "What's wrong in Indian Country and how do we fix it?" In contrast we focus on how Indigenous Peoples respond to colonial law in ways that promote thriving Indigenous communities and nations. Resilience is the key to understanding why legal battles continue. Resilience is why Indigenous Peoples will continue to fight the hard battle to regain their self-determination and sovereignty. It is why they will incorporate customary law into their institutions and will use international law and courts to fight the continuing colonialism that informs national law in colonized countries.

Another theme is that **Indigenous law is marginalized**, whether it is in the traditional, national, or international arenas. The criminalization of customary law was a key process used to further colonial exploitation of land and resources. There was "active hostility" by colonial governments toward customary law, as the Honorable Raymond D. Austin states, and this hostility still exists toward laws that might benefit Indigenous Peoples. This is despite federal legislation like the Indian Reorganization Act (1934) that purported to support the usage of customary law. Originally marginalization may have been the result of the devaluing by colonizers of unfamiliar legal structures since they disregarded any laws but their own (and sometimes even those), but more likely it was the need to delegitimize Indigenous law to justify the imposition of Euro-based colonial law.

This marginalization continues today. Even laws to protect sacred sites, as described by Jocks, are ignored or devalued in order to justify economic exploitation. As James W. Zion and the Honorable Robert Yazzie state in their chapter, American laws "generally presume against the validity of Indian law." Yet **traditional law remains relevant and is resurging** locally and globally, as described in chapters by Jocks, Austin, and Zion and Yazzie. As Austin points out, the more customary laws are used, the more their use becomes precedent for tribal courts. The ineffectiveness of the European-based legal system in dealing with Indigenous issues calls for another path, one that traditionally was found in customary law. As Fox, Leonardo J. Alvarado, and Kurt Siedschlaw point out, Indigenous and non-Indigenous laws and justice institutions can inform each other, and the latter can work to cooperate and coordinate their services. This resurgence is arguably a result of Indigenous community capacity-building (as defined by Nielsen in chapter 7) and the persistent work and success of Indigenous legal scholars.

Another theme is the **use of European-based law to destroy Indigenous human rights** by enacting laws about forced assimilation, political disenfranchisement, and the destruction of social institutions. The few Euro-based cases such as *Johnson v. M'Intosh* (1823), *Cherokee Nation v. Georgia* (1831), and *Worcester v. Georgia* (1832), collectively known as the Marshall Trilogy, intended (perhaps) to aid Indigenous people but more likely to further federalism over states' rights, had unintended negative consequences (see in general the chapters by Zion and Yazzie, Siedschlaw, and Alvarado). On the other hand, Indigenous human rights are being **operationalized** through the United Nations Declaration on the Rights of Indigenous Peoples (UNDRIP) and incorporation into domestic laws as discussed by Anaya (1996) and in this book by Alvarado. They are also being operationalized through day-to-day justice provision as discussed by Nielsen. According to international conventions such as UNDRIP, Indigenous people have the **right to make and use their own laws and justice institutions**. Alvarado in his chapter describes the importance of the international arena in gaining recognition of Indigenous rights, justice, and law, despite the resistance of many colonial governments. There are still issues, however, with the United States' acceptance of this declaration (see the chapter by Zion and Yazzie).

Law can be a tool of exploitation. It has been used to justify slavery, massacres, land and resource theft, and fraud in treaty-breaking. International bodies recognize treaties as legitimate international law, but colonial governments regularly break them. As Alvarado points out, current legal relations continue to perpetuate colonial-era ideology, exploitive goals, and oppression. When treaty rights are upheld, however, they can be **a tool to protect and preserve** the natural resource rights, cultural rights, political rights, and economic rights of Indigenous Peoples.

Another theme is that laws affecting Indigenous Peoples were and are developed in **complex legal environments** based in the interplay of politics, religion, economics, and entrepreneurship. Attitudes based in patriarchy and a sense of European/non-Indigenous superiority continue to inform law today so that in the United States there continue to be jurisdictional issues in the operation of tribal, state, and federal laws. There also needs to be recognition, as Fox and Alvarado point out, of the **differential impacts** on men and women, youth, children, and disabled people. To this tangle must be added the pressure on colonial governments to conform to international treaties and conventions (see the chapter by Alvarado). These complex legal environments, however, can sometimes **create opportunities** for negotiation, originality, and new strategies such as Jocks describes.

There is a profound **lack of cultural awareness by non-Indigenous legal experts** such as judges and lawyers about Indigenous values, spirituality, and laws. Too many of them use cultural stereotypes about the nature and content of customary laws and Indigenous justice systems. Traditional law and non-Indigenous law do have different views of justice— one is focused on healing and harmony, the other on sentencing and punishment. Zion and Yazzie and Jocks describe some of these important differences. Out of ignorance and sometimes indifference, lawmakers may negatively impact Indigenous religious freedoms. Legal personnel who practice in border towns and communities with large Indigenous populations may incorrectly apply federal legislation to certain kinds of cases. State governments and courts in particular do not understand the legal foundations and spirit of sovereignty, applying their non-Indigenous values of justice instead. Siedschlaw in his chapter describes how this has occurred with the application of the Indian Child Welfare Act. While this is still an issue, the continuing use of traditional law by Indigenous justice systems, as well as the opportunity for cultural legal competency provided by the growing legal literature written by Indigenous legal scholars, may in time counterbalance this.

The importance of **international comparisons is another theme**. Colonization followed similar patterns in the countries colonized mainly by Britain (in the case of this book), though of course with very different historical details. The impacts on Indigenous Peoples have also been similar. As Alvarado, Jocks, and Nielsen illustrate, Indigenous Peoples have created innovative solutions to their common issues that could be shared directly or modified to be more culturally and situationally effective.

Another theme is that the development of law by and for Indigenous Peoples is another **way to exercise sovereignty**, as Austin points out. Sovereignty, or the right to make decisions about one's own citizens, is one of the most important themes shared by the chapters. Grassroots efforts can get laws changed, but it is an uphill battle. Law from the top down benefits colonial interests; law from the bottom up benefits Indigenous sovereignty. International law provides the context for such sovereignty: as Alvarado states in his chapter, "the effective exercise of Indigenous justice and law is essential for the internationally recognized rights of Indigenous Peoples." Indigenous-designed and -operated organizations and programs have been formed to operationalize the laws and to turn their promise into reality. Nielsen in her chapter describes examples of seven justice service organizations in four countries that were designed by and for Indigenous Peoples and individuals. They are examples of the on-the-ground, pragmatic community application of the principles of the United Nations Declaration on the Rights of Indigenous Peoples. The Navajo peacemaking program referred to by Austin, Zion and Yazzie, and Nielsen in their chapters is a well-known example of sovereignty in action.

Related to sovereignty is the theme of **capacity-building in Indigenous communities and nations**. Because of marginalization created by colonization, Indigenous communities are among the poorest in each colonized country (see Coates 2004). In order to provide educational, social, economic, justice, and other basic services to their members, Indigenous communities and nations need resources such as physical infrastructure, skilled work forces, an economic base, a solid cultural foundation, and not least of all, a fair and equitable legal structure that recognizes and promotes customary law and human rights and can operate within the legal limitations (no matter how discriminatory) imposed by colonial governments.

These themes will be discussed further in the concluding chapter to the book.

THE BOOK

This is the second book in the Indigenous Justice series from University of Arizona Press. The first book focuses on crime and social justice in Indian Country. The next one reports on new research in the area of environmental justice for Indigenous Peoples. This book on Indigenous justice focuses on the intersection of law, colonialism, and community responses by Indigenous Peoples, especially in the United States, though some of its chapters have an international focus, including issues in Canada (Jocks and Nielsen), Latin America (Alvarado), and New Zealand and Australia (Nielsen). More importantly, the book describes successful ways in which Indigenous communities and nations use law to enact change.

NOTES

1.   For excellent histories from an Indigenous point of view, see, for example, Walker (1990) for New Zealand; Mudrooroo (1995) for Australia; Monchalin (2016) for Canada, and Dunbar-Ortiz (2014) for the United States. A good overview of colonization globally is Coates's (2004) book, *A Global History of Indigenous Peoples: Struggle and Survival*. For information on the relationship between colonization and current Indigenous justice issues, see for example, the Truth and Reconciliation Commission (2015) for Canada; and the National Inquiry . . . (1997) for Australia.

2.   Indian Country is defined as "(a) all land within the limits of any Indian reservation under the jurisdiction of the United States government, notwithstanding the issuance of any patent, and, including rights-of-way running through the reservation, (b) all dependent Indian communities within the borders of the United States whether within the original or subsequently acquired territory thereof, and whether within or without the limits of a state, and (c) all Indian allotments, the Indian titles to which have not been extinguished, including rights-of-way running through the same" (18 USCA §1151 [1948]).

REFERENCES

Anaya, S. James. 1996. *Indigenous Peoples in International Law*. Oxford: Oxford University Press.

Bluehouse, Philmer, and James W. Zion. 2009. "Hozhooji Naat'aanii: The Navajo Justice and Harmony Ceremony." In *Navajo Nation Peacemaking: Living Traditional Justice*, edited by Marianne O. Nielsen and James W. Zion, 156–64. Tucson: University of Arizona Press.

Calavita, Kitty. 2016. *Invitation to Law and Society: An Introduction to the Study of Real Law*. 2nd ed. Chicago: University of Chicago Press.

Cardani, John. 2009. "The Jurisdictional Jungle: Navigating the Path." In *Criminal Justice in Native America*, edited by Marianne O. Nielsen and Robert A. Silverman, 114–33. Tucson: University of Arizona Press.

Coates, Ken S. 2004. *A Global History of Indigenous Peoples: Struggle and Survival*. New York: Palgrave Macmillan.

DeJong, David H. 2015. *America Indian Treaties*. Salt Lake City: University of Utah Press.

Dunbar-Ortiz, Roxanne. 2014. *An Indigenous Peoples' History of the United States*. Boston: Beacon Press.

Echo-Hawk, Walter. 2010. *In the Courts of the Conquerors: The 10 Worst Indian Law Cases Ever Decided*. Golden, CO: Fulcrum.

Getches, David H., Charles F. Wilkinson, and Robert A. Williams Jr. 1998. *Cases and Materials on Federal Indian Law*. 4th ed. St. Paul, MN: West.

Kirmayer, Laurence J., Megha Sedev, Rob Whitley, Stephanie F. Dandeneau, and Colette Isaac. 2009. "Community Resilience: Models, Metaphors, and Measures." *Journal of Aboriginal Health*, November 2009: 62–117.

Macdonald, Theodore. 2009. "Introduction." In *Manifest Destinies and Indigenous Peoples*, edited by David Maybury-Lewis, Theodore Macdonald, and Biorn Maybury-Lewis, 1–19. Cambridge, MA: Harvard University Press.

Monchalin, Lisa. 2016. *The Colonial Problem: An Indigenous Perspective on Crime and Injustice in Canada*. Toronto, ON: University of Toronto Press.

Morse, Bradford W., ed. 1989. *Aboriginal Peoples and the Law: Indian, Métis and Inuit Rights in Canada*. Revised 1st ed. Ottawa, ON: Carleton University Press.

Mudrooroo. 1995. *Us Mob: History, Culture, Struggle: An Introduction to Indigenous Australia*. Sydney, NSW: Angus and Robertson.

National Inquiry into the Separation of Aboriginal and Torres Strait Islander Children from Their Families. 1997. *Bringing Them Home: National Inquiry into the Separation of Aboriginal and Torres Strait Islander Children from Their Families*. Sydney, NSW: Human Rights and Equal Opportunity Commission.

Nichols, Roger L. 2009. "National Expansion and Native Peoples of the United States and Canada." In *Manifest Destinies and Indigenous Peoples*, edited by David Maybury-Lewis, Theodore Macdonald, and Biorn Maybury-Lewis, 145–69. Cambridge, MA: Harvard University Press.

Nielsen, Marianne O. 2009. "Introduction to the Context of Native American Criminal Justice." In *Criminal Justice in Native America*, edited by Marianne O. Nielsen and Robert A. Silverman, 1–17. Tucson: University of Arizona Press.

Nielsen, Marianne O., and Karen Jarratt-Snider, eds. 2018. *Crime and Social Justice in Indian Country*. Tucson: University of Arizona Press.

Nielsen, Marianne O., and Linda M. Robyn. 2019. *Colonialism Is Crime*. New Brunswick, NJ: Rutgers University Press.

Nielsen, Marianne O., and James W. Zion, eds. 2005. *Navajo Nation Peacemaking: Living Traditional Justice*. Tucson: University of Arizona Press.

Nies, Judith. 1996. *Native American History*. New York: Ballantine Books.

Pommersheim, Frank. 2009. *Broken Landscape: Indians, Indian Tribes, and the Constitution*. New York: Oxford University Press.

Porter, Robert Odawi. 2005. *Sovereignty, Colonialism and the Indigenous Nations: A Reader*. Durham, NC: Carolina Academic Press.

Prucha, Francis P. 1984. *The Great Father: The United States Government and the American Indians*. Vol. 1. Lincoln: University of Nebraska Press.

Statistics Canada. 2015. "Table 3: Distribution of First Nations People, First Nations People with and Without Registered Indian Status, and First Nations People with Registered Indian Status Living on or off Reserve, Canada, Provinces and Territories, 2011." https://www12.statcan.gc.ca/nhs-enm/2011/as-sa/99-011-x/2011001/tbl/tbl03-eng.cfm.

Truth and Reconciliation Commission of Canada. 2015. *Final Report of the Truth and Reconciliation Commission of Canada*. Vol. 1: *Summary*. Toronto: James Lorimer.

U.S. Department of Health and Human Services. 2018. "Profile: American Indian/Alaska Native." https://minorityhealth.hhs.gov/omh/browse.aspx?lvl=3&lvlid=62.

U.S. Department of Justice. 2018. "Department of Justice Releases Annual Report to Congress on Indian Country Investigations and Prosecutions." Press Release, November 21, 2018. https://www.justice.gov/opa/pr/department-justice-releases-annual-report-congress-indian-country-investigations-and.

Vera, Kim Benita. 2012. "From Papal Bull to Racial Rule: Indians of the Americas, Race, and the Foundations of International Law." *California Western International Law Journal* 42:453–73.

Walker, Ranguini. 1990. *Ka Whawhai Tonu Matou: Struggle Without End*. Auckland, NZ: Penguin.

Wilkins, David E., and K. Tsianina Lomawaima. 2001. *Uneven Ground: American Indian Sovereignty and Federal Law*. Norman: University of Oklahoma Press.

Williams, Robert A., Jr. 1983. "The Medieval and Renaissance Origins of the Status of the American Indian in Western Legal Thought." *Southern California Law Review* 57:1–100.

————. 1990. *The American Indian in Western Legal Thought: The Discourses of Conquest*. New York: Oxford University Press.

————. 1997. *Linking Arms Together: American Indian Treaty Visions of Law and Peace 1600–1800*. New York: Oxford University Press.

————. 2005. *Like a Loaded Weapon-The Rehnquist Court, Indian Rights, and the Legal History of Racism in America*. Minneapolis: University of Minneapolis Press.

LEGAL RESOURCES

Bull "Inter caetera divinae" (1493)

Cherokee Nation v. Georgia, 30 U.S. 1 (1831)

Doctrine of Conquest

Doctrine of Discovery

Indian Child Welfare Act 99 Stat. 3069 (1978)

Indian Reorganization Act 25 U.S.C. ch. 14, subch. V § 461 et seq. (1934)

Johnson v. M'Intosh 21 U.S. 543 (1823)

Lyng v. Northwest Indian Cemetery Protective Association 108 S.Ct. 1319 (1988)

Major Crimes Act U.S. Statutes at Large, 23:385 (1885)

Oliphant v. Suquamish Indian Tribe, 435 U.S. 191 (1978)

Tribal Law and Order Act Pub. L. 111–211, H.R. 725, 124 Stat. 2258 (2010)

United Nations Declaration on the Rights of Indigenous Peoples (2007)

U.S. v. Kagama 118 U.S. 375 (1886)

Violence Against Women Reauthorization Act Public Law 113–4 (2013)

Worcester v. Georgia 31 U.S. (6 Pet.) 515 (1832)

PART I

TRADITIONAL LAW

INTRODUCTION BY MARIANNE O. NIELSEN AND KAREN JARRATT-SNIDER

Traditional or customary law is the root of a legal renaissance in many Indigenous nations and communities as they incorporate it into the legal and justice systems imposed upon them by colonial powers.[1] It is a tool for Indigenous cultural resurgence and a form of de facto sovereignty.

An important context for this section is the nature of traditional law. It was not a separate social institution but was woven into the everyday community life of Indigenous people. This paradigm was radically different from codified European-based laws (see Dumont 1996).

For about two hundred years after the arrival of the settler-colonists, customary law was allowed to continue unmolested, but as the stakes got higher (more settlers, more demand for resources) Indigenous customary law as represented in ceremonies and governance practices was criminalized (Dunbar-Ortiz 2014; and see Austin in this section). Its unfamiliarity and "un-Christian" and unwritten nature made it the target of missionaries and government officials who had stakes in replacing it with supposedly superior European-based colonial law, law that also just happened to justify the acquisition of Indigenous lands and resources. Customary law was attacked through assimilationist policies and practices such as boarding/residential schools and colonial laws forbidding spiritual ceremonies and traditional Indigenous government structures. An unfortunate consequence was the internalization of oppression by some Indigenous individuals so that they, too, lost respect for traditional law. Customary law continued, however, albeit underground. Over time, it has been reemerging in communities and nations where it was not destroyed by colonial oppression and tragically lost (see Lucas 1985).

Issues continue today in the recognition and implementation of customary law. Most settler-colonist lawmakers and political leaders either do not understand customary laws or deliberately choose to ignore them. Many non-Indigenous scholars lack knowledge of them as well. As Calavita (2016, 107) points out, some legal scholars still doubt that Indigenous law is law, but as she writes, somewhat tongue in cheek, "the very fact that the formalized law of the colonial powers and the indigenous justice systems of colonized peoples—some of which were decentralized, informal, and uncodified—crossbred seems to suggest (if my rudimentary biology is correct) that they are of the same species."

Traditional law as part of spirituality needs more protection than it currently receives. For Indigenous cultures to thrive they need freedom of religion as it is guaranteed for all citizens in the U.S. Constitution and promised to American Indians, specifically in the American Indian Religious Freedom Act (1978). In general, though, non-Indigenous individuals and governments ignore this right because of their lack of understanding of and respect for American Indian spirituality. For example, in U.S. prisons, Native American prisoners are often denied access to religious ceremonies and medicine people because of "safety and security concerns" that could be based in stereotypes or discrimination (Archambeault 2009). The Sacred Peaks/Snowbowl controversy in Arizona is another example. The courts recently denied that American Indian Peoples that hold the San Francisco Peaks as sacred had more sway than economic interests. The county court declared that "the use of reclaimed water by Snowbowl is not unreasonable or illegal under the circumstances, nor is there a likelihood that it will result in irreparable harm to the plaintiff" (Judge Moran, cited in Locke 2016). The issue of lack of protections for Indigenous Peoples' religious freedom is also discussed by Jocks in part II.

On the whole, in most settler-colonist countries, including those outside the United States, traditional law is marginalized, ignored, and at best devalued by lawmakers and the settler-colonial justice system. For example, the Australian Law Reform Commission in the mid-1980s studied and recommended the incorporation of some Indigenous Australian customary law into the Euro-based Australian system. Their efforts met with very little legal success. A later government task force in Western Australia looked at the recognition of Aboriginal customary criminal and civil law, including family law, hunting and fishing rights, and community governance. It recommended that Indigenous customary law be recognized, although it added, disappointingly, "to a certain extent the recognition of Aboriginal law must be subjugated to the dominant interests of the state and the international community" (Law Reform Commission 2006, 11). Indigenous customary law in the United States has not been honored by being the subject of a government-sponsored task force.

In Indigenous communities and nations, traditional law is opening up a path of community and nation resistance against colonial laws and institutions, as the authors within this section demonstrate. Zion and Yazzie's chapter and Austin's chapter are important for understanding the impact of traditional law, not only on the everyday lives of Indigenous Peoples, but on the amelioration of issues in their communities and nations. These chapters focus on law as an integral part of the fabric of healthy, stable, and functioning Indigenous communities and nations.

Zion and Yazzie use the political and legal activism surrounding the Dakota Access Pipeline as a jumping off point to discuss the place of customary law in international law and the resulting potential for the creation of new systems of customary law and dispute resolution within Indigenous communities. Such dispute resolution systems focus on restoring harmony to the community and resolving the underlying issues that caused the dispute. Peacemaking and other Indigenous forms of dispute resolution are growing in number across the world. The

Native American Rights Fund website is an excellent resource, for example, on dispute resolution programs operating in the Navajo Nation, Hawai'i, and Canada (https://peacemaking.narf .org/about-peacemaking/).

Austin's chapter also advocates for the incorporation of customary law and traditional dispute resolution mechanisms into Indigenous justice systems, and thereby provides a blueprint for Indigenous nations to "do sovereignty." He focuses on the incorporation of traditionally based dispute resolution, peacemaking, into the Navajo Nation justice system and describes how it has been incorporated into the tribal code. Customary law and its role in nation-building is further explored in the final chapter of this book.

NOTE

1. It should be noted that the terms *traditional laws* and *customary laws* are used interchangeably in this book.

REFERENCES

Archambeault, William G. 2009. "The Search for the *Silver Arrow*: Assessing Tribal-Based Healing Traditions and Ceremonies in Indian Country Corrections." In *Criminal Justice in Native America*, edited by Marianne O. Nielsen and Robert A. Silverman, 191–206. Tucson: University of Arizona Press.

Calavita, Kitty. 2016. *Invitation to Law and Society: An Introduction to the Study of Real Law*. 2nd ed. Chicago: University of Chicago Press.

Dumont, James. 1996. "Justice and Native People." In *Native Americans, Crime, and Justice*, edited by Marianne O. Nielsen and Robert A. Silverman, 20–33. Boulder, CO: Westview.

Dunbar-Ortiz, Roxanne. 2014. *An Indigenous Peoples' History of the United States*. Boston: Beacon Press.

Lucas, Phil. 1985. *The Honour of All*. Part 1 (film). Kelowna, BC: Filmwest Associates.

Law Reform Commission of Western Australia. 2006. *Aboriginal Customary Laws: The Interaction of Western Australian Law with Aboriginal Law and Culture, Final Report.* http://www.lrc.justice.wa.gov .au/_files/p94_fr.pdf.

Locke, Katherine. 2016. "Hopi Tribe Lawsuit Dismissed." *Navajo-Hopi Observer.* www.nhonews.com/news/2016/aug/23/hopi-tribe-lawsuit -dismissed/.

LEGAL RESOURCES

American Indian Religious Freedom Act, Public Law No. 95–341, 92 Stat. 469 (1978).

1

REVISIONING TRADITIONAL INDIGENOUS JUSTICE IN LIGHT OF THE UNITED NATIONS DECLARATION ON THE RIGHTS OF INDIGENOUS PEOPLES

JAMES W. ZION AND THE HONORABLE
ROBERT YAZZIE

BSERVERS OF American Indian law and policy in 2018 note a transition in the political and legal climate where American Indian and Indigenous issues came to a dead end in United States policy due to, first, varying political perspectives on the nature of Indians and their law in this country, and second, to a new period marked by a presidential administration that is hostile to equal protection and minority issues.[1] Indigenous activists, lawyers, and supporters put a lot of time and effort into elaborating a comprehensive statement of Indigenous rights in the Declaration on the Rights of Indigenous Peoples that was adopted by the United Nations General Assembly in its Resolution No. 61/295 (September 13, 2007). The Declaration has not prompted the changes that Indigenous Peoples and organizations hoped for, certainly in the United States, and there continues to be opposition and obstructionism over Indigenous rights from the leaders of this and other settler States and corporations. The term *settler States* refers to settlement, colonies, and other modes of entry into the Americas, Asia, and elsewhere to supplant Indigenous governance and law with alien governance, law, and religion—new models that are imposed rather than consensual. Interest and advocacy on Indigenous issues were prompted by modern concerns over civil rights and minority rights and aggressive activism in the 1960s and 1970s. That advocacy led to this UN General Assembly resolution, which looks like a codification of international Indigenous rights law but is without a formal statement that the Declaration is "law" as such (or "hard" law).

When the Declaration was adopted over the objections of the United States, Canada, Australia, and New Zealand (the major settler States in English-speaking regimes) those States took differing positions on how they would comply (or not) with the declaration. The United States gave lukewarm "recognition" by the U.S. State Department without attribution to its source in a vague general acceptance statement by President Barack Obama, accompanied by policy statements that are in fact evidence of an intent to violate a great deal of the Declaration. That document is being given varying degrees of recognition globally, but the primary emphasis for purposes of this chapter will be on the United States' treatment of the declaration and the associated field of American Indian affairs law (as it is called by the American Bar Association), as these relate to the #NODAPL conflict.

An organization known as the Dakota Access Pipeline acquired (contested) rights to run a pipeline to carry oil from the Bakken oil fields in western North Dakota to southern Illinois, and the flashpoint was the insistence of the leadership and members of the Standing Rock Indian Reservation in North Dakota that the energy company did not have necessary permissions from the federal government, the tribe, and others to lay pipe, and that such activities damaged physical cultural heritage (i.e., graves and sacred sites) and disrupted tribal life. There was a confrontation at the north edge of the Indian reservation where camps were established to block pipeline activities starting in April 2016 and continuing through February 23, 2017, when the North Dakota National Guard and company enforcers evicted Indians and others who self-identified as "#NODAPL," meaning "no Dakota Access Pipeline."

One of the unique things about the NODAPL movement is that it involved American Indian lawyers, mostly women, who went on site to coordinate opposition, legal defense, and legal initiatives. Although the protesters were evicted from the site, they carried the fight to investment companies and investor organizations in an attempt to block or remove funding for pipelines. Discussions included how to use investor advocacy to highlight many of the past arguments about Indigenous property and cultural rights as they are based in various provisions of the declaration.

This conflict illustrates what is different today in legal issues: Indigenous Peoples themselves are active in advocating their rights in nontraditional forums (i.e., places other than courts or legislatures) using both longstanding statements of positive (i.e., "hard") law and new conceptions that target new aspects of international human rights law such as relations with foreign governments and religious institutions. The question is sorting out the utility of centuries of State practice as it impacts Indigenous Peoples, and new international standards, laws, and forums (both governmental and nongovernmental) that are developing now.

This chapter will examine the history of the recognition (or not) of Indigenous law in the global legal system to show how it has been marginalized and disregarded, how it is now treated in international human rights law, and what the possibilities might be if the activism of young American Indians translates into action to prompt new forms of law and justice that might respond to what young Indians (and mature supporters) are trying to tell us. Past arrangements to accommodate Indigenous law, institutions, and self-determination have failed, so a new approach is needed. Accordingly, this chapter will (1) lay out the history of Indigenous law in colonial societies that are the product of conquest, including "recognition rights"; (2) discuss the current position of Indigenous law in the international human rights and legal system; and (3) speculate on a potential new vision of Indigenous law and justice that is, in fact, a revisioning of recent developments in the creation of new systems of customary law and Indigenous dispute resolution that foster human rights.

DEVELOPMENT OF THE RECOGNITION RIGHT

The history of the "Western Legal Tradition" and comparative law legal history excludes mention of principles of the laws of Indigenous Peoples other than in discussions of "custom" (for example, see Berman 1983; Glendon, Gordon, and Osakwe 1982). The texts usually address the major non-Indigenous fields of civil law, based generally on Roman law sources;

"Common Law," a system of case precedents in English-speaking jurisdictions; and the "Socialist Law Tradition," largely based on or mirroring
the Roman civil law tradition (Glendon, Gordon, and Osakwe, 1982). As
can be seen, the Roman law system made significant contributions to all
three systems, and therefore to laws affecting Indigenous Peoples.

"Law," in the arena of Indigenous Peoples and many other societies,
is a means of ordering and regulating societies and relationships among
Peoples and is largely based on conquest or the domination of one group
of peoples over others (as in the capitalist economic and social system).
While there have been major conflicts involving powerful States and
conquered peoples since the beginning of recorded history, the most
prominent colonial system of expansion for our purposes is the Roman
Empire. It was a post-republic movement of authoritarian imperial
Rome for about fifteen hundred years, approximately terminating with
the sacking of Rome by the Visigoths in 410 and Vandals in 455 in the
Western Empire, and the fall of the Eastern Empire to the Ottoman
Turks in 1453. One of the realities of empire for the development of
Roman law was what to do with colonial holdings after conquest was
secured.

The conquest and colonizing process used a system of placing local
governors in charge of territories; the local governors held official Roman
power that included rights to judge and issue edicts. However, that power
was exercised pursuant to a policy that localities could retain their own
laws and have institutions to exercise their own authority so long as their
local laws did not conflict with the real or perceived rights of Romans
(Morey 1900, 67–68). The practice of allowing some local autonomy and
relative independence provided an incentive to stay in good standing with
Rome through its governors, and Roman law respected *mos regionis*, a
"regional tradition" or "law of the [particular] land," so that local law and
its application could maintain social stability (Garnsey and Seller 1987,
107–11; Potter 2009, 181, 184–85).

The history of the interplay of Roman law and practice with the customs and institutions of the various "barbaric" peoples the legions encountered in today's Western Europe is still being written so as to more clearly
identify the laws and practices of the conquered groups, but the first modern European State to engage in the conquest of Indigenous Peoples of
the Western Hemisphere was Spain. Its variation of the Roman policy of

recognition in order to manipulate conquered populations is the primary contributor to today's inadequate and insufficient legal policy.

Spain was the crossroads of major clashes between imperialist empires, namely Carthage and Rome, and various other societies that occupied the Iberian Peninsula. The Romans drove the Carthaginians out of power by 205 BC, and the "Spanish tribes were conquered" by 19 BC, so that there was relative stability in the peninsula in a "Pax Romana" (Crow 1963, 28–29). The troops that occupied what we today call Spain spoke a Latin dialect known as "vulgar Latin" that evolved into the Spanish language, and Roman occupation led to the conclusion by historians that "Roman law and customs were adopted throughout the land" (Crow 1963, 53–54).

That conclusion grossly overstates the reality that the history of Spain is one of ongoing conflict among different nationalities, religions, cultures, and regions, so that conclusions that Roman law was adopted or prevailed there are inaccurate. The fact is that when Roman domination ended, "Spanish culture and psychology were polarized in two opposing tendencies: on the one hand, the Roman feeling for union, centralization, and imperium, and on the other, the African tendency toward disunion, tribalism, and separation. Throughout the following centuries the people of Spain have expressed themselves by moving first in one of these directions, only to swing suddenly in an about-face and move in the other. This essential dichotomy has never been resolved by democratic compromise for more than the briefest periods" (Crow 1963, 35).

Columbus petitioned Queen Isabella and King Ferdinand for charters, permissions, and monies for exploration as the royal couple laid siege to the city of Granada at the gates of Santa Fe, and he got two such permissions on April 27 and 30, 1492. In the meantime, Granada fell and the Catholic monarchs moved to pacify their subject populations in the Alhambra Decree of March 31, 1492, expelling Jews from Spain and allowing the Catholic Inquisition to weed out heresy and religious difference (Kamen 2005). That was the political situation in Spain when Columbus set off on his expedition on August 3, 1492.

Columbus returned to Barcelona and landed on March 15, 1493, but he posted a letter to Luis de St. Angel (known as the "San Angel Letter"), the treasurer of Aragon (the "grant manager" in today's usage), before landing in Spain. That "relation" of the results of the expedition set a precedent for a series of such reports to Spanish monarchs, full of speculations, exaggerations, pious lies, and other distortions of the situation encountered in the Americas. Columbus left the impression he could communicate with the Indians in their own languages, and he also reported that the inhabitants were not opposed to exploitation, as the letter stated that there were riches in gold, spices, and other products, as well as lands to be taken. Columbus boasted about his navigation and diplomatic skills and told of one meeting with the report that "I am so friendly with the king of that country that he was proud to call me brother and hold me as such." Columbus's fawning report, made to justify to the Spanish monarchs the great rewards he expected (and that they reneged on, as monarchs are wont) was timely for their needs. The Catholic monarchs finally won the religious war for Spain and they were in the process of consolidating the power of their kingdoms of Castile and León over all of the peninsula, but they had a major problem: Catholic Spain had been at war between at least 711 and 1492, and that created a militarist culture with (largely) men who had to use their military skills elsewhere. That meant that they were dumped into the Americas (Kamen 2005).

It is said that most of the Spanish conquistadores, or "conquerors," were from the region of Extremadura in southwestern Spain. There wasn't much there for combatants in the religious wars to go home to because the region was dry and poor, and the males of the time had the choices of inheriting poor land, if they were the eldest son, or becoming a priest, leaving other sons with no place to go. This included the war princes of the Americas: Hernán Cortés (Mexico), Francisco Pizarro (Peru), and Hernando de Soto (Florida), and other prominent military commanders or explorers (Burns 2001). The time was right for them to find adventure, get power, and return with riches.

Their relations with Indigenous Peoples of necessity led to the development of new laws. While Roman law was accepted wholesale or in large part on the continent of Europe as the Civil Law System, Spain had a unique position because its Roman code was *Las Siete Partidas* ("The Seven Divisions") promulgated by Alfonso X (the "Wise" or "Learned") who was the king of Castile from 1221 through 1284 (Burns 2001, vi:xi). Given the cultural divide in Spain, Alfonso knew that "his custom law feudal kingdom would resist the professional, sophisticated, and academic nature of the *Partidas*," he also realized "that the modern world then bursting upon Castile would make such a law inevitable" (Burns 2001, vi:xi). The code is written in an essay format and sets out principles and discussions of policy, law, and jurisprudence, and its style is alien to the English-American statutory format that is essentially a form of legislative commands or micromanagement by elected politicians. It is in four volumes that still make good reading and is still strictly part of the law and jurisprudence in the areas of the United States taken or stolen from Mexico under the Treaty of Guadalupe Hidalgo of 1848. Neither Roman law nor the *Partidas* give code guidance for questions of the recognition of local law and decision-making processes, and that omission was filled in through a series of policy debates on what to do with or to Indians once they were subdued, and in Indian-specific royal decrees (Burns 2001).

When Spain began settlement on islands in the Caribbean, unemployed veterans, adventurers, and freebooters were among the settlers, and the non-Christian locals were badly exploited by Christians who pushed them off their lands, captured them as a labor force, starved them, inflicted European diseases upon them, and generally devastated local populations. On the Sunday before Christmas in 1511 Antonio de Montesinos ascended to a church pulpit to face his Christian congregation and strongly demanded, "Tell me, by what right do you keep these Indians in cruel servitude? . . . You are in mortal sin for the cruelty and tyranny you deal out to these innocent people. . . . Are these not men? Have they not rational souls?" (Fuentes 1992, 125). As it is with today's conflicts over expansion, settlement, and resource extraction, the answers essentially were "What right do you have to ask," "Why are you ragging on us," and "No, they are not human or worthy of respect." The settlers made loud complaints to the Spanish Crown and Montesinos's fiery sermon set off decades of debate over the humanity of Indians and their rights to be free of exploitation and abuse.

Given the dominance of the Catholic Church in Spain and its control over knowledge and the learned professions, the Crown looked to academics who were also lawyers for advice and guidance. One of them was Francisco de Vitoria, a respected graduate of the University of Paris, known for his wisdom in theology, political policy, and law. He wrote two tracts to answer questions put to him about the rights of Indians that were published later, namely, *De Indis* (1532) ("concerning the Indies" and the rights of Indians) and *De Jure belli Hispanorum in barbaros* (author's translation: "concerning the Spanish law of war with barbarians") (Vitoria

1991, 231–92, 293–328). They laid out principles of just war and the need for justification for war against Indians, and generally stated that the Indians had legal rights to their own systems of governance and property that could not be denied except through "just war" or specific consent.

Political factions led by cleric-lawyer experts sprang up, and the people who supported the settlers chose Juan Ginés de Sepúlveda, who published a tract on "war with the Indians," to justify their actions. A faction of pro-Indian Spaniards looked to lawyer-cleric Bartolomé de las Casas to articulate their position. Las Casas had the advantage of good connections, family who sailed with Columbus, and the experience of having held Indian slaves in Cuba before he got a divine wake-up call to reform. There was a standoff between the two advocates in a series of debates at the University of Valladolid in 1550 and 1551 where they debated their relative positions before royal representatives, and the essential question was whether or not the Indians of the Americas were "human" and thus entitled to respect for their governance, laws, and property (Casas [1542] 1979). Las Casas "won" the debates, which led to royal policies and decrees that required consensual dealings with Indian leaders and fair treatment and respect for Indian governance, laws, and property; however, because of the distance from seats of power, there were arguments over regulation and deregulation (the ultimate argument being settled by revolution in Spanish America) and blatant disregard for the law or directives. Clerics advocated and got laws to protect Indians, but the colonists defied those laws and Spain ultimately was unable to enforce them.

There was another precedent for royal policy on local law and institutions. In Spain there were distinct communities of Christians, Moors, and Jews, and Christians and Jews under Moorish control were allowed to continue to use their own laws (including customary laws and practices) in their own communities. There was also some tolerance for distinct local practices. Christians generally followed the same (practical) policy, so there was a degree of autonomy in Moorish and Jewish communities with respect for their laws and customs. That was also part of the reality that Roman law had in respecting the *mos regionis*, or "law of the land," and in the recognition by Alfonso X in promulgating the Seven Divisions that custom and practice would resist regulation. Spain was not alone in the push-and-pull of opposing tendencies of union, centralization, and imperium against disunion, "tribalism," and separatism. Those oppositions are realities in modern societies as well. Central governments cannot, or will not, intervene when the rights of Indians to enjoy their own cultures are threatened, or when they need protection for violations of their property and civil rights. This is exemplified in the confrontation at the Standing Rock Indian Reservation in North Dakota, where local law enforcement agencies and pipeline company thugs were permitted to abuse Indians and their supporters when they attempted to block a pipeline venture of dubious legality (Zion 2017). In sum, the development of Spanish law established principles that underlie notions in the recent United Nations Declaration on the Rights of Indigenous Peoples that Indigenous Peoples have basic and overriding human rights to self-determination, and to local decision-making that is binding on central authorities.

English law followed a similar path. England was foreclosed from exploration and settlement in the Americas due to papal decrees and a treaty between Spain and Portugal respecting lands in the Americas, but that changed with the Protestant Reformation and the establishment of the Church of England. Bartolomé de las Casas penned an account of Spanish atrocities against Indians in 1542 (Casas [1542] 1979), a great deal of which was based on what he saw and participated in while he was a plantation co-owner in Cuba, and it was quickly translated into other European languages and used to bash the Spanish. The English version was published as *Tears of the Indians* in 1656, and the dedication to dictator Oliver Cromwell hinted that Spanish policies and practices toward Indians should be used in dealing with the Irish (Phillips [1542] 1970). The English common law of dealing with Indian custom and local law developed at approximately the same time.

The first lead decision in English law was *The Case of Tanistry* (1608), where Lord Coke ruled on the validity of Irish customary law, after noting that Indigenous principles may survive British rule if they are "reasonable, certain, of immemorial usage and comparable with crown sovereignty." His 1608 decision in *Calvin's Case* (upholding citizenship by birth) set out the principle that while Christian laws survive, those of infidels do not. Coke's limited view on Christian versus infidel was rejected in the case of *Omichund v. Barker* (1744) as being "contrary to scripture, common sense and humanity." There was an unreported arbitration decision in longstanding litigation that Indians, as a distinct people, had a property interest in land, and royal charters to others did not invalidate Indian title until there was a fair and honest purchase (Smith 1950). The question of the validity of Indigenous law and decisions was finally closed in a case interpreting the British *Royal Proclamation of 1763* that the laws of an acquired territory remain in force until altered by Crown action (*Campbell v. Hall* 1774).

Some American court decisions follow the English precedents. The first U.S. case was *Johnson v. M'Intosh* in 1823 where the U.S. Supreme Court ruled that "a person who purchases lands from the Indians, within their territory, incorporates himself with them, so far as respects the property purchased; holds their title under their protection, and subject to their laws." The question of the binding nature of Indian decisions that are "criminal" in nature, with a ruling that Indian criminal law does apply in "Indian Country" was set in the case of *Ex Parte Crow Dog* (1883). Law in the nature of probate property law was affirmed in the case of *Jones v. Meehan* (1899). The Supreme Court ruled that Indian nations have exclusive jurisdiction over domestic relations matters under their own law in *United States v. Quiver* (1916).

The general line of case law on Indian law supplanting non-Indian law on questions of jurisdiction has not fared well in the latter part of the twentieth century and the beginning of the twenty-first, so that prior precedents in favor of exclusive or primary Indian jurisdiction have been supplanted by decisions that generally presume against the validity of Indian law and its application by American Indian tribunals. Consistency and grounding in basic human rights principles is not necessarily a hallmark of U.S. law. There are emerging events that hopefully will change that shortcoming.

THE CONTEMPORARY INTERNATIONAL HUMAN RIGHTS POSITION

The various international human rights conventions do not generally address Indigenous rights and jurisdiction, but the beginning point of any discussion of that is the International Covenant on Civil and Political Rights (ICCPR). It is important because of its recognition (in Article 1[1]) that "all peoples" have the right to self-determination. That finally put to rest the settler State insistence that Peoples in colonized lands had no such right. Of particular importance is the provision in Article 27 of ICCPR that persons who belong to ethnic, religious, and linguistic "minorities" retain a right to "enjoy their own culture."

Lawyers for Indigenous Peoples and groups generally reject the notion that they are "minorities," as in Article 27 of ICCPR, because of the long history and background of Indigenous sovereignty and nationhood. That objection was noted in a November 1979 report of the Commission on Security and Cooperation in Europe, a U.S. agency tasked with the duty of assuring U.S. compliance with the Helsinki Final Act of 1975. The Helsinki Final Act is not a "treaty" as such, according to experts, but it carries treaty-like responsibilities to respect human rights. There were commission hearings in 1979 where criticism was directed at the United States for its treatment (or rather, maltreatment) of American Indians with the objection that they are citizens of Indian nations and tribes and not simply members of minority groups (CSCE 1979, 149). The 1979 report corrected the historical record, noting that Indians had citizenship and nationhood, and added that American Indians do have a status as "a racially distinct minority group" and also status as "sovereign, domestic dependent nations" so that their human rights are secured by both Principle VII of the Helsinki Final Act that addresses the rights of national minorities, and by Principle VIII, "which addresses equal rights and the self-determination of peoples" (CSCE 1979, 148–49). The back story on this report is that there was a meeting of signatories of the Final Act in Yugoslavia where the United States was heavily criticized by the Soviet Union for violations of the human rights of American Indians. As a result, a U.S. State Department employee, Dr. Shirley Hill Witt, was called to a meeting in Madrid by the Attorney General of the United States to write a lengthy description of the good treatment of American Indians, including the conclusions above (pers. comm.).

Another important document is the Universal Declaration of Human Rights adopted by the United Nations in 1948. The Commission on Human Rights that was established to implement it established a Sub Commission on Prevention of Discrimination and Protection of Minorities in 1947. The specially appointed rapporteur studied the rights of persons who belong to ethnic, religious, and linguistic minorities and published the study in 1979 (Capotorti 1979). It states, "The right of persons belonging to ethnic minorities to preserve the customs and traditions which form an integral part of their way of life constitutes a fundamental element in any system of protection of minorities" (Capotorti 1979, 67). The report's recommendations included "constitutional recognition of the existence of distinct groups and of the right to their members to a special regime [of law]," such recognition in "ad hoc international juridical instruments," and other forms of recognition (Capotorti 1979, 96).

The Capotorti report means that Indigenous Peoples can claim rights under their own laws, as enunciated by their own legal institutions, under the rubric of the "right to culture" in those States (and there are many) that have ratified the covenant. The reference to "ad hoc international juridical instruments" means those adopted for a particular purpose, and that means rights and interpretations adopted for specific subject matters, such as a General Assembly resolution that was approved twelve years following the work of the United Nations Declaration on the Rights of Indigenous Peoples (UNDRIP) working group. The working group was open to members of the United Nations, including the major settler States that were previously exempted from international law provisions on non-self-governing nations as such, and including Indigenous nations and groups, Indigenous nongovernmental organizations, and Indigenous civil society in general.

UNDRIP supports the right to have one's own law and legal institutions and to have that law and decisions under it recognized in several articles:

> Article 1 assures the enjoyment, by both individuals and groups, of "all human rights and fundamental freedoms as recognized in the Charter of the United Nations, the Universal Declaration of Human Rights and international human rights law";
> Article 3 upholds the centuries-old right of self-determination and reaffirms enjoyment of the right under the ICCPR;
> Article 4 assures the Indigenous "right to autonomy or self-government in matters relating to their internal and local affairs, as well as ways and means for financing their autonomous functions";
> Article 11(1) preserves "the right to practice and revitalize . . . cultural traditions and customs" and (2) requires States to "provide redress through effective mechanisms to secure those rights";
> Article 12 generally guarantees the right to "manifest, practice, develop and teach" customs;

Article 18 affirms "the right to participate in decision-making in matters
which would affect their rights";

Article 27 requires States to establish and implement "a fair, independent,
impartial, open and transparent process, giving due recognition to
indigenous peoples' laws, traditions, customs and land tenure systems,
to recognize and adjudicate the rights of indigenous peoples pertain-
ing to their lands, territories and resources";

Article 28(1) establishes a broad "right to redress, by means that can
include restitution or, when this is not possible, just, fair and equitable
compensation, for the lands, territories and resources which they have
traditionally owned or otherwise occupied or used"; and

Article 34 provides that "Indigenous peoples have the right to promote,
develop and maintain their institutional structures and their distinctive customs, spirituality, traditions, procedures, practices and, in the
cases where they exist, juridical systems or customs, in accordance
with international human rights standards."

Indigenous rights to make and have laws that must be respected and
implemented that are clearly set out in international law in ICCPR, the
Helsinki Final Act, and UNDRIP are not simply a pious wish, a touchy-
feely hope, or a profound state of feeling, but binding international law.
Returning to the statute of the International Court of Justice on what
comprises "international law," the rights described above are stated in
international conventions, international custom, general principles of
law "recognized by civilized nations" (an ironic term), and even "judicial
decisions and the teachings of the most highly qualified publicists of the
various nations, as subsidiary means for the determination of rules of law"
(International Court of Justice 1945).

UNDRIP is generally recognized in international forums and in
United Nations treaty bodies and has been interpreted in the federal court
of Canada as stating recognized international law standards. UNDRIP
is applied in United Nations institutions such as the treaty bodies (e.g.,
the Human Rights Council and the United Nations Committee on the
Elimination of Racial Discrimination), and there is a special body that
has authority to address UNDRIP issues and make recommendations on
how specific topics should be handled when applying it. It is the Expert
Mechanism on the Rights of Indigenous Peoples that meets each year in

Geneva, Switzerland, and the reports that apply to justice issues include the "Final Report on the Study on Indigenous Peoples and the Right to Participate in Decision-Making" (2011), "Access to Justice in Promotion and Protection of the Rights of Indigenous Peoples" (2013), and "Access to Justice in the Promotion and Protection of the Rights of Indigenous Peoples: Restorative Justice, Indigenous Juridical Systems and Access to Justice for Indigenous Women, Children and Youth, and Persons with Disabilities" (2014).

CURRENT STATE OF INDIAN LAW IN THE UNITED STATES

The United States spent decades attempting to block or delay UNDRIP and voted against it in the General Assembly. President Obama issued a statement that the United States was "lending support" to UNDRIP on December 16, 2010, but the document posted on the U.S. State Department website was not "signed" by the president or the secretary of state and it has now disappeared from that website (along the lines of Orwell's novel, *1984*). The undated Department of the Interior policy on consultation with Indian tribes permits only "consultation" on some proposed decisions affecting Indians and their nations and it excludes comment by Indian leaders who are not elected officials, Indian tribes that are not formally recognized, non-reservation-dwelling Indians (who are approximately 75 percent of the American Indian population), Indian civil society, or the many Indigenous groups that are present in the country in significant numbers (U.S. Census 2012). The census data uses self-definition for the definition of "American Indian," so that the majority of American Indians includes people who are not enrolled as Indians, people who consider themselves to be "Indian" because they are living a traditional life as such, and even Indians from other countries who relate to each other as such.

On the point of legal acceptability of traditional Indian law, the U.S. Court of Appeals for the Ninth Circuit rejected a decision of the Crow Tribal Court on grounds that did not squarely address it in *Burlington North Railroad Company v. Red Wolf* (1999), and the Tenth Circuit Court of Appeals issued an opinion with a concurring opinion that mocked the application of Navajo common law in the case of *Atkinson Trading Company, Inc. v. Shirley* (2000). Given the history of the use of Indian law in American jurisprudence, those appellate courts could not say that it is not "law" or that Indian courts cannot apply their own law, but Indian customary law is essentially a dead letter.

Those larger policy-level obstructions are in place despite warnings to the central government of serious problems. For example, when Bill Clinton was president of the United States, he had a progressive attorney general who implemented an Office of Tribal Justice within the U.S. Justice Department to focus on American Indian issues and among her initiatives was an order to the Bureau of Justice Statistics to compile a statistical analysis of problems in Indian Country. It published a sensational report in February 1999 that painted a picture of severe violence in Indian Country, including extremely high victimization of Indian women and inordinately high levels of interracial crimes against American Indians (Bureau of Justice Statistics 1999). As justice planners whose focus is Indian Country took a closer look at the foundations of the statistics and the report's conclusions, it became apparent that the bureau did not do a good job. It failed to note that the databases of the more than four hundred federally "recognized" Indian tribes of the United States were poor in both design and function (due to federal neglect), that state databases that track criminal offenses and victimization of Indians were poor, and that the bureau rushed to publication as a public relations move on the part of the U.S. Justice Department.

Whether this report was accurate or not, when the prior authorization statute for the Violence Against Women Act (VAWA) expired, there was a great deal of debate not only over its impact on the sovereignty of American Indian nations but over statistical indications that American Indian women were being sexually assaulted in grossly disproportionate numbers and whether there was a need to do something about that. One of the issues was the interracial sexual assaults on American Indian women and the obvious means to address that, which would have been to return statutory recognition to American Indian tribal jurisdiction over all offenders within tribal "Indian Country," which had been taken away by the Major Crimes Act (1885) and the *Oliphant* decision (an important discussion prevented here by space limitations). There was also the issue of providing adequate financial support for policing, prosecution, criminal defense,

Indian courts, and incarceration or probation systems. Instead, the 2013 Violence Against Women Act legislation and the Tribal Law and Order Act (2010) provided that rather than recognize American Indian law and justice systems as they were touted to do, there would be only limited support in competitive grants for those Indian tribes that amended their statutes to provide for procedural protection for Indian defendants (Tribal Law and Policy Institute 2016). There are other issues as well: the Federal Bureau of Investigation, which handles offenses in Indian Country, puts a low priority on Indian Country cases; U.S. attorneys who are political appointees find no glory in prosecuting crime in Indian Country; and the federal legislative and justice bureaucracy neglects American Indian tribes. There is also a lot of legislative hostility to Indian tribes by the American political Right.

THE VIABILITY OF INDIGENOUS JUSTICE INSTITUTIONS

There is a serious question about the viability of American Indian or Indigenous self-governance in general, and justice institutions in particular. With the way that Indian law and institutions have been consistently denigrated, the serious question is if they can continue to persist. The answer is, "Yes, maybe."

World War II was a watershed for Indian self-governance and law because it marked the start of the industrialization of Indian reservations, dilution of on-reservation populations, and major language and culture loss. Despite that, it cannot be said that upcoming generations of American Indians do not care about their inherited languages and traditions or think Indian culture and law are gone. One of the most striking pieces of evidence of that reality, as mentioned earlier, is the spontaneous movement of Indians (and supporters) of all generations to the Standing Rock Indian Reservation in North Dakota for an unsuccessful attempt to block a petroleum pipeline. Even so, the movement against DAPL continues with renewed and improved plans to continue the struggle—attempts to deny funding for the pipeline, criminal defense of the arrests made there, and new legal and nonlegal initiatives that show that Indian America intends to revive itself into something vibrant.

Two problems affecting this promise of cultural and legal resurgence are the intrusion of alien law and institutions in Indian Country affairs and the fact that non-Indian promises for the support of Indian institutions (such as Westernized tribal courts; emerging customary systems like Navajo peacemaking; and the bureaucratic machinery of tribal police and social service agencies) are not responsive to Indian needs or desires. Twentieth-century progressivism is a failure. The Indian Reorganization Act of 1934 was intended to recognize tribal government so that it would have the governmental power to control affairs in Indian Country under local law. Hostility to Indian government following World War II led to a statute popularly referred to as "Public Law 280" that gave some states mandatory criminal and civil jurisdiction in Indian Country and other states discretionary criminal and civil jurisdiction (Pub. L. No. 280 [1953]). This law greatly restricted tribal criminal and civil jurisdiction over their own lands. So while the Indian Reorganization Act authorized tribal governmental power, the United States, through the states, kept control over the provision of governmental functions and services in Indian Country.

American Indian activism in the late 1960s and early 1970s prompted a move to shift monies for essential governmental services to Indian tribes so they could deliver them, but the Indian governments were never funded at the same levels as when services were provided by federal agencies and bureaucracy limited the scope of tribal governmental functions. When it came to tribal policing, prosecution and defense functions, courts, and corrections, the funding was never sufficient to address the actual need and Indian tribes either did not have the income to fund those functions or had to devote income such as monies from resource development to other needs. American Indian nations continue to survive in extreme poverty and the methods of federal allocations of funding, coupled with permitting unconscionable business practices in resource extraction (including massive environmental damage by extraction industries), make it impossible for Indian nations to compete in resource development by using Western law and justice methods. Additionally, these extraction methods are alien to tribal cultures, and aside from being inefficient and wasteful, they often conflict with Indigenous perceptions of right and the wants and needs of communities. Other remedies are necessary, as #NODAPL illustrated, where the alien powers of the U.S. government interfere to hinder Indigenous law and Indigenous methods of justice.

WHAT IS TO BE DONE?

There have been attempts in Indian Country to nourish Indigenous law and justice methods. Indigenous justice still exists, although it has been ignored or excluded from the practice of international comparative law despite more than five centuries of contact and recognition of it. Attempts to use Western-styled tribal court systems to articulate traditional law in written decisions in the English language are frustrated by rejection of customary law and decisions by federal courts (for example, *Burlington Northern Railroad v. Red Wolf* [1999] and *Atkinson Trading Company* [2000]), interference with the exercise of criminal or civil jurisdiction over non-Indians, and dependence on federal funding that will not come.

Two approaches are needed if the obstructions are to be addressed. The first has to do with will and the second has to do with institutions. There is a common situation in Indian Country where Indian adults bemoan the fact that their children and grandchildren do not speak their own languages, do not know their own cultures, and do not practice the ancient ceremonies. One of the struggles of American Indian justice institutions is finding monies from various sources, but it is possible. When the Navajo Nation Judicial Branch bootstrapped American moral panic about gangs, it received a grant to study gangs in the Navajo Nation using a traditional law approach that sees gangs as *naayéé*, or a Navajo "monster" ("thing that gets in the way of a successful life") (Zion 2000). The Navajo Nation is divided into geographic areas called "agencies," and the grant was used to hold public focus group meetings in each area. The meetings in four agencies were attended largely by adult service providers and community leaders, but the hearings in one also featured a turnout of high school aged youth. The consensus of the meetings as a whole was that the young have lost their language and traditions and the most obvious defect was the failure of adults to personally foster language and culture. Outside education (boarding schools) and inroads on Navajo culture prompted those adult shortcomings, but the need was recognized.

Many young Navajos defied this consensus of loss when they went to Standing Rock, North Dakota, to confront the police and pipeline drillers, and many of them went with parents, aunts and uncles, and elders. They returned with a lot of zeal and energy, but they are now being frustrated. There was a meeting of youth and parents in one New Mexico community where the youth expressed their desire to confront the situation in the Navajo Nation but elders expressed their fear of the specter of the army returning (anonymous informant 2017). That fear is still strong and it hinders community organizing against either the "White Father" or his Navajo adherents. The issue with "will" is the need for a conscious community effort, possibly prompted by energetic and intelligent young Indians, to reach out to their elders to give them the courage to lead and teach.

The second action is reflected in two institutional needs: The first is for existing "institutions," by way of traditional leaders who have the knowledge of community lore and values, to get recognized and supported in a revival movement. That movement can be nourished by existing American Indian community colleges and Indians at nearby state institutions who can fund means to support community activities. Second, the Standing Rock movement is, consciously or unconsciously, nourished by mobilization in other parts of the world—Latin America in particular— around revival movements. Indians in Mexico and Bolivia were active in negotiating and promoting the Declaration on the Rights of Indigenous Peoples and we see a lot of movement in Mexico and Bolivia in support of community initiatives and political organizing.

There are no firm recommendations in this chapter because these actions are nascent. Those who participated in the drafting of the declaration, who work in Indigenous communities, and who actively pursue Indigenous law and government can see what is happening with the youthful and mature campaigners from Standing Rock and in developments in Latin America. One of the lessons is that it is possible to break free of the bureaucratic restraints of leadership that are overly amenable to forces that are inimical to true Indian interests and an impediment to positive change.

Freedom to revive and maintain true Indigenous law and to build new institutions to use it will not come from the central government nor from tribal bureaucracies. We know from history that Indigenous law and institutions were excluded from the canon of comparative law, but some inroads are being made. The only real value to this is that Indigenous law and institutionalization are now being recorded so they can be disseminated through Indigenous youth. The groundwork is there and an Indigenous cadre can be nourished to make it bear fruit (see, for example, Fanon 1963; Debray 1967; Freire 1997; Davis 2016).

The possibility for advancement in the United States may come from a greater appreciation of the historical underpinnings of Indian law in past decisional law (recognizing the defects in a lot of statutory law) and newly developing initiatives. For example, there is a soft law process in the development of uniform standards for business practices that comply with human rights law, and UNDRIP is in fact being recognized as its principles are applied to business regulation, standards for human rights for business, planning based on surveys of need, and proposals to meet needs or violations of rights. International human rights law is now developing outside the usual model of State practice, as agreed-upon international standards to measure the application of rights-granting documents are being negotiated in informal international fora. The concluding points of this chapter are that there are centuries of law and practice in favor of Indigenous rights, and as traditional Indigenous principles are being rediscovered and discussed, they are being incorporated in contemporary agreements and understandings with the active participation of Indigenous leaders and their own lawyers.

NOTE

1.   There is a more technical and detailed treatment of the precedents discussed in this section in James W. Zion and Robert Yazzie (1997). The article was prepared as a briefing for an inter-American conference on implementing the constitutional right to Indigenous law and institutions in Bolivia, Prevención de Conflictos y Solución en Comunidades Indígenas, Cochabamba, Bolivia, March 21–23, 1995, where there was a presentation on Navajo peacemaking as an Indigenous dispute resolution model.

REFERENCES

Berman, Harold J. 1983. *Law and Revolution: The Formation of the Western Legal Tradition*. Cambridge, MA: Harvard University Press.

Bureau of Justice Statistics. 1999. *American Indians and Crime*. Washington, DC: Government Printing Office.

Burns, Robert I., ed. 2001. *Las Siete Partidas*. 5 volumes. Translated by S. P. Scott. Philadelphia: University of Pennsylvania Press.

Capotorti, Francesco. 1979. *Study on the Rights of Persons Belonging to Ethnic, Religious and Linguistic Minorities*. New York: United Nations No. E/CN.4/Sub. 2/384/ Rev. 1.

Casas, Bartolomé de las. (1542) 1979, translator J. P. (1656). *Tears of the Indians: Being an Historical and True Account of the Cruel Massacres and Slaughters of Above Twenty Millions of Innocent People Committed by the Spaniards in the Islands of Hispaniola, Cuba, Jamaica, Etc.: As, Also, in the Continent of Mexico, Peru, and Other Places of the West Indies, to the Total Destruction of Those Countries*. London: J. C. for Nath. Brook.

Commission on Security and Cooperation in Europe. 1979. *Fulfilling Our Promises: The United States and the Helsinki Final Act*. Washington, DC: The Commission. https://www.csce.gov/international-impact/publications/fulfilling -our-promises-united-states-and-helsinki-final-act-2.

Crow, John A. 1963. *Spain: The Root and the Flower*. Berkeley: University of California Press.

Davis, Angela. 2016. *Freedom Is a Constant Struggle*. Chicago: Haymarket Books.

Debray, Régis. 1967. *Revolution in the Revolution?* New York: Grove Press.

Fanon, Frantz. 1963. *The Wretched of the Earth*. New York: Grove Weidenfeld.

Freire, Paulo. 1970. *Pedagogy of the Oppressed*. New York: Continuum.

Fuentes, Carlos. 1992. *The Buried Mirror: Reflections on Spain and the New World*. Boston: Houghton Mifflin.

Garnsey, Peter, and Richard R. Saller. 1987. *The Roman Empire*. Berkeley: University of California Press.

Glendon, Mary Ann, Michael W. Gordon, and Christopher Osakwe. 1982. *Comparative Legal Traditions*. St. Paul, MN: West Publishing.

Kamen, Henry. 2005. *Spain, 1469–1714: A Society of Conflict*. 3rd ed. Harlow, UK: Pearson Longman.

Morey, William C. 1900. *Outlines of Roman Law*. New York: G. P. Putnam's Sons.

Phillips, John. (1542) 1970. "Preface." In *Tears of the Indians: Being an Historical and True Account of the Cruel Massacres and Slaughters of Above Twenty Millions of Innocent People Committed by the Spaniards in the Islands of Hispaniola, Cuba, Jamaica, Etc.: As, Also, in the Continent of Mexico, Peru, and Other Places of the West Indies, to the Total Destruction of Those Countries*, by Bartolome de las Casas [translator J. P. 1656]. London: J. C. for Nath. Brook.

Potter, David 2009. *Ancient Rome: A New History*. New York: Thames & Hudson.

Smith, Joseph H. 1950. *Appeals to the Privy Council from the American Plantations*. New York: Columbia University Press.

Tribal Law and Policy Institute. 2016. "Guide for Drafting or Revising Tribal Laws to Implement the Tribal Law and Order Act (TLOA) Enhanced Sentencing and the Violence Against Women Act Reauthorization of 2013 (VAWA 2013), Special Domestic Violence Criminal Jurisdiction." Los Angeles: The Institute.

U.S. Census. 2012. *The American Indian and Alaska Native Population: 2010.* Washington, DC: U.S. Census Bureau.

Vitoria, Francisco. 1991. *Vitoria Political Writings.* Edited by Anthony Pagden and Jeremy Lawrance. Cambridge: Cambridge University Press.

Zion, James W. 2000. "Finding and Knowing the Gang *Nayee*—Field-Initiated Gang Research Project." Window Rock, AZ: Judicial Branch of the Navajo Nation.

———. 2017. "Confrontation at Standing Rock: The Future of Indigenous Resistance in the United States." *Verdict* 23 (2): 3–13.

Zion, James W., and Robert Yazzie. 1997. "Indigenous Law in North America in the Wake of Conquest." *Boston College International & Comparative Law Review* 20:55–84; reprinted in Porter, Robert, ed. 2005. *Sovereignty, Colonialism and the Indigenous Nations*, Durham, NC: Carolina Academic Press.

LEGAL RESOURCES

Atkinson Trading Company, Inc. v. Shirley 210 F.3d 1247 (10th Cir. 2000)

Burlington North Railroad Company v. Red Wolf 196 F.2d 1059 (9th Cir. 1999)

Calvin's Case 77 Eng. Rep. 377, 398 (K.B. 1608)

Campbell v. Hall, 1 Cowp. 204, 209, 98 ER 1045 (K.B. 1774)

The Case of Tanistry 80 Eng. Rep. 516, 520 (K.B. 1608)

Ex Parte Crow Dog 109 U.S. 556, 572 (1883)

Helsinki Final Act (1975)

Indian Reorganization Act 25 U.S.C. ch. 14, subch. V § 461 et seq (1934)

International Court of Justice (1945)

International Covenant on Civil and Political Rights. resolution 2200A (XXI) (1976)

Johnson v. M'Intosh, 21 U.S. (8 Wheat.) 543, 543–6. 2 (1823)

Jones v. Meehan 175 U.S. 1, 29 (1899)

The Navajo Treaty (1868)

Omichund v. Barker 125 Eng. Rep. 1310, 1312 (Ch. 1744)

Public Law 280. 18 U.S.C. § 1162, 28 U.S.C. § 1360, and 25 U.S.C. §§ 1321–1326 (1953)

Royal Proclamation (1763)

Statute of the International Court of Justice 33 UNTS 933 (1945)

Tribal Law and Order Act 124 Stat. 2258 (2010)

United Nations Declaration on the Rights of Indigenous Peoples. Resolution No. 61/295 (2007)

United States v. Quiver 241 U.S. 602, 606 (1916)

Violence Against Women Reauthorization Act. Public Law 113–4 (2013)

2

TRADITIONAL AMERICAN INDIAN JUSTICE

THE HONORABLE RAYMOND D. AUSTIN

THIS CHAPTER will cover two major topics that are normally seen as the core of traditional American Indian justice in the United States: (1) tribal customary law and its use in dispute resolution and (2) traditional dispute resolution forums and their role in modern Indian nation justice systems. Traditional justice institutions like peacemaking and modern institutions like courts and alternative dispute resolution mechanisms such as mediation and arbitration are found in American Indian nation dispute resolution systems. The general term "American Indian peacemaking" identifies the traditional, nonadversarial justice institution that the Indian people invented and established to resolve disputes. In addition, American Indian justice is affected by the U.S. Supreme Court's active hostility toward Indian customary law and the modern tribal courts' exercise of jurisdiction over non-Indian litigants as defendants. Apparently, the Supreme Court is working toward the day when Indian nations will have absolutely no adjudicatory and regulatory jurisdictions over non-Indians on Indian reservations.

We should first put this chapter in perspective. Although many tribal codes authorize use of customary law (or Indian common law), few federally recognized Indian nations in the United States actually use it, and even fewer have a functioning traditional justice institution to complement their courts. The federal government now recognizes 573 American Indian nations as federally recognized tribes (USDOI n.d.). More than half of these Indian nations have their own laws and dispute resolution systems, including courts and peacemaking. Some of these Indian nations have also retained their unique customs and traditions to varying degrees, so one should not point to a custom and declare it applicable to all Indian nations.[1] Incorporating Indian custom into tribal court decision-making is primarily (perhaps 90 percent) procedural, and the rest involves application of the custom to facts to resolve the issue before the court.

I rely primarily on the methods that the Navajo Nation courts use to incorporate and empower its customary law (or Navajo common law). I also discuss Navajo peacemaking to show how traditional process and customs are used as part of traditional Indian justice. The world knows the Navajo Nation has a well-developed body of customary law and a highly regarded peacemaking program. The Navajo Nation is at the forefront of Indigenous peoples' efforts to revitalize and use customary law and traditional methods of dispute resolution in modern dispute resolution and community problem-solving.

AMERICAN INDIAN CUSTOMARY LAW

We begin by examining the traditional Navajo perspective of law. The Navajo word for law is *bee haz'áanii*. A literal interpretation of *bee haz'áanii* could be stated in English as "by it which a certain condition or state exists" (Austin 2009, 41). The words "condition" and "state" refer to the state of things at a given time in the universe, in the world, or in a human society. The desired condition or state that Navajos strive for individually and in Navajo society as a whole is *hózhó*. The English words "peace, balance, and harmony" are close describers of *hózhó* (Austin 2009, 53–56 [discussing *hózhó*]). Witherspoon (1975, 8) states, "The Navajo concept of '[*hózhó*]' refers to that state of affairs where everything is in its proper place and functioning in harmonious relationship to everything else." The problem with trying to translate Navajo concepts into English is that there is usually no equivalent concept in English. The "it" in my interpretational phrase above refers to the doctrines, principles, norms, customs, and traditions that maintain the desired condition or state at a given time.

The condition of *hózhó* is not static but full of energy, movement, activity, and progression. Navajos believe in the existence of doctrines, principles, and rules that promote, adjust, and maintain relations and relationships among all things and beings in the universe, in the world, and in a human society, including Navajo society. Relations and relationships are important concepts embedded in American Indian cultures because they are central to societal cohesion and solidarity. Most American Indians, including Navajos, believe in universal kinship or the traditional principle that everything in the universe is interconnected, interrelated, and interdependent. Universal kinship directs the effects of any activity, or its energy, to travel along the kinship connections to impact other things and beings throughout the relations. At the human level, conflict among members of a community affects each disputant's family, extended relatives, and members of the community.

Although traditional Navajos—and there are a few still around—know *bee haz'áanii* as the norms, customs, and traditions that underlie, repair, and maintain *hózhǫ́*, the modern meaning of the term encompasses statutory law, court-made law, administrative regulations, and consuetudinary law (values, norms, customs, and traditions, or American Indian common law).² *Hózhǫ́* is a preeminent doctrine and drives the Navajo world; thus, peace, harmony, and balance are emphasized in ceremonies and everyday life and *hózhǫ́* is the ultimate goal of all relations and relationships in Navajo society. When strife appears, customary law and peacemaking, a traditional reconciliation process, are used to restore *hózhǫ́* by repairing and healing relationships between the disputants and their families, relatives, and clans.

The Navajo dispute restoration process is referred to here as the Navajo jurisprudence model. The Navajo jurisprudence model contains the essentials that apply in traditional Navajo peacemaking (called *Hózhǫ́ǫ́jí Naat'áanii*) and in the modern Navajo Nation courts. The model works this way: first, there is the state of *hózhǫ́* (harmony, balance, and peace); second, *hózhǫ́* is disrupted by *anáhóót'í*, meaning a disrupter (*naayéé'*) has caused a problem or issue to arise; third, law (either modern or consuetudinary) is applied to resolve the problem or issue; and finally, the state of *hózhǫ́* is restored. The overall goal of traditional dispute resolution (i.e., peacemaking) is restoring positive relationships so all individuals affected by the dispute can return to a life of peace, balance, and harmony. Traditional dispute resolution also benefits participants through airing of grievances, acknowledgment of wrongs, apology between disputants and relatives, and healing of all. Good relationships among members allow an Indian society to function in peace, balance, and harmony.

People not familiar with American Indian cultures usually want to know where one finds Indian customary law. The answer to this question is neither quick nor easy. America's past relationship with American Indians is littered with federal Indian policies, including the Indian removal policy, reservation policy, assimilation policy, allotment policy, and termination policy, that have extensively damaged, and in most cases irreparably damaged, Indian languages, cultures, religions, property holdings, and the lives of generations of American Indians.

Most federal Indian policies were carried out with a malignant intent to eradicate American Indian tribalism—that is, terminate Indian identity, languages, cultures, and religious practices—using a civilizing and Christianizing strategy. The federal government's Indian assimilation policy is a prime example of this destructive intent. The assimilation policy produced the federal Indian boarding school system to strip children of their Indian identity, the allotment system to break up reservation lands and make them available to white people, and the use of law in the Court of Indian Offenses to ban Indian cultures.

In 1883 the Commissioner of Indian Affairs, without statutory authorization (and probably without constitutional authorization) and without the consent of Indian nations, established the Court of Indian Offenses, a system of criminal laws and courts designed to operate under a set of rules and procedures created by the Bureau of Indian Affairs (BIA). A federal district court said the Court of Indian Offenses was not a real court but rather another government tool to "civilize" the Indians. According to *United States v. Clapox* (1888):

> These "courts of Indian offenses" are not the constitutional courts provided for in section 1, art. 3, Const., which congress only has the power to "ordain and establish," but mere educational and disciplinary instrumentalities, by which the government of the United States is endeavoring to improve and elevate the condition of these dependent tribes to whom it sustains the relation of guardian. In fact, the reservation itself is in the nature of a school, and the Indians are gathered there, under the charge of an agent, for the purpose of acquiring the habits, ideas, and aspirations which distinguish the civilized from the uncivilized man.

The rules were actually a criminal code that "criminalized traditional Indian dances, traditional marriage and divorce, community and social gatherings, traditional probate, traditional burials and mourning practices, and religious practices of medicine men" (Austin 2011, 356; see also Prucha 1973, 300–305; Hagan 1980, 104–25). Included in the federal government's ban of Native cultures was the use of customary law and traditional dispute resolution methods. Punishment for committing any of these "Indian crimes" ranged from incarceration and fines to hard labor and denial of food.

The direct attack on Indian cultures and traditional practices throughout America resulted in a substantial loss of customary law, traditions, and practices—the essentials of traditional dispute resolution and use of customary law. The huge challenge for Indian nations today is rediscovering, revitalizing, and using traditional laws and methods in the modern dispute resolution context and in community problem-solving. Some Indian nations today do not use customary law or traditional dispute resolution methods because either they are not interested or no one in the community knows them. Even lack of knowledge of customs and norms, while challenging, should not deter use of customary law. American Indian Peoples have some common customs, norms, and traditions that can be tapped, including the concepts of balance, harmony, respect, relations, and relationships, including kinship networks. Other Indian nations may have members who know fragments of old customs and norms that can be revitalized and used. Some Indian nations have retained a substantial amount of language, culture, and religious narratives that supply customary law to their legal systems and governments. The latter kind of Indian nation usually has a large number of speakers of the tribe's language. While I frequently advocate for use of customary law in tribal court decision-making, it is up to each Indian nation, as a sovereign, to decide for itself if it wants to do so.

American Indian customary law for the most part is not written or categorized under indexed headings in books on a particular tribe's culture, religion, and traditional governing institutions. Scholarship on Indian customary law is still small, and both a developed body of customary law and scholarship on the subject should increase as more American Indians revitalize their customs and norms and utilize them in their modern government operations, dispute resolution forums, and daily lives. The following books contain excellent scholarship on American Indian customary law and traditional dispute resolution methods: Austin (2009), Llewellyn and Hoebel (1941), Richland (2008), Strickland (1975), and Nielsen and Zion (2005). Indian customary law and traditional dispute resolution methods, including peacemaking, fall under the oral tradition; a longstanding and valuable tradition that causes the U.S. Supreme Court to suspect unfairness when the courts of American Indian nations exercise jurisdiction over non-Indians.[3] Part of Justice Souter's concurring opinion in *Nevada v. Hicks* (2001) summarizes this suspicion:

> Tribal courts . . . differ from other American courts . . . in their structure, in the substantive law they apply, and in the independence of their judges. Although some tribal courts . . . "are guided by written codes, rules, procedures, and guidelines," tribal law is still frequently unwritten, being based instead "on the values, mores, and norms of a tribe and expressed in its customs, traditions, and practices," and is often "handed down orally or by example from one generation to another." The resulting law applicable in tribal courts is a complex "mix of tribal codes and federal, state and traditional law," which would be unusually difficult for an outsider to sort out. [Citations omitted]

White Americans are suspicious of people who "won't assimilate." The people who "won't assimilate" allegedly diverge from the so-called values of the dominant American society. In spite of what the non-Indian world thinks, the oral tradition is deeply embedded in American Indian thinking, cultures, languages, religions, and ways of life. Until we find abundant writings on American Indian customary law, the oral tradition will remain the most important and reliable access to that knowledge.

Customary law is important to litigation in tribal courts and tribal court decision-making. The Indian people should work to revitalize and preserve their cultures, and that includes their traditional laws and dispute resolution methods. The constitutions, codes, and court rules of many Indian nations contain a choice of law rule that requires their court to use customary law to interpret the constitution, statutes, and administrative regulations. In the absence of any applicable statutory law, the choice of law provision usually authorizes use of customary law as substantive law to apply in a case. For example, the Navajo Nation choice of law statute sets forth these requirements:

A. In all cases the courts of the Navajo Nation shall first apply applicable Navajo Nation statutory laws and regulations to resolve matters in dispute before the courts. The courts shall utilize Diné bi beenahhaz'áanii (Navajo Traditional, Customary, Natural or Common Law) to guide the interpretation of Navajo Nation statutory laws and regulations. The courts shall also utilize Diné bi beenahhaz'áanii whenever Navajo Nation statutes or regulations are silent on matters in dispute before the courts.

B. To determine the appropriate utilization and interpretation of Diné bi beenahhaz'áanii, the court shall request, as it deems necessary, advice from Navajo individuals widely recognized as being knowledgeable about Diné bi beenahhaz'áanii. (7 N.N.C. § 204[A]–[B])

The Hoopa Valley Tribe's choice of law provision is probably one of the most detailed among tribes, but its preference for use of customary law is similar to that of Navajo and other Indian nations. First, the parties can stipulate to have the case resolved "by tribal law and custom" and "agree to abide by the decision" (Hoopa Valley Tribal Code 2008). This provision should allow non-Indian parties to stipulate to the use of customary law. The provision then declares the tribe's traditional law to be its common law and requires its court to apply relevant common law to the issue before the court (Hoopa Valley Tribal Code 2008). The choice of law provision next requires the court to give initial preference to the Hoopa Valley Tribe Constitution and Bylaws and statutory laws (Hoopa Valley Tribal Code 2008). Thereafter, if "no written Tribal law applies to a cause of action or the issues involved in an action, the Court will look to the Tribe's traditional law and if it finds the traditional law to be applicable in settling the dispute, will base its decision on traditional Tribal law" (Hoopa Valley Tribal Code 2008).

The customary law provision that appears in most tribal codes can be traced to the BIA law and order regulations for the Court of Indian Offenses. For example, the law and order regulations approved by the secretary of the interior on November 27, 1935, and reissued in 1937, provided as follows:

"161.23 Law applicable in civil actions. In all civil cases the Court of Indian Offenses shall apply . . . any ordinances or customs of the tribe, not prohibited by . . . Federal laws."

Where any doubt arises as to the customs and usages of the tribe the Court may request the advice of counsellors [sic] familiar with these customs and usages (25 C.F.R. § 161.1 [1938]).

The Court of Indian Offenses used the law and order regulations as laws and procedural rules in its proceedings. Indian nations were encouraged to adopt constitutions and tribal codes following passage of the 1934 Indian Reorganization Act. Consistent with the policy behind the Indian Reorganization Act—giving Indians control of their own affairs—the BIA attempted to reverse the damage done to Indian cultures by encouraging tribes to use their customs and traditions in proceedings before the Court of Indian Offenses. Even then, many Indian nations lacked the expertise and resources to draft new laws based on their culture so they adopted provisions of the BIA law and order regulations "as their initial laws on domestic relations, criminal offenses, and court procedures" (Austin 2011, 363). For instance, in 1959, the Navajo Nation adopted the BIA law and order regulations as Navajo law: "Pending the adoption by the Navajo Tribe and approval thereof by the Secretary of the Interior of a permanent law and order code, the law and order regulations of the Department of the Interior, 25 CFR 11, . . . are hereby adopted as tribal law" (Navajo Tribal Council Resolution No. CJA-1–59 [Jan. 6, 1959]). The Indian nations that adopted the customary law provision from the BIA law and order regulations retained its original intent, if not the actual wording, when they wrote the provision into their codes.

If an Indian nation's code is silent on whether customary law should be used in its court, should the litigants present customary law and ask the court to apply the custom? I have been asked this question and my response is worth repeating:

> We live in a world of the written word, which has conditioned some people to believe that the written word is more valuable and credible than the oral tradition. When tribal court judges cannot locate a written provision, such as in the tribe's constitution, code, or court rule, authorizing them to use

customary law, they might conclude that they do not have authority to do so. This reasoning is not consistent with either the ruling in *Williams v. Lee*, that Indian nations possess a right to make their own laws and be ruled by them, or the modern federal policy of self-determination[.] It would also mean tribal court judges are denying the use of Indian customary law by allowing western concepts on the application of law to control what is essentially tribal court decision making. Modern Indians and tribal government officials can, at times, think like the ancestors to construct frameworks to apply to internal problems. Relying on traditional thinking to construct methods and solve problems is "doing sovereignty" the American Indian way. (Austin 2011, 361)

Traditional thinking, or "thinking like an Indian" means pondering how disputes were settled in American Indian societies before Western ways came to dominate. The old-time, traditional peacemaker did not have to ask the chief or the council for authorization to apply customs, norms, or traditions to settle disputes in the community. The authorization "was inherent in the tribe's culture and longstanding dispute resolution practices. In other words, disputes had to be settled so harmony, peace, and positive relationships prevailed within the community. . . . The past provides assurance that a modern court of an Indian nation can tap its own culture and traditional dispute resolution practices for authorization to use customary law" (Austin 2011, 361). A tribal court judge can and should incorporate customary law into tribal court jurisprudence even if the tribal code is silent on the matter. Each time a tribal court judge applies custom and writes it into the court's decision, customary law is identified, written down, and preserved. "Thinking like an Indian" ensures that American Indians are "doing sovereignty" using their own ways—the Indian way.

The process that different tribal courts use to incorporate Indian customary law into tribal court jurisprudence usually advances along a familiar procedural path. The initial task is locating the custom, norm, or tradition that would apply to the problem. The next task is introducing the custom, norm, or tradition into litigation through written materials, or through the testimony of an expert witness on unwritten customary law, or through judicial notice, or a combination of these methods. Finally, if the customary law is relevant, the court will apply it.

Although the task of finding customary law may appear monumental to the layman, it is not difficult for lawyers because as skilled researchers they know how to discover written and unwritten materials. In fact, lawyers who practice in the Navajo Nation courts find and argue Navajo customary law, not only in the Navajo Nation courts, but also in state and federal courts.[4] Indian customs, norms, and traditions can be unwritten (again due to the oral tradition), but that does not mean it cannot be found. Similar to "other kinds of legal research, a tribe's customary law can be found in literature (e.g., books, research studies, articles, or court cases) or by locating individuals, usually elders, who carry that knowledge" (Austin 2011, 363).

Knowledgeable Indian elders are valuable sources on norms, customs, and traditions that serve as customary law. Knowledgeable Indian elders are the "tribal encyclopedia" because they carry the tribe's history, culture, language, and religious tenets and practices in their heads. Other individuals who have knowledge of customary law are peacemakers (they work extensively with customary law to settle disputes), retired tribal court judges, ceremonial practitioners (people non-Indians call medicine men or medicine women), and individuals who live a traditional lifestyle. Once the custom or norm is identified, it must be examined for relevancy and then formally introduced into litigation. If the custom or norm will be used for a purpose other than litigation, it should still be relevant to the problem at hand.

A person who carries traditional knowledge can be qualified as an expert witness and testify on relevant customs, norms, or traditions before a tribal court. Before going further, it is worth noting that a guide for finding and determining customary law and for introducing that law into litigation should be written and made available to court practitioners and the Indian nation's judges. The guidelines can be placed in the code, court rules, or in an appellate court opinion. In the case of *In re Estate of Belone* (1987), the Navajo Nation Supreme Court set forth guidelines on locating and using Navajo customary law in the Navajo Nation courts.

The procedure for getting customary law before the court involves a few steps. First, the trial judge maintains discretion over the qualifying of an expert and admitting of customary law. The proposed expert's knowledge of custom and the manner of acquisition of that knowledge are two crucial inquiries made during the qualifying of an expert. Second, the party seeking to introduce customary law must demonstrate its relevance to the issue before the court. A custom or norm that is relevant should help the judge or jury understand the facts and issues better. Finally, if a dispute about the proffered customary law arises, the court has discretion to convene a panel of knowledgeable experts, as established in most tribes' choices of law statutes, to discuss the matter and advise the court. Most tribal courts follow this general procedure for introducing customary law into court proceedings. There are, however, times when a knowledgeable person will refuse to disclose customs, norms, or traditions.

In the past, American Indian elders freely disclosed cultural knowledge, including sacred religious tenets, to non-Indian anthropologists, ethnologists, and social scientists. Free flow of cultural knowledge from the Indian to the non-Indian is not the norm today, especially among knowledgeable Navajo elders, because of non-Indian tendencies to mock and ridicule Indian beliefs by calling them myths, fantasies, and superstitions. Any Indigenous knowledge should be analyzed and understood within the context of the culture it comes from. The person who wants to elicit customs, norms, or traditions from an Indigenous knowledge holder should explain the reasons for seeking the knowledge and how it will be used. An Indian knowledge holder may refuse to disclose certain knowledge to anyone, Indian or non-Indian, because of its sacredness (called guarded knowledge). Sacred knowledge can only be disclosed in ceremony or to certain persons (like an apprentice) or between knowledge holders. Nonetheless, Indian elders usually identify customs, norms, or traditions that are applicable to solving legal issues or community problems because they know these cultural norms promote positive relationships and maintain harmony in the community.

Customs, norms, and traditions can be found in creation narratives, clan narratives, fundamental doctrines, tribal history, maxims, traditional stories, ceremonies, songs, prayers, and language. Sources of customary law can also be found in narratives about places, such as geographical features and special places where important and sacred things happened (Basso 1996). The Indian elder taps these sources to identify the applicable customary law.

Language is a rich source of customary law because many Indian languages are verb-based and descriptive. For example, the Navajo word *bił ch'íníyá* literally means "something has slipped past a person" due to the person's carelessness or inattentiveness. Implicit in the word is the understanding that one has control over the matter such that the person can prevent it from escaping. In the legal sense, this word means a party has "failed to take advantage of an opportunity" (see *In re Estate of Kindle* 2006). A missed deadline for filing documents with a court is one such failure. *Bił ch'íníyá*, as Navajo customary law, has the same legal effect as res judicata and finality in American law. Res judicata means a matter conclusively decided by a court is final and cannot be relitigated.

Written materials are other sources of American Indian customary law. The most valuable are tribal appellate court opinions that apply customary law to an issue in the case. Appellate court opinions have precedential value, contribute to a developing body of customary law, and transform oral norms, customs, and traditions into written law. Academic writings by anthropologists, ethnologists, American Indian studies professors, and federal Indian law professors; writings by Indian traders and explorers of the 1800s and 1900s; and writings by Indian authors are also good sources of Indian customary law. Finding customary law takes time but it is worth the effort because Indian customary law provides a unique insight into non-Western ways of thinking about law. Books and articles written on a specific tribe's culture, creation narratives, language, and religious practices and beliefs can contain valuable information on customary law.

The courts of Indian nations, like Western courts in general, have the judicial notice doctrine at hand to recognize relevant Indian norms, values, customs, and traditions as customary law and apply them. Generally, judicial notice means a court can accept a well-known and indisputable fact without requiring a party to prove that fact (*Black's Law Dictionary* 1999). In *In re Estate of Belone*, the Navajo Nation Supreme Court declared that a Navajo Nation judge can take judicial notice of a Navajo custom: "[I]f a custom is generally known within the community, or if it is capable of accurate determination by resort to sources whose accuracy cannot reasonably be questioned, it is proven. . . . [I]n other words, 'judicial notice may only be taken of those facts every damn fool knows.'" *Hopi Indian Credit Association v. Thomas* (1996), the leading Hopi court decision on judicial notice, requires the Hopi trial courts to take judicial notice of "Hopi custom, tradition or culture when it is applicable." The Hopi appellate court also used the general language of judicial notice to establish its rule: "A court may dispense with proof of the existence of Hopi custom, tradition or culture if it finds the custom, tradition or culture to be generally known and accepted within the Hopi Tribe" (*Hopi Indian Credit Association v. Thomas* 1996).

The judicial notice doctrine is a valuable tool that Indian nation courts can use to develop a body of written customary law. A tribe's culture and dispute resolution goals should inform the tribal court's use of the judicial notice doctrine. A tribal court judge who speaks the tribe's language has an advantage over a nonspeaker because the speaker is embedded in the tribe's culture and is uniquely qualified to extract the full meaning and understanding of the tribe's norm, custom, or tradition to determine whether judicial notice is appropriate. Even if the judge is sure a norm, custom, or tradition is customary law, he or she should still allow the litigants to be heard on the matter to ensure that the customary law is not outdated, irrelevant, or in conflict with, say, a clan custom or local custom.

After the customary law has been introduced into court proceedings, the tribal court has the duty of applying the customary law. This is an important duty because recognition of customary law creates precedent and contributes to growing a body of customary law. The judge should do a thorough analysis and explain to the reader why the norm, custom, or tradition is customary law; explain the origin and source of the customary law such as a creation narrative, clan narrative, or the tribe's language; interpret or describe the custom or norm; and explain how and why the custom would apply to the facts and issue at hand. A clear analysis provides future litigants and Indian nation courts with a model to build a body of customary law.

Customary law has been used in traditional Indian dispute resolution since time immemorial. The Bureau of Indian Affairs prohibited traditional dispute resolution during the heyday of the Court of Indian Offenses along with other cultural practices. In spite of the bureau's efforts, some Indian nations retained this method of dispute resolution, called peacemaking today, and are actively using it in conjunction with or alongside their modern tribal courts. Peacemaking is a fundamental part of traditional American Indian justice.

AMERICAN INDIAN TRADITIONAL
DISPUTE RESOLUTION

Navajo Nation peacemaking is the standard bearer for American Indian peacemaking in the United States. The term peacemaking is used here to refer generally to the various methods Indian nations employ as nonadversarial traditional dispute resolution. Traditional dispute resolution and the customary laws and cultural traditions that are used in that forum are unique to each Indian nation that uses them. American Indian peacemaking comes from the old ways of resolving disputes—ways that were firmly grounded in culture and well established long before the federal government imposed the adversarial system of courts, known as the Court of Indian Offenses, on Indian nations. Some Indian nations, including Navajo, have annexed peacemaking to their court systems, while others keep it independent of the adversarial court system.

Peacemaking, at least Navajo peacemaking, is premised on the belief that parties in dispute and their relatives and respected community members can join together to resolve the dispute at their local community in a nonadversarial setting. A peacemaker, usually a respected member of the community, guides the peacemaking participants during the peacemaking session and on to a consensual solution. Indian values, norms, customs, and traditions are applied to the issue or problem during the peacemaking session. For example, the Oneida Indian Nation of New York requires use of its "religious or other traditional ways of mediation and problem-solving" in peacemaking sessions (Oneida Indian Nation). It is also possible to apply modern statutory law and case law in peacemaking.

Scholars of Navajo common law have noted that nonadversarial methods of dispute resolution such as traditional Indian peacemaking and non-Indian mediation are horizontal systems of justice (Bluehouse and Zion 1993). Equality, maintaining relationships, and making adjustments to bargaining positions among parties to achieve equality are the essential elements of a horizontal system of justice. In a horizontal system of justice, the disputants, with the guidance of a third-party mediator or peacemaker, are assured an active voice in the decision-making process, and the process is not hampered with rigid rules of evidence and procedure. In contrast, the adversarial method of justice, such as courts and other adjudicatory bodies, is a vertical system of justice. The vertical system of justice uses hierarchies of authority, power, and punishment to achieve finality. The vertical system of justice relies on a powerful decision maker (the judge) to make decisions for others (the disputants) based on facts developed through evidence rules and the application of the rule of law. The final decision is enforced through coercive power or the government's police power. American Indian peacemaking and the traditional methods of dispute resolution of most Indigenous Peoples fit the horizontal system of justice.

American Indian peacemaking, as a horizontal system of justice, relies primarily on relationships to restore disputants and their relatives to harmony with each other and maintain peace in the community. A dispute may affect the community and even the entire tribe if the membership is small because relationships forged through kinship connect members of the community. Navajos, and most American Indians, are communally oriented so they view the world from a community perspective. American Indian nations are composed of a set of communities tied together and maintained through relationships such as kinship and the extended family. Because relationship is central to the well-being of community in American Indian societies, traditional dispute resolution's ultimate goal is restoration of positive relations between disputing parties, their families and clans (if the tribe has a clan system), and their community.

Again, using Navajo as an example, relationship is the driving force of the Navajo clan system (called k'éí) and is expressed through kinship terms. Navajos trace descent through their mother's side, so their mother's clan, the "born-of clan," is their clan. The father's clan, the "born-for clan," is the secondary clan. The other two clans are the maternal and paternal grandfathers' clans, which are third and fourth in importance. The clan system plays a vital role in Navajo peacemaking because it regulates the relationships and duties and obligations toward kin that give identity to the Navajo people and provides the dynamic force that maintains Navajo society and culture.

Harmony, balance, and peace, included in the concept of hózhó, prevail when relationships, including kinship, are durable and stable within a community. Disputes among community members upset relationships and disharmony results. A wise and respected peacemaker's services and guidance are then needed to restore harmony, balance, and peace within the community. The peacemaker, usually an elder and a clan relative of the disputants, need not be independent and impartial like a court judge. The parties expect their peacemaker to have prior knowledge of the events causing the dispute and its impact on their families and community. The local communities appoint local individuals as Navajo peacemakers so they have an interest in the community's well-being. Navajo peacemaking, as a dispute resolution program based on tradition, returns and invests dispute resolution functions in the local communities.

These are the general steps the Navajo Nation court system uses to get a case before a peacemaker: (1) a party files a complaint and serves the defendant with the complaint; (2) the defendant may file an answer to the complaint; (3) the court clerk advises both parties that they can consent to peacemaking; (4) after their consent to peacemaking, the parties agree on a peacemaker; (5) the case file goes to the peacemaker and the trial court steps away from the case; (6) the peacemaker sets a date, time, and place of peacemaking and encourages the disputants to invite relatives, elders, and respected community members to the peacemaking session; (7) the peacemaking session is held and a final solution is agreed on and written; and (8) the trial judge reviews the written agreement, and once satisfied, turns it into a final court order. A peacemaking agreement cannot be appealed because the disputants participated in discussions concerning the problem and contributed to the final agreement.

Navajo peacemaking is a traditional justice ceremony, so prayer is used to start and end a session. Authority and power are absent from a peacemaking session because the peacemaker is not a judge and peacemaking is not adversarial. A peacemaker uses persuasion during the session and ensures that everyone has an opportunity to speak to the problem and contribute to a consensual agreement. A peacemaker, respected and skilled with words, cites norms from creation narratives, religious tenets, and rules of kinship to guide a peacemaking session. Navajos believe in participatory democracy, a traditional principle used in peacemaking that ensures free-flowing discussion and allows interested parties a voice in the decision-making process. Peacemaking is essentially egalitarian and nonadversarial, so a peacemaker does not decide or rule on issues for the disputants.

Disputes are highly emotional with attendant animosity between the disputants and their families. An experienced peacemaker uses kinship terms, cultural values, and humor to maintain an amicable and relaxed environment during the session. A peacemaker uses persuasion to keep participants focused on the issues because participants can quickly stray to nonessential topics that divert attention from the main problem. A peacemaker encourages "talking things out" (free-flowing discussion) and use of norms, customs, and traditions to arrive at a consensual solution. Peacemaking is also used to "teach" participants the Navajo cultural values that promote kinship and relationships (called *k'é*). Elders and knowledge holders are encouraged to do the "teaching" using creation narratives, clan stories, religious tenets, history, and personal experiences. The parties and participants arrive at a solution to the problem through consensus.

Depending on the case, solutions can be varied and multiple. For example, if a case involves a party (offender) who has committed assault while drinking, the parties might agree on payment of restitution to the person assaulted (victim); additional compensation to the victim's family to restore positive relations between the families; a traditional ceremony, paid for by the offender's family, to restore the victim's mind, body, and spirit to harmony; and alcohol counseling or admission to an alcohol rehabilitation facility for the offender. Restitution does not have to be monetary, so it can be material items, including jewelry and livestock. Restitution can also be labor for the benefit of the victim's family or service to the community.

Family members and extended relatives are essential participants in peacemaking because they enforce the final agreement by making sure its terms are fulfilled and by keeping the offender in line, especially if the offender has problems with alcohol or drugs. If a party is not adhering to the peacemaking agreement, the relatives will request another session to address the lack of compliance. American Indian peacemaking, although practiced according to each tribe's ways, is flexible and conforms to the parties' and relatives' expectations of justice according to American Indian ways.

CONCLUSION

There are presently 573 American Indian nations that have the political status of federally recognized tribes. Federally recognized tribes have a government-to-government relationship with the United States. We do not know the exact number of recognized Indian nations that have formal governments (i.e., a government that performs executive, legislative, and judicial functions). We also do not know the exact number that have an operating dispute resolution system. The BIA estimates that it provides funding and technical assistance to 225 Indian nations that have a dispute resolution system of some kind (BIA n.d.; see also Kronk 2010, 242n46). The BIA also states that it operates twenty-three Courts of Indian Offenses for tribes that do not operate a court system (BIA n.d.).

Unfortunately, a majority of those 225 American Indian nation court systems do not actively use either or both customary law and a traditional dispute resolution forum based on the nation's own culture. There are various reasons for this. Some Indian nations have lost their culture completely, including language, creation narratives, religious beliefs and practices, and traditional rules of kinship, so no one within the nation can be a source of customary law. Some Indian nations have retained some culture, but there is not enough in the culture to rebuild a body of common law and traditional dispute resolution methods, so attorneys and judges simply ignore them. Some Indian nations may have a provision in their code that allows their courts to use customary law only if all parties are nation members or if the case concerns only a specific area like a juvenile matter. See, for example, the Little River Band of Ottawa Indians Tribal Code (2012). The jurisdiction of the Little River Band's courts is limited to members.

Whatever the reasons for the little use of customary law and traditional methods of dispute resolution, Indian nation officials need to understand that use of traditional ways is "doing sovereignty" the American Indian way. Relying on customary law and traditional methods of dispute resolution ensures perpetuation of American Indian cultures and allows Indian nations to use their own traditional ways of doing things to solve community problems. Hopefully, more and more American Indian nations will see the need to use customary law and traditional methods of dispute resolution and actually use them in the self-governing process.

NOTES

1.　This does not mean that we should discount a modern phenomenon—an emerging use of intertribal common law in the Indian nation courts. See as an example, *Rave v. Reynolds* (1996) (the issue before the court concerned legal standing to challenge the constitutionality of the rules established for the tribe's elections). On intertribal common law, the court states, "The tradition of most Indian tribes in the United States . . . encourages participatory and consensual resolution of disputes, maximizing the opportunity for airing grievances (i.e., hearing), participation, and resolution in the interest of healing the participants and preventing friction within the tribal community."

To what extent scholars and tribal court judges will recognize intertribal common law as another source of law in the tribal courts is presently unknown.

2.   The Navajo Nation Supreme Court explains *bee haz'áanii* in *Bennett v. Navajo Board of Election Supervisors* (1990) this way: "The Navajo word for 'law' is *bee haz'áanii*. While we hear that word popularly used in the sense of laws enacted by the Navajo Nation Council . . . it actually refers to higher law. It means something which is 'way at the top': something written in stone so to speak; something which is absolutely there; and, something like the Anglo concept of natural law. In other words, Navajos believe in a higher law, and as it is expressed in Navajo, there is the concept similar to the idea of unwritten constitutional law."

3.   I have worked with Indian nation courts and American Indian customary law for more than thirty years, and during that time I have not seen a case where an Indian nation court ruled for an Indian party simply because the opposing party was a non-Indian. In fact, an intensive study found that non-Indians won nearly half of the cases they litigated against Navajos in the Navajo Nation courts (Berger 2005).

4.   Members of the Navajo Nation Bar Association are licensed to practice law in the Navajo Nation courts and administrative forums. Members of this association are required annually to take refresher courses on Navajo history and culture, including Navajo common law (customary law), to maintain their licenses.

REFERENCES

Austin, Raymond D. 2009. *Navajo Courts and Navajo Common Law: A Tradition of Tribal Self-Governance.* Minneapolis: University of Minnesota Press.

———. 2011. "American Indian Customary Law in the Modern Courts of American Indian Nations," *Wyoming Law Review* 11 (2): 351–73.

Basso, Keith H. 1996. *Wisdom Sits in Places.* Albuquerque: University of New Mexico Press.

Berger, Bethany R. 2005. "Justice and the Outsider: Jurisdiction over Nonmembers in Tribal Legal Systems." *Arizona State Law Journal* 37:1047–125.

Black's Law Dictionary. 1999. 7th ed. "Judicial Notice." St. Paul, MN: West Publishing Co.

Bluehouse, Philmer, and James W. Zion. 1993. "Hozhooji Naat´aanii: The Navajo Justice and Harmony Ceremony." *Mediation Quarterly* 10 (4): 327–37.

Bureau of Indian Affairs (BIA). n.d. Last accessed August 3, 2017. https://www.bia.gov/FAQs/index.htm.

Hagan, William T. 1980. *Indian Police and Judges.* Lincoln: University of Nebraska Press.

Kronk, Elizabeth Ann. 2010. "American Indian Tribal Courts as Models for Incorporating Customary Law." *Journal of Court Innovation* 3 (2): 231–46.

Llewellyn, Karl N., and Adamson Hoebel. 1941. *The Cheyenne Way: Conflict and Case Law in Primitive Jurisprudence.* Norman: University of Oklahoma Press.

Nielsen, Marianne O., and James W. Zion, eds. 2005. *Navajo Nation Peacemaking: Living Traditional Justice.* Tucson: University of Arizona Press.

Prucha, Francis Paul, ed. 1973. *Americanizing the American Indians: Writings by the "Friends of the Indian," 1880–1900.* Lincoln: University of Nebraska Press.

Richland, Justin B. 2008. *Arguing with Tradition: The Language of Law in Hopi Tribal Court.* Chicago: University of Chicago Press.

Strickland, Rennard. 1975. *Fire and the Spirits: Cherokee Law from Clan to Court.* Norman: University of Oklahoma Press.

U.S. Dept. of the Interior (USDOI) Indian Affairs. n.d. "Programs and Services." Accessed June 21, 2018. https://www.bia.gov/programs-services.

Witherspoon, Gary. 1975. *Navajo Kinship and Marriage.* Chicago: University of Chicago Press.

LEGAL RESOURCES

Bennett v. Navajo Board of Election Supervisors, 6 *Navajo Reporter* 319, 324 (Nav. Sup. Ct.) (1990)

Hoopa Valley Tribal Code, § 2.1.04(a), .05 (Oct. 2.) (2008)

Hopi Indian Credit Association v. Thomas, slip op. at 4, No. AP-001–84 (Hopi Ct. App., Mar. 29) (1996)

Indian Reorganization Act 25 U.S.C.A. § 461 *et seq.* (1934)

In re Estate of Belone, 5 *Navajo Reporter* 161, 165 (Nav. Sup. Ct.) (1987)

In re Estate of Kindle, No. SC-CV-40–05, slip op. at 5–6 (Nav. Sup. Ct., May 18) (2006)

Little River Band of Ottawa Indians Tribal Code, Tribal Courts Ordinances, §§ 6.01, 6.02, and 7.01 (2012)

Navajo Nation Code, 7 N.N.C. § 204(A)-(B) (2005)

Nevada v. Hicks, 533 U.S. 353, 383–85 (2001)

Oneida Indian Nation of New York, Peacemaking Rules, Rule 5(b).

Rave v. Reynolds, 23 *Indian Law Reporter* 6150, 6157 (Winnebago Tribe of Nebraska Supreme Court) (1996)

United States v. Clapox, 35 F. 575, 576 (D. Or.) (1888)

PART II

NATIONAL LAW

INTRODUCTION BY KAREN JARRATT-SNIDER AND MARIANNE O. NIELSEN

Most colonial governments were quite experienced in using national law to control and exploit Indigenous nations, as mentioned in the book's introduction, and as also mentioned, Indigenous people are attempting to use national laws to benefit their communities. Colonial authorities learned the power of law before reaching the "new world," for example, in England's colonization of Scotland and Ireland (Zion 2006). As part of their colonial ideology, the colonists judged the law of Indigenous Peoples to be inferior or nonexistent. Indigenous law interfered inconveniently in the serious business of colonial land and resource acquisition.

It could be argued that today Indigenous Peoples are constrained by more laws than any other diverse group, and many of these laws are discriminatory (Williams 2005). There are many human rights and justice-related issues that are unique to Indigenous America because of the special legal status of Indigenous Americans, and the highly complex jurisdictional issues that resulted from colonial ideologies being institutionalized into federal law and policy (see the introduction to the book). This jurisdictional maze impacts the lives of Indigenous Peoples nearly every day. The authors in this section describe how Indigenous communities have responded in innovative ways by, for example, using health-based legislation to protect sacred sites (Jocks), using tribal elders as expert witnesses in state courts (Siedschlaw), and developing community-level activism to improve services and support legislation to protect Native American women from violence (Fox).

There are some important legal and political contexts for understanding the challenges that Indigenous communities face in these ameliorative efforts. In this introduction we provide context for the issues and resolutions described by the authors. First, we describe the concept of federalism, which at times erodes sovereignty—such as in the Termination Policy era when criminal jurisdiction transferred to certain states under Public Law 280. It also can offer opportunities for Native nations to regain and expand sovereignty, as Siedschlaw and Fox discuss in their chapters. We also discuss Canadian and American differences in national law regarding Indigenous Peoples.

FEDERALISM AND U.S. FEDERAL INDIAN POLICY

U.S. federal Indian policy, when viewed at a glance, seems contradictory. That is to say that the actions in one particular policy era are reversed or contravened in another. In fact, until the current era of self-determination in federal Indian policy, each shift in policy ushered in a new idea on how to resolve what policymakers described as "the Indian problem." Careful examination of the history of federal Indian policy fills volumes on the topic (Deloria and Lytle 1984; Deloria 1985). So vast is the topic that particular works examine a single policy era, such as Fixico (1986) does in his book on the termination and relocation era. Others focus on federal Indian policy affecting a single Native nation, such as the Navajo Nation, or offer overviews of federal Indian policy as it affects and is affected by federal Indian law

(Getches, Wilkinson, and Williams 1998) or a particular Native nation's politics and law (Wilkins 2003). When discussing how national laws impact the lives of Indigenous Peoples as the topic relates to chapters in this section by Jocks, Siedschlaw, and Fox, a brief discussion of U.S. American Indian self-determination policy offers useful background and insights into the examples these authors discuss.

After World War II, Congress attempted to deal with "the Indian problem" once and for all by terminating the special trust relationship (also known as the ward-guardian relationship) that grew out of three U.S. Supreme Court cases known collectively as the Marshall Trilogy—*Johnson v. M'Intosh* (1823), *Cherokee Nation v. Georgia* (1831), and *Worcester v. Georgia* (1832). The other part of the termination and relocation policy was to assimilate American Indians by relocating American Indian individuals or families to metropolitan areas (see Fixico 1986). This time, Native peoples had had enough. The termination and relocation policy galvanized American Indians across the country into action in opposition to the policy. The National Congress of American Indians (NCAI) was created in the 1940s (Getches, Wilkinson, and Williams 1998). By this time, the Civil Rights Movement was well under way, bringing attention at the national level to discrimination against African Americans. By the 1970s these and other groups, including Hispanic Americans and American Indians, brought issues affecting their groups to the forefront of national conversations around issues of discrimination and disparate treatment in the U.S. political system. In 1960, President Nixon addressed Congress, recommending "self-determination without termination" and called for an end to the termination policy. In his message Nixon declared, "The time has come to break decisively with the past and create the conditions for a new era in which the Indian future is determined by Indian acts and Indian decisions" (Getches, Wilkinson, and Williams 1998, 253). The era of American Indian self-determination not only brought an end to termination (and saw it rescinded for some tribes and in some states) but it also included the passage of Public Law 93–638—the Indian Self-Determination and Education Assistance Act (1975), which provided, among other things, for American Indian nations to contract with the federal government to provide their own essential programs and services in education, law enforcement, and many other areas. The Indian Child Welfare Act (1978) soon followed, as well as the American Indian Religious Freedom Act (1978) and many more congressional acts supporting American Indian self-determination. Additionally, many presidential executive orders followed, including Executive Order 13175 (2000), requiring federal agencies to consult and coordinate with federally recognized American Indian tribes, and Executive Order 13007 (1996) on Indian sacred sites.

The American Indian self-determination policy meant understanding the American federalist system differently. Federalism is often referred to as intergovernmental relations and is the division of powers between national (or central or federal) and subnational units of governments such as state and local governments (see, for example, Denhardt 1999 or Stillman 2000). Tribal nations are frequently missing from such definitions and discussions even though tribal nations have a status higher than states (*Native American Church v. Navajo Tribal Council* [1959]) and—with 573 federally recognized tribes—outnumber state governments by more than an 11:1 ratio (Bureau of Indian Affairs n.d.). Perhaps this is because American Indians are mentioned only twice in the U.S. Constitution: once where American Indian individuals are excluded for purposes of counting people for determining state representation in Congress (Section 2), and as tribes in what is often referred to as the Indian Commerce Clause (Article 1, Section 8). The latter serves as the sole explicitly stated authority of Congress over Indian affairs. As Shattuck and Norgren (1991) noted some time ago, "Since Congress' authority over Indian tribes was placed in the same category as its power over 'foreign nations' and the 'several states,' it served as the underpinning for the understanding that federal legislative authority over Indian affairs was plenary" (Shattuck and Norgren 1991, 125–26). Ironically, both the passage of time and periods of devolving federal authority over certain items to states has resulted in state incursions upon Indigenous sovereignty, resulting in what Corntassel and Witmer (2008) refer to as "forced federalism." These same authors discuss intergovernmental relations between tribal nations and other governments in the U.S. system, referring to the expansion of intergovernmental relations as "new federalism."

American Indian sovereignty has survived both state and federal assaults, in part through employing Indigenous community responses (see, for example, Nielsen and Jarratt-Snider 2018, 185–92) and in part by seizing opportunities by assuming authority for programs and services that would otherwise be devolved to state governments. Also, as Siedschlaw shows in his chapter on the Indian Child Welfare Act and Nebraska, with astute political advocacy and the right circumstances (particularly state officials willing to work with Indigenous Peoples and nations), intergovernmental relations between American Indian nations and states can occasionally yield positive results for American Indians. He offers an example of the increasing frequency of intergovernmental relations between these two groups in the development of state-level Indian child welfare services.

Further evidence of intergovernmental relations between American Indian nations and the United States lies in the practice by the United States of making treaties with tribal nations, a practice that governments use for making agreements with sovereign governments, yet once U.S. federal Indian policy entered the current policy era of American Indian self-determination (in the 1970s), more and more tribal nations are included in various pieces of legislation where they are recognized as governments and where intergovernmental relations occur. In fact, today it is not uncommon to find legislation where intergovernmental relations include federally recognized American Indian tribes and Alaskan Native villages. See for example, the Tribal Forest Protection Act (2004) and of course, as Fox shows in her chapter, the Violence Against Women Reauthorization Act (VAWA) (2013).

The sovereignty of tribal nations is recognized in general legislation such as VAWA, but while tribal nations have the authority to administer these programs and services, challenges still remain in their implementation, as discussed in Fox's chapter. She describes how the *Oliphant v. Suquamish* (1978) decision creates difficulties for Indigenous nations in fully implementing the goal of VAWA to reduce violence against women. In *Oliphant*, the court held that American Indian tribal courts do not have jurisdiction over non-Indian offenders, a decision that escapes logic. Typically, criminal jurisdiction is based on either territory or subject matter (see the book's introduction), whereas in *Oliphant* the court based criminal jurisdiction on race. Fox discusses how this case created difficulties in enforcing the law for crimes against Indigenous women on Indigenous lands. She describes how VAWA addresses only some of the violence against Native women even though it provides tribal nations with the authority to strengthen their responses and (to some extent) address areas in the jurisdictional maze that were lacking before these additions were made to the legislation.

Jocks's chapter focuses on national laws in the United States and Canada and their (for the most part) failure to protect sacred places of Indigenous peoples. He also discusses negotiation with federal entities as a strategy for protecting sacred places of Indigenous Peoples. In the United States that failure constitutes discrimination against Native peoples by denying them one of the sections of the U.S. Constitution held most dear by many American citizens—the right to religious freedom.

CANADA AND U.S. NATIONAL LAWS

An important context for Jocks's chapter is the difference between national laws in the United States and Canada that affect Indigenous Peoples, and to which Indigenous Peoples must respond. The following overview focuses on just a few of the important legal differences (see Reynolds 2018 for a detailed critical analysis of Aboriginal legal status in Canada). In Canada, Aboriginal people are 4.3 percent of the population and a rapidly increasing demographic (Statistics Canada 2011) compared to the United States, where American Indians and Alaska Natives are

2.0 percent of the population (U.S. Department of Health 2018). The "existing Indigenous and treaty rights" of Aboriginal Peoples (a term that includes First Nations, Inuit, and Métis) (First Nations 2009b), are recognized in Section 35 of the Constitution of Canadian (1982). This legal recognition, it is important to note, enables First Nations to exercise more control in their responses to the issues caused by colonialism and colonial law such as the acquisition of Indigenous land that contains sacred sites.

Despite questions about how self-interested the interpretations by the Canadian government are of the Canadian treaties, the treaties have been affirmed by the Canadian Supreme Court (Hall and Abers 2017). In the United States there was a trail of broken treaties (Nielsen and Robyn 2019) where many Indian nations were forced off the reservation lands that had been guaranteed to them by treaty, for example with the Cherokee, Choctaw, and many others (Nies 1996). Unlike the United States where treaty-making stopped in 1871, in Canada treaty-making is still occurring because large portions of Canada are unceded Indian territory (Hall and Abers 2017). This provides more opportunities for First Nations to regain their land and resources (and sacred sites) than in the United States.

Just like the United States, Canada has had and still has discriminatory laws. The Indian Act, a particularly paternalistic law that has been revised numerous times since its first enactment in 1876, over the years served to oppress Aboriginal individuals, especially women. Until 1985, for example, if an Aboriginal woman married a non-Aboriginal man, she lost her Indian status, including treaty and health benefits and the rights to live on and be buried on the reserve; if a non-Aboriginal woman married an Indian man, she became Indian (First Nations 2009a). The Indian Act divided Aboriginal people into many categories, including status and non-status Indians, treaty and nontreaty Indians, registered and nonregistered Indians, Métis, and Inuit. This was no accident. Each of these groups had different rights and issues, which meant that it was difficult for them to work together to legally challenge the colonial and later the federal government on important issues such as the protection of sacred sites.

Despite the less violent interactions between Aboriginal nations and the colonial government compared to the United States, these were still times of intense suffering, death, and dispossession for Canada's Aboriginal people, which must not be ignored (see, for example, Monchalin 2016). However, the current prominence of Aboriginal people as the largest "minority group" in Canada gives them more political and social visibility and power than Native Americans in the United States, a fact that could be contributing to the results found in Jocks's chapter.

In general the future for the issues, especially in the United States, raised by the authors in this section is mixed, illustrating both the challenges and the opportunities provided by federalism, or intergovernmental relations. Each of the authors in this section brings examples of community-based responses to important issues that affect lives every day of Indigenous people in the United States in their communities and nations.

REFERENCES

Bureau of Indian Affairs. n.d. "United States Department of Interior, Indian Affairs." bia.gov/bia.

Corntassel, Jeff, and Richard C. Witmer. 2008. *Forced Federalism: Contemporary Challenges to Indigenous Nationhood.* Norman: University of Oklahoma Press.

Deloria, Vine, Jr., ed. 1985. *American Indian Policy in the Twentieth Century.* Norman: University of Oklahoma Press.

Deloria, Vine, Jr., and Clifford M. Lytle. 1984. *The Nations Within.* New York: Pantheon Books.

Denhardt, Robert B. 1999. *Public Administration: An Action Orientation.* 3rd ed. Orlando, FL: Harcourt Brace.

First Nations and Indigenous Studies, University of British Columbia. 2009a. "The Indian Act." https://indigenousfoundations.arts.ubc.ca/the_indian_act/.

———. 2009b. "Terminology." https://indigenousfoundations.arts.ubc.ca/terminology/.

Fixico, Donald Lee. 1986. *Termination and Relocation: Federal Indian Policy, 1945–1960.* Albuquerque: University of New Mexico Press.

Getches, David H., Charles F. Wilkinson, and Robert A. Williams, Jr. 1998. *Cases and Materials on Federal Indian Law.* 4th ed. St. Paul, MN: West Publishing.

Hall, Anthony J., and Gretchen Abers. 2017. "Treaties with Indigenous Peoples in Canada." *The Canadian Encyclopedia.* www.thecanadianencyclopedia.ca/en/article/aboriginal-treaties.

Monchalin, Lisa. 2016. *The Colonial Problem: An Indigenous Perspective on Crime and Injustice in Canada.* Toronto, ON: University of Toronto Press.

Nielsen, Marianne O., and Karen Jarratt-Snider. 2018. *Crime and Social Justice in Indian Country.* Tucson. University of Arizona Press.

Nielsen, Marianne O., and Linda M. Robyn. 2019. *Colonialism Is Crime.* New Brunswick, NJ: Rutgers University Press.

Nies, Judith. 1996. *Native American History.* New York: Ballantine Books.

Reynolds, Jim. 2018. *Aboriginal People and the Law: A Critical Introduction.* Vancouver: University of British Columbia Press.

Shattuck, Petra T., and Jill Norgren. 1991. *Partial Justice: Federal Indian Law in a Liberal Constitutional System.* New York: Berg Publishers.

Statistics Canada. 2011. "Aboriginal Peoples in Canada: First Nations People, Métis and Inuit." https://www12.statcan.gc.ca/nhs-enm/2011/as-sa/99-011 . . . /99-011-x2011001-eng.cfm.

Stillman, Richard J., II. 2000. *Public Administration: Concepts and Cases.* 7th ed. Boston: Houghton Mifflin.

U.S. Department of Health and Human Services. 2018. "Profile: American Indian/Alaska Native." https://minorityhealth.hhs.gov/omh/browse.aspx?lvl=3&lvlid=62.

Wilkins, David E. 2003. *The Navajo Political Experience.* New York: Rowman and Littlefield.

Williams, Robert A., Jr. 2005. *Like a Loaded Weapon: The Rehnquist Court, Indian Rights, and the Legal History of Racism in America.* Minneapolis: University of Minnesota Press.

Zion, James W. 2006. "Justice as Phoenix: Traditional Indigenous Law, Restorative Justice, and the Collapse of the State." In *Native Americans and the Criminal Justice System,* edited by Jeffrey Ian Ross and Larry Gould, 51–65. Boulder, CO: Paradigm.

LEGAL RESOURCES

American Indian Religious Freedom Act Public Law 95-4-341 (1978, 1996)

Cherokee Nation v. Georgia 30 U.S. 1 (5 Pet.) (1831)

Constitution of Canada (1982)

Executive Order of the President 13007, signed May 24, 1996. "Indian Sacred Sites."

Executive Order of the President 13175, signed November 6, 2000. "Consultation and Coordination with Indian Tribal Governments."

Indian Child Welfare Act, Public Law 95–608

Johnson v. M'Intosh 21 U.S. (Wheat) 543, L.Ed. 681 (1823)

Native American Church v. Navajo Tribal Council 272 F.2d. 131 (1959)

Oliphant v. Suquamish Indian Tribe 435 U.S. 191, 98 S. Ct. 1011 55 L.Ed. 2d 209 (1978)

Tribal Forest Protection Act. Pub. L. 108–278. (2004)

U.S. Constitution (1788)

Violence Against Women Act 42 U.S.C. 13701 (1994, 2000, 2005, 2013)

Worcester v. Georgia 310 U.S. 515, 6 Pet. 515, 8 L.Ed. 438 (1832)

3

RESTORING CONGRUITY

Indigenous Lives and Religious Freedom in the
United States and Canada

CHRIS JOCKS

O UT OF *respect for Indigenous protocols, I will begin by telling you who my people are. My mother was Patricia O'Donoghue, whose mother came to Brooklyn, New York, from Germany, and whose father came to Brooklyn from Ireland. My father was Conway Jocks, a Kanien´kehá:ka (Mohawk) man from Kahnawà:ke. His mother was Margaret Beauvais Jocks, of the Bear Clan; his father was Joseph Jocks, of the Wolf Clan. A person of mixed ancestry, I have chosen to live as an Indigenous person. When I stay in Kahnawà:ke I participate in the doings at the Mohawk Trail Longhouse, where I sit with the Bear Clan. I am married into the Diné (Navajo) family of Robyn Jackson, whose first clan is Tó´áhani. They live in the Wheatfields area, in the Chuska Mountains of the Navajo Nation. I am writing these words at the foot of a deeply revered being, Dook´o´oosłííd, also known as the San Fran-cisco Peaks, on land Aboriginally known and cared for by many Indigenous Peoples, including the Hopi, Diné, Yavapai, Havasupai, and Apache.*

For more than four hundred years in the United States and Canada, Indig-enous nations have confronted settler regimes intent on gaining control of the lands and resources of Turtle Island (a name used by many Indigenous people for North America). From the beginning, settler colonial strategy included forced subversion of Indigenous relationships with the beings Native people often regarded as elders on their territories: plants, animals, and for lack of a better term, spirit beings—attacks, in other words, on culture and religion. Indigenous resistance has taken many forms, from military to political to ceremonial to artistic. This chapter surveys and analyzes the history of legal efforts to protect Native peoples' revered and beloved places and the beings who live on them, focusing on the failure of U.S. and Canadian courts to grant protection under their own doctrines of religious freedom. My purpose is not to mourn or bemoan this failure, which was predictable and now appears intractable. Rather, it is to instigate critical reflection on the deep structural incongruities it is built upon, and then gesture toward newer strategies built on other foundations.

FENCING THE HERD, OR PROBLEMS WITH THE CATEGORY OF "RELIGION"

Years ago I was talking with a young Onondaga man about my dissertation research, which concerned the evolution of Longhouse tradition at Kahnawà:ke. He asked which academic discipline I was approaching this from, so I told him my training was in religious studies. He answered without a pause, but with a hint of scorn, "The Longhouse is not a religion." By then I had learned enough not to be surprised by this point of view. I thought I understood it. I was ready with a well-considered reply built around a broader, more holistic, more inclusive definition of religion. We got along decently enough—I seem to remember us joking about this whole "religion" thing—but I don't think he ever relented, and he was right. He wasn't right in an absolute sense, because English words like "religion" are indeed fences that can be moved. But he was right because no matter how the religion fence is repositioned, I am now convinced that the Indigenous animals will not be found inside. I will come back to this.

This is a problem in the academic study of religion, or at least it should be, but it's an even greater problem for religious freedom law, which means it is a problem for Indigenous Peoples. Religious freedom has been a bedrock constitutional principle in the United States since 1791, and in Canada since 1982 (1960 if you count the Canadian Bill of Rights; 1947 if you count the Saskatchewan Bill of Rights). Yet it has afforded very little protection to the beliefs and practices of Indigenous Peoples who live within the external boundaries of these invading-settler nations. This is particularly true in cases involving Indigenous efforts to protect revered and beloved places—also known as sacred sites—from harm. The elaborated principles and precedents of U.S. and Canadian religious freedom law have been of almost no use to Indigenous Peoples in these instances.

In the United States, critics such as Vine Deloria Jr. (1992, 1994), and Brian Edward Brown (1999) have explained this failure in terms of the precedence of property rights over human rights in American jurisprudence, a theory that is as important today as it was when Deloria proposed it. As they and others have amply demonstrated, Justice O'Connor's 1988 ruling in *Lyng v. Northwest Indian Cemetery Protective Association* caps a long line of judicial decisions that leave little room for any other explanation. In Canadian case law, as I will explain below, no crass reference to the Crown's superior rights as property owner will be found. Judges asked to rule on Indigenous demands for protection of sacred sites on traditional Indigenous territory Canada claims to own are required to balance the needs of Indigenous Peoples with those of the non-Indigenous Canadian public, including logging and mining and utility operators and their employees. As Michael Lee Ross (2005) has demonstrated, these rulings usually end up with the same result: permission for commercial developers to disrupt and despoil these revered places.

Ross and Brown make reasoned yet impassioned pleas for judges to dig deeper, to educate themselves or be educated about the true foundations and depth of Indigenous beliefs and practices, with the hope that the courts will then be compelled to extend religious freedom protections to these sacred sites. This sounds like a noble cause. Religious freedom is a fundamental component of almost every national and international formulation of basic human rights, from the United States Constitution (1791) to the Universal Declaration of Human Rights (1948) to the United Nations Declaration on the Rights of Indigenous Peoples (2007). Achieving standing on this platform would seem to offer the ultimate, most indisputable guarantee available for Indigenous Peoples. But realistically, given the legal history referenced here, such an achievement in the United States or Canada seems unlikely to occur in our lifetimes. The centuries-long erosion of canyon walls is an apt metaphor for the slow decomposition of the opposing walls of industrial civilization's certainty, ethos, and power.

Consequently, Indigenous Peoples are exploring and employing other strategies in their fight to stay alive in relation to their lands: strategies such as historical preservation, cultural survival and sustainability, public health, and assertion of the rights of nature. Some of these strategies will be discussed in more detail below. The irony is that the arena of religious freedom was an awkward fit from the beginning. Tisa Wenger's *We Have a Religion* (2009) illustrates this incongruity in the context of the Pueblo Indian Dance Controversy of the 1920s. Beginning with her discussion, I will suggest that the concept of religion itself is intrinsically alien to Indigenous ways of life—practices, ontologies, epistemologies, and values. Those who use the word religion and think with it have proven unable to escape its categorical separation of "matter" and "spirit." The result is that, as applied to Indigenous lives, the ideal of religious freedom cannot apprehend what it pretends to protect. The operation and its operand are incommensurable. The animals flee the very scent and sound of the corral.

RELIGIOUS FREEDOM AND INDIGENOUS LANDS IN THE UNITED STATES

The origin of religious freedom in the United States appears to owe as much to tactical politics as it does to lofty idealism—probably more (Lambert 2006; Holmes 2006). The First Amendment did not resolve the tug-of-war between high church and low church Protestants, Catholics, and Deists, but it did remove it from the federal arena. In this contest, Jews and Muslims were invisible bystanders. Indigenous Peoples were not even in the ballpark. Most Americans would have laughed at the notion that Indians had religion at all, an opinion first voiced three hundred years earlier by Columbus (Casas 1827, 36). As Peter Nabokov asserts, "When white men first witnessed Indians impersonating animal spirits in costume and dance, and worshiping rocks and rainbows, they failed to see this as a form of deep religious expression. To their Christian minds, these were deplorable pagan rites. Worship of more than one deity, and sacrificial offerings directed at the natural world, stamped Indians as a misguided, lesser form of mankind. Here were Christless heathens crying to be rescued from eternal damnation" (Nabakov 1999, 50–51). We might pause and look more closely at this statement because it illustrates the difficulty of incommensurability I am suggesting. Phrases such as "impersonating animal spirits," "worshiping rocks and rainbows," and "sacrificial offerings," carry associations straight from the European study of world religions, connotations that do not contain or even encounter the Indigenous animals, the Indigenous sense of the animals as Indigenous people know and understand and relate to them. To suggest but one example for further thought, I have heard more than one participant, in what an anthropologist might denote as "Indigenous ritual impersonation," describe the experience not as impersonating an animal spirit, but as being temporarily animated by, or sharing an intensification of being with a revered spirit being, associated with an animal relative.

It is not until 1882 that Indigenous ways of living were recognized as religion by the U.S. federal government—recognized, that is, in order to outlaw them. The Code of Indian Offenses, announced in Interior Secretary Henry M. Teller's Annual Report of 1883, focused on traditional ceremonial dances as degrading relics of barbarism that promote idleness, sexual license, and—horror of horrors—the giving away of property (Teller 1883; Burke 1921, 1923). The era encompassed by these pronouncements was the era of forced assimilation, under which the federal government sought to accelerate the erasure of treaty obligations as well as traditional Indigenous identity, knowledge, practice, languages, and land. As a result of allotment, demoralization, and federal abrogation of treaties under the doctrine of plenary power, many revered and beloved places were removed from Indigenous care. Most were transferred to federal ownership and control, under which they were ripe for natural resource extraction. The taking of the Black Hills (Hé Sápa to the Lakota people) is a prototypical case (Ostler 2010; also see Inouye 1992 for a concise overview of religious discrimination against American Indians).

The federal prohibition against ceremonial dances was lifted during John Collier's term as commissioner of Indian Affairs (1933–1945), an interlude of progressive but paternalistic reform, but the work of protecting revered and beloved places had only begun. After World War II the United States commenced a period of unprecedented economic growth fueled by extensive and massive public works projects engineered to extract energy and redirect the flow of water. At the same time, prosperity for working-class mainstream (mostly white) Americans was harnessed into unprecedented demand for travel, leisure, and recreation opportunities on public lands. Both trends threatened to overrun, submerge, dig up, and wreck the integrity of a long list of places held in reverence by Indigenous Peoples and individuals, who turned to the U.S. courts for relief. A series of cases were filed beginning in 1960, leading up to the catastrophic *Lyng* ruling in 1988. See table 3.1 for a list, spanning fifty years from 1958 until 2008.

TABLE 3.1 American Cases, 1958–2008

1. *Seneca Nation of Indians v. Brucker* (1958) **Claim:** The Seneca Nation disputed the use of eminent domain to take land from the Allegany Seneca Reservation, to be flooded by the Allegheny Reservoir behind Kinzua Dam, in violation of the 1794 Treaty of Canandaigua. The flooded land would include the Cornplanter Grant, a place revered by many Seneca and other Haudenosaunee (Iroquois) people as the site of the prophet Handsome Lake's visions.	**Disposition:** Under the plenary power doctrine, the U.S. Congress has the authority to supersede treaties to implement decisions made in the public interest. The dam was constructed in 1960. **Sources:** Hauptman 2014
2. *Sequoya v. Tennessee Valley Authority* (1980) **Claim:** Tellico Dam project would flood ancient village sites within a valley regarded as sacred homeland by the Cherokee people. This would be a violation of the Free Exercise Clause of the First Amendment.	**Disposition:** Plaintiffs' claim denied. Reverence for the site is not central enough to Cherokee religion to qualify for First Amendment protection. The dam was completed in 1979. **Sources:** Stambor 1982; Brown 1999, 9–38
3. *Badoni v. Higginson* (1981) **Claim:** Flooding of Glen Canyon would disturb the area around Rainbow Bridge, preventing Diné (Navajo people) from the practice of their religion. The Bureau of Reclamation was being asked to honor a provision of the dam's enabling legislation, which promised that the Rainbow Bridge site would be protected from the rising waters of Lake Powell.	**Disposition:** Plaintiffs' claim denied because (a) they have no property interest in the location, and (b) the public benefit created by the dam outweighs the burden on Diné free exercise of religion. The rising waters were allowed to reach the base of Rainbow Bridge, where a boat landing was constructed for tourists. **Sources:** Stambor 1982; Brown 1999, 39–60

(continued)

TABLE 3.1 *continued*

4.	*Wilson v. Block* (1984) **Claim:** Development of a commercial ski operation on the slopes of the San Francisco Peaks, held sacred by Diné (Navajo), Hopi, Havasupai, and other Indigenous peoples, would irrevocably damage the free exercise of their religion.	**Disposition:** Plaintiffs' claim denied. The court ruled that the plaintiffs had not proven that the Peaks were indispensable to their religion, and further ruled that the sacredness of the Peaks is confined to the summits, thus not relevant to the ski area below. **Sources:** Brown 1999, 61–92
5.	*Lyng v. Northwest Indian Cemetery Protective Association 108 S.Ct. 1319* (1988) **Claim:** Construction of a logging road by the U.S. Forest Service in proximity to sacred prayer sites would irreversibly destroy the ability of Indigenous people of the Karuk, Yurok, and Tolowa Nations from the free exercise of their religion.	**Disposition:** Plaintiffs' claim denied. The destructive impact on Indigenous religious practice is acknowledged. However, as the decision to permit the road construction would only *indirectly* burden the plaintiffs' religious practice, the rights of the United States as property owner supersede religious freedom claims on public land. **Sources:** McAndrew 1989; Deloria 1992, 1994, 267–82; Brown 1999, 119–70
6.	*Manybeads v. United States* (1989) **Claim:** Diné residents of the Big Mountain area who refused to cooperate with U.S. government-ordered relocation brought suit claiming that relocation would leave them unable to practice their religion.	**Disposition:** Plaintiffs' claim denied. Citing *Lyng*, the court ruled that the U.S. government has no obligation to prove compelling interest or to otherwise accommodate free exercise of religion claims on federal land.
7.	*Navajo Nation v. U.S. Forest Service* (2008) **Claim:** Members of six Indigenous nations sued the U.S. Forest Service and Arizona Snowbowl ski resort regarding their plan to use recycled wastewater to make artificial snow. The resort is located on the slope of the San Francisco Peaks, which are sacred to thirteen Indigenous nations. Plaintiffs claimed that the presence of treated wastewater on the sacred mountain would illegally burden and in fact make impossible their free exercise of religion.	**Disposition:** Plaintiffs' claim denied. The court found that the artificial snowmaking did not constitute a substantial burden on their practice of religion, but merely offended their "subjective spiritual experience" and their "feeling about their religion."

To belabor the obvious, in every one of these cases U.S. courts permitted commercial development interests to burden, and in some cases, "virtually destroy" the free exercise of Indigenous practices on public land (Brown 1999, 172). Unfortunately, the precedent set in *Lyng* appears to be rock solid. How many generations will it take for judges to slowly realize this and stop exercising their powers as arbiters of religion in the lives of Indigenous people? Who is even starting to do this work? For the foreseeable future, we are stuck with the precedent criticized in Justice Brennan's dissent: "The Court does not for one minute suggest that the interests served by the G-O Road are in any way compelling, or that they outweigh the destructive effect construction of the road will have on [the Indians'] religious practices. Instead, the Court embraces the Government's contention that its prerogative as landowner should always take precedence over a claim that a particular use of federal property infringes religious practices" (*Lyng v. Northwest Indian Cemetery Protective Association* [1988]).

As Brian Edward Brown writes, "For in the view of the courts, unresponsive to the fundamental claim of a holy presence consecrating it, land functioned as mere locale, the scene or setting, 'the background' where religious practices were conducted in their various tribal expressions" (Brown 1999, 175).

The inability of a single federal court *over fifty years*, at the appellate or Supreme Court level, to discern anything like what Brown alludes to suggests a deep, bedrock incongruity. It is built on a keen understanding and appreciation for the civilizing effects of property, as Deloria (1992, 1994), Brown (1999), Loesch (1993), and many others have observed. And it is built on a corresponding lack of understanding and appreciation—or even awareness—of Indigenous ways of practical kinship with land, sky, animals, plants, and one another. More fundamentally the Euro-American/ Western understanding of property presupposes the dichotomy of matter and spirit. Under this worldview matter is property and is meant to be turned to profit. It serves spirit but shares nothing with it. Spirit is insubstantial and also, in modern times, a completely optional stipulation. Religion refers to beliefs and practices concerning spirit. Nice if you're that kind of person, but perfectly irrelevant for the siting and building of a dam.

THE CANADIAN CONTEXT

It turns out that religious freedom is a topic of significant debate in Canada today (Waldron 2013; Buckingham 2014; Joustra 2014). On one side are strong secularists convinced that in a pluralistic society religious arguments can only damage the political process, which must remain essentially rational. Only a Canadian *laïcité*, they assert—a reference to French secularism—can prevent the kind of toxic confluence of religion and politics they see increasingly evident in the United States, in which political valorization of a perceived Judeo-Christian heritage slides into politically sponsored initiatives of domestic and international Christian theocracy and evangelization (Joustra 2014, 41–44). Secularists maintain that the only bulwark against all forms of religious fanaticism and violence is a society in which religion is treated exclusively as a private matter. Robert Joustra cites three contemporary Canadian intellectuals who urge us to question whether religious freedom is a worthy ideal at all in the twenty-first century (Joustra 2014, 41–42).

On the other side are those who affirm the status quo, accept and in some cases embrace the Judeo-Christian roots of Canadian political culture, and insist that Canada would betray its identity if it allowed an immoderate hypersecularism to prohibit all public religious arguments: "The evidence of this is historical, legal, political, and cultural: Canada's two founding nations, French/Catholic and English/Protestant; the inscribed privilege of those traditions in Canada's Constitution and law and precedence; and finally the influence of American Judeo-Christian secular conservatism on the Canadian Conservative party" (Joustra 2014, 44, with reference to Buckingham 2014).

For these "Judeo-Christian secularists," religious freedom is properly regarded as the first liberty. Raymond de Souza, writing in the *National Post*, asserts that "[i]f a person is not free before God, is not free in his conscience, then there is no basis for his freedom before the state, and his property and other rights are of little avail" (de Souza 2013, quoted in Joustra 2014, 45). Dr. Joustra goes on to propose a third alternative, however, which he denotes "principled pluralism" (Joustra 2014, 47–52). It conceives of a pluralistic society that is held together by principles arrived at by consensus. All beliefs and convictions, secular or religious, would be welcomed as sources for these principles, but the principles themselves would be universalized, sanitized of their ideological origins. Joustra references a saying attributed to modern Catholic theologian Jacques Maritain about the debates leading to the adoption of the United Nations Universal Declaration of Human Rights in 1948: "Yes, we agree about the rights, but on condition that no one asks us why."

What does all this mean for First Nations people? First, we can observe that Joustra and Buckingham's above affirmation of Canada's Judeo-Christian origins refers to Canada's *two* founding nations. They seem to have missed the memo that Canada now acknowledges *three* founding nations, First Nations being collectively regarded as the first. In fact, the incommensurability of "religion" and religious freedom law in reference to First Nations is further evidenced by the fact that no document, book, or article I could locate on religious freedom in Canada makes any reference to Indigenous people, with two exceptions: One is a five-paragraph discussion of church-run Indian residential schools, in the context of a chapter on the role of religion in Canadian education. There is a brief mention of abuse in these schools, but no mention of their crystal-clear intent to persecute and eradicate Indigenous ways of thinking and being in the world—religions, if you must—and replace them with Christianity (Buckingham 2014, 33–35). There is no mention either of the Indian Act's prohibition of the Potlach, which commenced in 1884—around the same time as the Sun Dance prohibition in the United States—but was not rescinded until 1951.

The second source is Michael Lee Ross's *First Nations Sacred Sites in Canada's Courts* (2005). Ross is an attorney, with an attorney's painstaking attention to detail. His book explores a series of court rulings, one in Ontario and the remainder in British Columbia, involving First Nations revered and beloved places, or sacred sites. See table 3.2 for a listing (the page numbers refer to Ross 2005).

The overall tally is almost encouraging, at least compared to the U.S. chart: five victories for First Nations plaintiffs, with six defeats. Yet as Ross points out, *claims were denied in all five cases where sites or areas were explicitly identified as sacred.* In the *High Falls* case—the only one not from British Columbia and the one with the most devastating outcome for the First Nations plaintiffs—the purported reason was essentially procedural:

TABLE 3.2 Canadian Cases, 1985–2004

1. *Meares Island* **Claim**: Injunction by Clayoquot and Ahousaht people against logging; claim of Aboriginal rights. **Claim of sacredness?** Not quite. Claim of longstanding cultural use, including "trees which are involved in traditional Native practices"; connection to the past.	**Disposition:** Protection achieved in 1985 (30–31).
2. *Deer Island* **Claim**: Injunction by Kwakwaka'wakw people against logging on private land within traditional territory; claim of Aboriginal and treaty rights. **Claim of sacredness?** No	**Disposition:** Protection achieved in 1987 (38).
3. *High Falls* **Claim**: Claim by Poplar Point Ojibwe of treaty rights prohibiting construction of a hydro dam that would flood a sacred waterfall, located on traditional lands. **Claim of sacredness?** Yes	**Disposition**: Protection denied in 1991 due to an earlier agreement by the chief to allow construction under conditions (61–62).
4. *Ure Creek* **Claim**: Claim by Lil'wat people of Aboriginal rights to prohibit logging on sacred grounds that are on traditional territory. Refers to an area where only medicine people normally went. **Claim of sacredness?** Yes	**Disposition**: Protection denied in 1991. Evidence was denied as not specific enough (55–56).
5. *Lower Tsitika Valley* **Claim**: Claim by Tlowitsis-Mumtagila people prohibiting logging based on Aboriginal rights. **Claim of sacredness?** Yes	**Disposition**: Protection denied in 1991. Evidence of sacredness was denied as weak and submitted too late in the process, raising suspicion that it was made up (52–53).

(continued)

TABLE 3.2 *continued*

6.	*Westar* **Claim**: Claim of Aboriginal rights by the Gitksan and Wet'suwet'en people to prohibit logging on undisturbed traditional territory. **Claim of sacredness?** No. Rather, the claim included the cultural value of leaving the Shedin area, which had never been logged, undisturbed.	**Disposition**: Protection was denied in 1990 on the basis that any claimed Aboriginal right could not be exclusive, given that the plaintiffs did not claim to have historically *used* the area (43–46).
7.	*Siska Creek* **Claim**: The Siska Indian Band sought to prohibit logging on traditional territory based on Aboriginal rights. The territory had religious significance and was used for ceremonies. **Claim of sacredness?** Yes	**Disposition**: Protection was denied in 1999. The Court ruled that the area was not sufficiently unique, and that no "site-specific infringement" by the logging operation had been identified (109).
8.	*Halfway River* **Claim**: The Dunne-Za people of Halfway River First Nation, signers of Treaty 8, sought to prohibit logging in the Tusdzuh area, on their traditional territory. **Claim of sacredness?** No, but cultural use was asserted.	**Disposition: Protection was achieved in 1999.** The Appeals Court ruled that treaty rights did not extinguish all Aboriginal rights. Judge Advocate Huddart's opinion further suggested that the Dunne-Za plaintiffs could have employed a freedom of religion argument in addition to one based on Aboriginal rights (125–38).
9.	*Twin Sisters* **Claim**: Four First Nations, signers of Treaty 8, sought to prohibit oil and gas exploration on a mountain and valley on traditional territory which they regard as sacred. **Claim of sacredness?** Yes. This is the only one of the eleven cases to make specific reference to the right of "freedom of conscience and religion" guaranteed in the Canadian Charter of Rights and Freedoms.	**Disposition**: Protection was denied in 2000. Plaintiffs had demonstrated that the area held "theological" value, but not any "practical religious use." Moreover, treaty rights to traditional territory only extend to subsistence, not "sacredness" (116–25).

(continued)

TABLE 3.2 *continued*

10. *Taku River* **Claim**: Tlingit people sought to prohibit a proposed mining operation and associated road, on a revered and undisturbed area of their traditional territory. **Claim of sacredness?** No, but the Tlingits did assert that protecting the area was necessary to assure their *sustainability as a people*.	**Disposition: Protection was achieved in 2004.** This protection extends for as long as it takes for the final claim of Aboriginal rights to be adjudicated (77–88).
11. *Haida Nation* **Claim**: The Haida Nation sought to prohibit logging on Graham Island, part of Haida traditional territory, based on Aboriginal rights. **Claim of sacredness?** No	**Disposition: Protection was achieved in 2004.** This protection extends for as long as it takes for the final claim of Aboriginal rights to be adjudicated. The decision emphasized the mandate for reconciliation between the Crown and First Nations, based on "the honor of the Crown" (89–97).

by signing the earlier permission to allow construction, the chief had (inadvertently) forever relinquished his peoples' Aboriginal rights. Aside from this, the other denials all focused on perceived deficiencies in the claim of sacredness: the claim was too vague, made too late in the process, or insufficiently documented.

According to Ross, this list of denials reveals more about the judges than it does about the First Nations claims. It reveals their lack of understanding, but also their lack of interest in understanding, which is to say, their bias (Ross 2005, 171–78). In particular, he found that judges sought and privileged evidence of "practical religious purposes," provided they are demonstrably site-specific, and peremptorily dismissed evidence showing reverence for more expansive places based on a sense of stewardship supported by "theological/cosmological beliefs." The decision of Taylor in the *Twin Sisters* case asserts that Section 2(a) of the Canadian Charter of Rights and Freedoms, which guarantees "freedom of conscience and religion," "did not protect a concept of stewardship of a place of worship under the protection of religious freedom" (cited at Ross 2005, 124). This should remind us of the two rulings on the San Francisco Peaks, which held first that their sacredness was confined to the very top of the peaks and could not be conceived as applying to the entire mountain (*Wilson v. Block*), and second that the injuries reported by Indigenous plaintiffs from the application of treated wastewater on the mountain amounted to mere emotional discomfort rather than a burden on the exercise of religion (*Navajo Nation v. United States Forest Service*).

Equally significant for our study are the factors that contributed to successful claims of protection. The most important evidence is that which demonstrates a strong basis for Aboriginal title, especially evidence of longstanding and cultural and practical use of an area. Interestingly, the *Halfway River* plaintiffs succeeded when they *refrained* from making a religious or sacredness argument in asking that the Tusdzuh be left undisturbed. The *Taku River* case presented another interesting variation: the successful claim that protection was needed to guarantee the Tlingit First Nation's *sustainability as a people*. This is a small sample, but without the complete, transformative reeducation Ross recommends for judges and citizenry alike regarding Indigenous beliefs and practices, the record provides little basis for confidence in future religious freedom arguments.

CONCLUSION: COMPARISON AND ALTERNATIVES

In the United States, the Supreme Court ruling in *Lyng* appears to have closed the door on any prospect for the First Amendment to protect places revered and beloved by Indigenous Peoples, when American history and law have removed these places from Indigenous care (McAndrew 1989). Subsequent rulings in *Manybeads v. United States* (1989) and *Navajo Nation v. United States Forest Service* have removed any remaining hope, turned the lock, and thrown away the key. This will be disappointing to anyone still enthralled by fourth grade civics lessons about the heroic grandeur of the First Amendment's first guarantee. For the rest of us, in particular First Nations Peoples and their allies, fully aware of the gap between professed ideals and implementation in settler regime governments, we make a mental note and move on, to identify and work on other strategies. To fully research and chronicle these other strategies being developed and pursued at this time is beyond the scope of this chapter. Yet they are instructive. Here is a partial and preliminary list of some that have proven or may prove useful:

1. Historical preservation: The National Historic Preservation Act (NHPA) of 1966 has played a pivotal but also controversial role in the preservation of some sites, such as the Bighorn Medicine Wheel in northern Wyoming (Trope 1995; Chapman 2005). Amendments to the act in 1992 prioritized preservation of places of historical, cultural, and religious significance to Native nations and mandated tribal consultation in such cases. The actual implementation of these provisions have been criticized as weak, however, in competition with commercial development interests (Hinds 2017; Ore 2017).

2. Negotiation: Indigenous nations have occasionally negotiated rule and policy changes to accommodate Indigenous and broader public use of some sites, such as Bear's Lodge (Burton and Ruppert 1999) and the Badger-Two Medicine region (Ore 2017).

3. Congressional or executive action: The return of Blue Lake to Taos Pueblo in 1970 and, in 2016, the designation of Bears Ears National Monument by President Obama under the American Antiquities Act of 1906 are two examples of protection of revered and beloved places by political action, based on public pressure, rather than judicial ruling. In the case of Taos Pueblo the protection involved actual transfer of title to the Native nation seeking protection (Bodine 1973). It should be noted that it was executive and congressional action, not a decision of the courts, that finally rescinded in 1933 the Bureau of Indian Affair's policy that had for fifty years rendered the Sun Dance and other Native ceremonies as punishable "Indian Offenses." It must also be noted that in December 2017 the Trump administration drastically reduced the Bears Ears National Monument, demonstrating the vulnerability of executive branch protections.

Canadian law regarding Indigenous or Aboriginal rights, what they are and how they are to be secured, is still in formation. Canada's constitution is only thirty-five years old, including its recognition and affirmation of Aboriginal rights in Section 35(1). Canada is still making treaties with First Nations. A series of Supreme Court rulings from *Calder* (1973) to *Guerin* (1984) to *Sparrow* (1990) to *Delgamuukw* (1997) to *Tsilhqot'in* (2014) are like a door opening very, very slowly toward the possibility of realizing some measure of Indigenous rights. The form those rights will take and the structures that will recognize and protect them are nowhere near to being determined.

The *appearance* of goodwill on the part of the government can be relied upon. *"The honor of the Crown"* and reconciliation between Canada and its Aboriginal Peoples, are treated not as high sentiment but as legal principles. At the same time, for all the politeness and the honor of the Crown, and in spite of the handful of cases where unwanted commercial development was forestalled at the edge of Aboriginal territories, as of 2017 forests continue to be cut, rivers and lakes continue to be poisoned, and pipelines continue to be approved across First Nations lands without their consent and against their will. The majority of First Nations soldier on in remote locations or tiny squares of land, doing their best to resist and to keep building a future amidst deepening social and economic and medical and environmental disparities, disrupted daily with all the catastrophic expressions of intergenerational trauma. For some, protection of sacred sites may have to wait. And yet the success of cases such as *Meares Island, Deer Island, Halfway River, Taku River,* and *Haida Nation* suggest further strategies to add to the list (see table 3.2 for details).

4. Subsistence and sustainability: In Canada revered and beloved places are often places of subsistence as well as ritual or story, but the Canadian judiciary misunderstands when it distinguishes "practical religious use" from subsistence. *Subsistence on the land, in respectful give-and-take with plant and animal kin, is ceremony.* Protection of subsistence territory is protection of sacred territory. It ensures the sustainability of First Nations and Peoples. This is an avenue of legal strategy that seems ripe for further development.

5. Health: This is related to the previous point. Health is regarded as a basic right for all Canadians, not a privilege to be purchased, as in the United States. Yet even in the United States an obligation is recognized for the State to protect its citizens from toxic, life-threatening conditions. Revered and beloved places are sources of health for Indigenous people, in an industrialized world where it has become

unremarkable for economic development to entail significant, even catastrophic, health deficits. Protecting these places from harm and toxicity is the same as protecting the people from harm and toxicity. It is a public health issue. To name but one example, I have attended discussions in which Diné *hataałi* (traditional practitioners) discussed the direct impacts upon human physical, mental, and spiritual health, caused by the spraying of treated wastewater on that revered and beloved mountain-being, Dook´o´oosłííd.

6. Inherent rights of nature: In 2016 the Ho-Chunk Nation approved a constitutional amendment according rights to nature (CELDF 2016). That same year, New Zealand approved a legal process to accord legal personhood and rights to lands and rivers (Rousseau 2016). This year the first such accord has been approved: the Whanganui River is now a legal person under New Zealand law. A Māori minister of parliament is quoted to have said, "it's not that we've changed our world view but people are catching up to seeing things how we see it" (Haunui-Thompson 2017).

Categories such as history, subsistence, sustainability, health, and inherent rights of nature move the discussion away from the polarizing imperatives associated with the concept of religion. This does not guarantee that they will be any more successful as strategies for legal protection of revered and beloved places. The categorical sway of property rights and wealth generation in settler societies seems stronger than ever in 2018. Even so, these are categories that may resonate more easily with Indigenous practices in which matter and other-than-human beings and everyday living are suffused with spirit.

To solidify this point let me retell a short historical episode to further dislodge any undue lingering reverence about the category of religion, or the principle of religion—with a tip of the hat to my Onondaga friend. I found this account in Tisa Wenger's book, *We Have a Religion: The 1920s Pueblo Indian Dance Controversy and American Religious Freedom* (2009). She describes the 1920s as a time when tremendous external forces bore upon the Pueblo city-states of the Rio Grande Valley and surrounding region. Anglo and Hispano settlers demanded access to Pueblo lands they considered "surplus," as well as title to Pueblo lands already taken by previous generations of squatters. At the same time Protestant missionaries had commenced a breathless crusade to condemn and outlaw Pueblo ceremonial work, which they considered idolatrous, barbaric, and obscene. Missionaries lobbied Indian Affairs Commissioner Burke, who sympathized with their cause. But the Indians had allies too. A diverse collection of artists, anthropologists, tourist entrepreneurs, and social reformers led by the redoubtable John Collier, stood up for the Pueblos and hired lawyers to assist them (Wenger 2009).

This is where the story gets interesting. The lawyers and advocates were progressive Americans who naturally enough cast their defense of Pueblo traditions in terms of religious freedom, and with the help of a well-organized public campaign, their argument eventually won the day. A compromise was reached on the land issues—a compromise that stopped further land grabs but did little to restore what had already been taken—and the prohibition against their centuries-old ceremonial work was rescinded.

Yet an unintended side effect followed. Some progressive-minded Pueblos, mostly young school-educated adults, now refused to perform what their elders regarded as their ceremonial obligations, claiming that the time-honored practice of compelling them to do so would be an illegal violation of *their* freedom of religion (Wenger 2009, 98–101, and 183–85). To use a favorite analogy of legal scholars, the genie of American-style religious freedom, once summoned, could not be put back into its bottle.

In fact, Pueblo leaders in this period of 1923–24 might have recognized the incongruity of the religious freedom strategy. For them, religion—in Spanish, *religión*—signified Spanish Catholicism, an alien practice forced upon them in the seventeenth century with dire consequences but subsequently accommodated for two hundred years in the interest of coexistence. *Religión*, in other words, referenced a domain of external interference that was now managed. In contrast, their own ceremonial practices they referred to as *costumbres* (customs) (Wenger 2009, 5). Pueblo Peoples describe their practice to outsiders in practical, everyday terms, not strained with performances of piety or anxiety for the fate of souls. As Wenger states, "Pueblo tradition understood ceremonial participation as another form of community work, along with maintaining the irrigation ditches, roads, and other public spaces"

(Wenger 2009, 100). These *costumbres* are about participating in a vital communal-cosmic exchange of effort and identity that ensures the continuation of the Pueblo world. The Pueblo attitude says, "We do our work, we do our part, the rains come, everything grows and is happy, as it has always been." We can imagine these ceremonies as exchanges of energy—or to use another analogy, like a cosmic existence tax. Everyone needs to participate so that everyone can continue to be sustained by the collective benefits.

In 1923–24, Pueblo leaders were urged to obtain protection for their *costumbres* by recasting them as *religión*, which under the American system, arrived in unfamiliar guise as a domain of personal freedom. Protection was indeed obtained, but at a cost. Ceremonial participation became a personal religious choice rather than fulfillment of a cosmic social contract. The body of American constitutional law around the concept of religious freedom had developed no rules, no tools, no fences, no maps, that could more appropriately locate Pueblo *costumbres*.

It is early April as I conclude this study. It's time for the ditches to be cleaned.

REFERENCES

Bodine, John J. 1973. "Blue Lake: A Struggle for Indian Rights." *American Indian Law Review* 1:23–32.

Brown, Brian Edward. 1999. *Religion, Law, and the Land: Native Americans and the Judicial Interpretation of Sacred Land*. Westport, CT: Greenwood Press.

Buckingham, J. E. 2014. *Fighting over God: A Legal and Political History of Religious Freedom in Canada*. McGill-Queen's Studies in the History of Religion. Montreal, QC: McGill-Queen's University Press.

Burke, Charles H. 1921. "Circular No. 1665." Washington, DC.

———. 1923. "Supplement to Circular No. 1665." Washington, DC.

Burton, Lloyd, and David Ruppert. 1999. "Bear's Lodge or Devil's Tower: Intercultural Relations, Legal Pluralism, and the Management of Sacred Sites on Public Lands." *Cornell Journal of Law and Public Policy* 8:201–47.

Casas, Bartolomé de las. 1827. *Personal Narrative of the First Voyage of Columbus to America, from a Manuscript Recently Discovered in Spain*. Translated by Samuel Kettell. Boston: Thomas B. Wait and Son.

Chapman, Fred. 2005. "The Bighorn Medicine Wheel: Landscape Wars and Negotiating Native American Spirituality in the New West." In *Preserving Western History*, edited by Andrew Gulliford, 159–74. Albuquerque: University of New Mexico Press.

Community Environmental Legal Defense Fund (CELDF). 2016. "Ho-Chunk Nation General Council Approves Rights of Nature Constitutional Amendment." *Intercontinental Cry*. https://intercontinentalcry.org/ho-chunk-nation -general-council-approves-rights-nature-constitutional-amendment/.

Deloria, Vine, Jr. 1992. "Trouble in High Places: Erosion of American Indian Rights to Religious Freedom in the United States." In *The State of Native America: Genocide, Colonization, and Resistance*, edited by M. Annette Jaimes, 267–90. Boston: South End Press.

———. 1994. *God Is Red: A Native View of Religion*. Golden, CO: Fulcrum Publishing.

de Souza, Raymond J. 2013. "A Religious Canada, Strong and Free." *The National Post*, February 21, 2013. Accessed March 31, 2017. http://nationalpost.com/ opinion/father-raymond-j-de-souza-a-religious-canada-strong-and-free/ wcm/9ee6ac43–10fc-4037-bd3e-0f9208ad9f98.

Haunui-Thompson, Shannon. 2017. "Whanganui River to Gail Legal Personhood." *Radio New Zealand (RNZ)*. Accessed March 20, 2017. http://www .radionz.co.nz/news/te-manu-korihi/326689/whanganui-river-to-gain-legal -personhood.

Hauptman, L. M. 2014. *In the Shadow of Kinzua: The Seneca Nation of Indians Since World War II*. Syracuse, NY: Syracuse University Press.

Hinds, Brody. 2017. "Twenty-Five Years Later: The Amendments to the National Historic Preservation Act and Tribal Consultation." *American Indian Law Review* 41:141–71.

Holmes, David L. 2006. *The Faiths of the Founding Fathers*. New York: Oxford University Press.

Inouye, Daniel K. 1992. "Discrimination and Native American Religious Rights." *University of West Los Angeles Law Review* 23:3–19.

Joustra, Robert. 2014. "Three Rival Versions of Religious Freedom: What Canada's Office of Religious Freedom Can Teach Us About Principled Pluralism." *The Review of Faith and International Affairs* 12:41–54.

Lambert, Frank. 2006. *The Founding Fathers and the Place of Religion in America*. Princeton, NJ: Princeton University Press.

Loesch, Martin C. 1993. "The First Americans and the 'Free' Exercise of Religion." *American Indian Law Review* 18:313–77.

McAndrew, Stephen. 1989. "Lyng v. Northwest: Closing the Door to Indian Religious Sites." *Southwestern University Law Review* 18:603–29.

Nabakov, Peter, ed. 1999. *Native American Testimony: A Chronicle of Indian-White Relations from Prophecy to the Present, 1492–2000.* New York: Penguin Books.

Ore, Kathryn Sears. 2017. "Form and Substance: The National Historic Preservation Act, Badger-Two Medicine, and Meaningful Consultation." *Public Land and Resources Law Review* 38:205–44.

Ostler, Jeffrey. 2010. *The Lakotas and the Black Hills: The Struggle for Sacred Ground.* New York: Viking.

Ross, Michael Lee. 2005. *First Nations Sacred Sites in Canadian Courts.* Vancouver: University of British Columbia Press.

Rousseau, Bryant. 2016. "In New Zealand, Lands and Rivers Can Be People (Legally Speaking)." *New York Times,* July 13, 2016. https://www.nytimes.com/2016/07/14/world/what-in-the-world/in-new-zealand-lands-and-rivers-can -be-people-legally-speaking.html.

Stambor, Howard. 1982. "Manifest Destiny and American Indian Religious Freedom: Sequoyah, Badoni, and the Drowned Gods." *American Indian Law Review* 10:59–89.

Teller, Henry M. 1883. "Report of the Secretary of the Interior." Washington, DC.

Trope, Jack F. 1995. "Existing Federal Law and the Protection of Sacred Sites: Possibilities and Limitations." *Cultural Survival Quarterly* 19:30–35.

Waldron, Mary Anne. 2013. *Free to Believe: Rethinking Freedom of Conscience and Religion in Canada.* Toronto, ON: University of Toronto Press.

Wenger, Tisa. 2009. *We Have a Religion: The 1920s Pueblo Indian Dance Controversy and American Religious Freedom.* Chapel Hill: University of North Carolina Press.

LEGAL RESOURCES

CANADA (COURT CASE CITATIONS LIST FINAL DECISIONS ONLY)

Calder v. Attorney General of British Columbia S.C.R. *313* (S.C.C.) (1973)

Canadian Bill of Rights: S.C. 1960, c. 44 (1960)

Canadian Charter of Rights and Freedoms, Part I of the Constitution Act, 1, being Schedule B to the Canada Act (U.K.), c. 11 (1982)

Canadian Constitution Act (1982)

Delgamuukw v. British Columbia, 3 S.C.R. 1010 (S.C.C.) (1997)

Guerin v. The Queen 2 S.C.R. 335 (S.C.C.) (1984)

Haida Nation v. British Columbia (Minister of Forests), SCC 73 (2004)

Halfway River First Nation v. British Columbia (Minister of Forests), B.C.J. No. 1880 (B.C.C.A.) (QL) (1999)

Hunt v. Halcan Log Services (Deer Island) 34 D.L.R. (4th) 504 (B.C.S.C) (1987)

Kelly Lake Cree Nation v. Canada (Twin Sisters), F.C.J. No. 1942 (F.C.T.D.) (QL) (2000)

MacMillan Bloedel v. Mullin (Meares Island), 2 C.N.L.R. 54 (B.C.C.A.) (1985)

McCrady v. Ontario (High Falls), O.J. No. 2321 (Ont. Ct. Gen. Div.) (QL) (1992)

Mount Currie Indian Band v. International Forest Products (Ure Creek), B.C.J. No. 703 (B.C.S.C.) (QL) (1991)

R. v. Sparrow 1 S.C.R. 1075 (S.C.C.) (1990)

Saskatchewan Bill of Rights Act, S.S. 1947, c.35 (1947)

Siska Indian Band v. British Columbia (Minister of Forests) (Siska Creek), B.C.J. No. 2354 (B.C.S.C.) (QL) (1999)

Taku River Tlingit First Nation v. Tulsequah Chief Mine Project, B.C.J. No. 155 (B.C.C.A.) (QL) (2002)

Tlowitsis Nation and Mumtagila Nation v. MacMillan Bloedel, (Lower Tsitikas Valley) 2 C.N.L.R. 164 (B.C.S.C.) (1991)

Tsilhqot'in Nation v. British Columbia SCC 44 (2014)

Westar Timber v. Gitksan Wet'suwet'en Tribal Council, C.N.L.R. 151 (B.C.C.A.) (1990)

INTERNATIONAL

Universal Declaration of Human Rights (1948)

United Nations Declaration on the Rights of Indigenous Peoples (2007)

UNITED STATES (COURT CASE CITATIONS LIST FINAL DECISIONS ONLY)

American Antiquities Act Pub. L. 59–209, 34 Stat. 225, 54 U.S.C. § 320301–320303 (1906)

Badoni v. Higginson 638 F. 2d 172 (10th Cir. 1980), cert. denied, 452 U.S. 954 (1981)

Lyng v. Northwest Indian Cemetery Protective Association 108 S.Ct. 1319 (1988)

Manybeads v. United States 730 F. Supp. 1515 D. Ariz. (1989)

National Historic Preservation Act Public Law 89–665; 54 U.S.C. 300101 et seq. (1966)

Navajo Nation v. U.S. Forest Service 535 F.3d 1058 (9th Cir. 2008) (en banc) (2007)

Seneca Nation of Indians v. Brucker 262 F.2d 27 (1958)

Sequoya v. Tennessee Valley Authority 620 F.2d 1159 (1980)

U.S. Constitution (1791)

U.S. Department of the Interior, Office of Indian Affairs. *Rules Governing the Court of Indian Offenses*, by Hiram Price, Commissioner. Washington, DC (1883)

Wilson v. Block 708 F.2d 735, 758 (D.C.Cir.1983); 464 U.S. 1056 (1984)

4

RESPECT FOR THE INDIAN CHILD WELFARE ACT AND ITS REFLECTION ON TRIBAL SOVEREIGNTY

KURT D. SIEDSCHLAW

FOR THE past forty years I have worked with the tribes, reservations, and Native American organizations of South Dakota, Nebraska, and other states. Although not of Native blood, I have nephews and nieces who have married into the tribes, close friends and family who are members of the Lakota Nation, grand nephews and nieces who are members of the tribes, and I have developed strong friendships with both traditional and political leaders on the reservations. I have spent more than thirty-five years specifically seeking an understanding of traditional Indigenous ways and Indigenous justice, and I have assisted the Nebraska Commission on Indian Affairs and the Nebraska Department of Health and Human Services in facilitating and writing the Native American Family Preservation plan for the state. The issues related to the national Indian Child Welfare Act (ICWA) of 1978, and their resolutions, resonate with me. ICWA laws were formulated to stop state authorities from removing Indian children from their Indian homes and from their rightful participation in the tribe. The law was formulated not only to support Indian children and families but to preserve Indian nations. In a paper written for the Native American Rights Fund in 2001 that reviews the foundation of the federal ICWA states, Cedric Ian Hay says that the act was formulated over a period of time with "the expressed purpose of protecting the best interests of Indian children and to promote the stability and security of Indian tribes and families" (Hay 2001, 2). He goes on to say, "As a departure from prior assimilationist policies, and an affirmation of tribal sovereignty and self-determination, ICWA expressly recognized the vested interest that Indian tribes have in their children as essential to their collective existence and created the Act to protect this relationship" (Hay 2001, 2).

I realized after serving as a "qualified expert witness" for more than fifteen years and testifying in the first seven of fourteen cases for which I was called as a such a witness, that what I was actually telling the court about was the lack of knowledge and understanding of ICWA. I provided testimony related to the extended family concept and customs, but what I was really testifying to was the need for knowledge and understanding of the agencies and the court officers in regard to the failures of compliance related to the federal Indian Child Welfare Act and related state legislation. I spent much of my time on the stand educating the parties and the court in regard to definitions, terms, and concepts of ICWA. I found that no one, including me, knew enough about the law and the proper application of the law to properly be the expert witness, even when accepted by the parties and the court as such.

I was very relieved when the Indian Child Welfare Act specialist of the Nebraska Department of Health and Human Services, in cooperation with the Nebraska Indian Child Welfare Coalition (training program), initiated an effort in 2010 to prepare tribal elders to serve as expert witnesses in state court proceedings. The Qualified Expert Witness Program was a direct response to the failure of state authorities to understand and recognize that if an Indian child needs to be removed from their parental home in the child's best interest, that child is still an Indian, and whether formally enrolled or eligible to enroll, is a member of that tribe no matter what action the state court may take. These tribal elders may contribute a great deal to resolving the serious issues that will be detailed shortly.

In this chapter, the legal history that has necessitated such a program is described, including issues in selected state courts, issues with U.S. Supreme Court decisions, the negative impacts on Native communities, the negative impacts on tribal sovereignty, and finally, the tribal elders program. First, a look at tribal sovereignty.

AMERICAN INDIAN TRIBAL SOVEREIGNTY

There is a direct tie between a court's or agency's respect for the federal Indian Child Welfare Act and similar state laws and their understanding of tribal sovereignty. A review of state court proceedings involving Native American children reflects states' lack of understanding and respect for tribal sovereignty. That understanding is represented through the actions and failures to act by state agencies, governmental representatives, and the judiciary. The ICWA requires that the U.S. federal government, every state government, every Indian tribe, and all the territories of the United States give "full faith and credit to the public acts, records, and judicial proceedings of any Indian tribe applicable to Indian child custody proceedings to the same extent that such entities give full faith and credit to the public acts, records and judicial proceedings of any other entity" as reflected in the United States Code Section 25 U.S.C. 1912(d) 1988.[1]

While there are many definitions of sovereignty, *Black's Law Dictionary* (1979, 1252) defines sovereignty as "the supreme, absolute and uncontrollable power by which any independent state is governed; supreme political authority; paramount control of the constitution and frame of government and its administration; the self-sufficient source of political power, from which all specific political powers are derived; the international independence of a state, combined with the right and power of regulating its internal affairs without foreign dictation; also a political society, or state, which is sovereign and independent."

The courts' recognition of sovereignty is essential because American Indians were here first. Foreign settlers from a continent across the ocean came much later. The primary objects of the settlers were trade and land acquisition. Pommersheim (2009, 3) points out that the principal means of interactions between the colonies and the Indian tribes were diplomacy and war. He clearly explains that diplomacy and war often resulted in a treaty to settle the issue. Treaties are law. Treaties are binding contracts between two sovereign entities. After the colonies became the successor to the European states, the treaties were between the U.S. government and the individual sovereign tribes.

The foundation of the relationship between the government and the Indian tribes can be identified within the treaties, the Indian Commerce Clause of the Constitution, which reserved interactions and agreements with the tribes to a relationship between the federal government and those tribes, and the provisions to exclude "Indians not taxed" from citizenship and from determining the number of representatives that each state was entitled. The interaction between the U.S. government and the Indian tribes resulted in more than 350 treaties (Pommersheim 2009, 3). The common focuses of the treaties were land acquisition and commerce agreements. The U.S. government, in congressional legislation, executive branch executive orders, and Supreme Court decisions, has formulated laws and policies that have set the framework for the interaction of tribal, federal, and state governments, including in matters of American Indian welfare.

THE INDIAN CHILD WELFARE ACT AND STATE COURTS

Most of the scholarship on ICWA attacks state court resistance as unreasonably hostile to ICWA's statutory goals at best, and anti-Indian at worst. Barbara Ann Atwood (2002), in "Flashpoints Under the Indian Child Welfare Act: Toward a New Understanding of State Court Resistance," reviews aspects of the state court resistance to ICWA and strives to present a more nuanced understanding of the reactions of state court judges to its unique aspects. In addition to Atwood, Professor Christine Metteer argues forcefully that state courts have defied the plain language of the federal- and state-related ICWA laws because of their deep mistrust of tribal courts and their entrenched resistance to the concept of tribal sovereignty (Metteer 1998).

Metteer (1998) points out that the legislative history of the act is replete with examples of state courts employing white middle-class values as universal truths in assessing the fitness of Indian parents. State courts have formulated many theories to demonstrate "good cause" not to recognize or acknowledge the Indianness of a child, the child not being found to be part of an "Indian community," or not part of an "existing Indian family." State courts have consistently applied the incorrect rules of evidence and burden of proof in moving an Indian child to foster care or moving for termination of parental rights. State courts have incorrectly applied rulings that give the 1997 Adoption and Safe Families Act (ASFA) priority over the state or federal ICWA. As an example, Atwood (20012) points out that the South Dakota appellate court endorsed the distinct objectives underlying ICWA and ASFA, and agreed that ICWA's more demanding standard has control, but she also reflects that testimony before Congress in 1978, leading up to the ICWA, suggests that state courts suffered from ignorance, poor training, and cultural bias in deciding Indian child welfare matters. It is my argument that these negative findings about the 1978 congressional hearings still have validity in the functioning of state courts in 2017.

State courts still seem to resist the principles of ICWA. When proceedings involve Indian children not domiciled or residing within the reservation, ICWA mandates that the state court shall transfer the jurisdiction to the Indian child's tribe under 25 U.S.C. 1911 (b). This transfer can be blocked by either parent, by declination by the tribal court, or by a finding by the state court of good cause to the contrary (490 U.S. 30, 104 L. Ed. 2nd.). If jurisdiction is retained by the state court, ICWA authorizes the tribal court to intervene as a party with an interest in the state court proceedings, yet I have observed that state courts have often misunderstood a tribal motion to intervene as a motion to transfer custody and have denied the tribal motion.

Both federal and state ICWA-related legislation focus on three interlocking structural approaches to the jurisdictional problems. The statutes are jurisdictionally stringent in favor of tribal court jurisdiction, create minimum federal standards for the removal of Indian children from their homes by the state, and establish strict placement preferences that must be followed by state courts. The federal ICWA expressly rests on Congress's authority under the Indian Commerce Clause, plenary power, and its "responsibility for the protection and preservation of Indian tribes and their resources."

Thirty-five states have passed state legislation that mirrors the federal law. Some states have strengthened the state legislation to further affirm the rights of Indian children and the tribes. Oklahoma and Iowa have strong Indian Child Welfare Act laws; however, "many states have attempted to circumvent the application of the Act continuing to remove Indian children from their homes" (Hay 2001, 4). The following examples provide fodder for Metteer's (1998) earlier contention about state transgressions.

First, state courts have expanded on the "good cause" exception to not recognize the tribal interests and to retain exclusive jurisdiction of a case that clearly falls under the terms of ICWA. A second exception formulated by state courts is the "existing Indian family" exception adopted by the Kansas courts (*In re Baby L* 1982). In reviewing the various exceptions challenging the ICWA, Suziannne D. Painter-Thorne states, "One exception is the so-called 'existing Indian family' exception. Under this exception, courts refuse to apply ICWA in situations where a court deems the child is not part of a sufficiently Indian family. In relying on this exception, these state courts ignore ICWA's plain language and Supreme Court precedent" (Painter-Thorne 2008–09, 367).

A third exception is that state courts have also attempted to circumvent the intent of ICWA legislation in identifying a "not involved in Indian culture" exception, that is, that the child is not a member of an Indian community and thus is not subject to the cultural standards of the Indian community and extended family. For example, the Kansas Supreme Court, in *In re Baby Boy L* attempted to assess whether the child had sufficient ties to the tribal culture or the reservation. The child was clearly identified as being an "Indian child" under the law but the court clearly failed to research, assess, or apply the concepts of tribal membership, extended family, or the intent of ICWA (*In re Adoption of Baby Boy L* 1982). It is interesting that the child, in this case, was not old enough to have experienced his Indian culture, but the court denied him the opportunity to ever know his culture because he was deemed not to be part of an "existing Indian family" (thereby also pulling in the second exception). The child was born, relinquished to adoption the same day he was born, enrolled as a member of the Kiowa Tribe, and claimed by his tribe and extended family, yet was viewed by the court as not being applicable to ICWA because he was not part of an "existing Indian family."

State courts have raised the concept of youth "not involved in Indian culture" as a justification for an exception to involvement of the tribes and not allowing either intervention of the tribe or transfer of a case from state court to tribal court. A variation on this exception was used by a trial court in Michigan that held that expert testimony in an ICWA case was not needed because the mother and child were "not involved in Indian culture." The Michigan Court of Appeals held that the trial court erred when it found that no expert testimony was needed when terminating parental rights under ICWA (McEwen 2008).

The dynamics of removing children under the rationale that they are "not involved in Indian culture" or are not part of an "existing Indian family" should be the precise reason to fully enforce ICWA laws and assist in affirming or reestablishing those children and families with their tribes. To rule that an Indian child is not an Indian child defies logic and reason. When a state court so rules, such a ruling does not cause that child to stop being an Indian, nor does such a ruling mean that the child is not either traditionally or legally a member of the tribe. This failure of state courts is a direct reflection of a lack of knowledge of Indian cultures, the legislative intent of ICWA, and any concept of tribal sovereignty.

The interests of the tribes in ICWA cases, separate and apart from the parental interests, are not always recognized. The Utah Supreme Court, for example, did recognize that "[t]he tribe has an interest in the child which is distinct from, but on parity with, the interests of the parents. This relationship between Indian tribe and Indian children finds no parallel in other ethnic cultures found in the United States." The court further emphasized the critical nature of the involvement of the tribe in the decision-making processes of the courts, noting that "[f]ew matters are of more central interest to a tribe seeking to preserve its identity and traditions than the determination of who will have the care and custody of its children" (*In re Adoption of Halloway* 1986).

Similarly, a 2010 Kansas Supreme Court ruling held that the lack of testimony by a qualified expert witness cannot be considered harmless (*In re S.M.H.* 2005). The district court in Kansas had ruled that the state failed to comply with ICWA standards for termination of parental rights by proving beyond a reasonable doubt that termination of parental rights was necessary, including the testimony of a qualified expert witness, *but* that it was "harmless error" not to have testimony of an expert witness in an ICWA termination of parental rights proceeding (*In re M.F.* 2010). The Kansas Supreme Court held that a harmless error analysis is inappropriate when the court does not comply with ICWA (*In re M.F.* 1187–88). In the Kansas case the district court accepted the testimony of a social worker with no knowledge of Native American culture and one year of experience as a social worker as an "expert witness." The Kansas Supreme Court subsequently overruled the lower court and affirmed the necessity of having a qualified expert witness testify in the case of termination of parental rights of an Indian child's parent.

A detailed case review of court cases involving the Indian Child Welfare Act in Nebraska and other states reflects a historical lack of compliance with state and federal law, a failure of agencies to train their people, and a significant lack of understanding on the part of state agencies and judicial representatives. A review of court rulings indicates a consistent effort to disregard the clear intent of state and federal ICWA law to avoid involvement of the tribes, a flippant use of the concept of "good cause," and efforts to seek and create new exceptions that allow them not to follow ICWA. Creativity has gone into the creation of exceptions such as the Indian child "not involved in Indian culture" or not part of an "existing Indian family."

Many state court decisions reflect and generate a result that mirrors the original testimony that was a foundation for the ICWA. Testimony before Congress in hearings prior to the 1978 ICWA legislation identified

> The disparity in placement rates for Indians and non-Indians is shocking. In Minnesota, Indian children are placed in foster care or in adoptive homes at a per capita rate five times greater than non-Indian children. In Montana, the ratio of Indian foster care placement is at least 13 times greater. In South Dakota 40 percent of all adoptions made by the South Dakota Department of Public Welfare since 1967–1968 are Indian children in a state in which Indians represent 7 percent of the population. In 16 states surveyed in 1969, approximately 85 percent of all Indian children in foster care were living in non-Indian homes. (Byler 1974, 1)

For some, this is not at all new, but rather the latest update that harkens back to the era of (federal) boarding schools, when the primary goal, in the words of Richard Pratt, a leading educator and spokesman, was "to kill the Indian and save the man" (Pommersheim 2009, 243). These cases reflect the lack of knowledge and understanding of both ICWA and Native American culture and are a strong argument for the need for tribal elders as expert witnesses, as proposed by the Nebraska Department of Health and Human Services and NICWC.

THE U.S. SUPREME COURT AND ICWA

For all of the state court proceedings involving the Indian Child Welfare Act, only two court cases that tested the federal law have been presented to the U.S. Supreme Court. The first case was *Mississippi Band of Choctaw Indians v. Holyfield* (1989). Justice Brennan, in his opinion, affirmed the necessity to consider the case based upon a federal standard and identified two reasons why. First, there was Congress's desire for nationwide uniformity in the application of domicile for the child (or where the home of the child might be legally). Second, and more important, was Congress's intent to limit (not expand) state judicial authority in dealing with Indian children and the expectations of the Indian Child Welfare Act (Pommersheim 2009, 242). The holding in the Holyfield case stressed the need to protect the interests of the Indian community in retaining its children within its society and reaffirmed the act's intent to establish some uniformity with regard to the state courts' handling of adoption and placement of Indian children.

A more recent case considering the Indian Child Welfare Act reviewed by the U.S. Supreme Court was *Adoptive Couple v. Baby Girl* (2013), which originated in South Carolina state courts. The case did not actually deal with anything but a very narrow interpretation of the ICWA law and whether there ever was a "family" to protect. The case did not even consider tribal rights, concepts, or sovereignty. The court had before it two competing interpretations of ICWA: The more expansive version, advocated by the biological father, argued essentially that ICWA applies whenever a court is considering whether to terminate parental rights of an Indian parent. The competing interpretation, advanced by the adoptive parents, argues that ICWA's coverage is limited to the kinds of cases that Congress most likely had in mind when it passed ICWA—namely, those in which social workers and other government officials seek to remove Indian children from an existing Indian family (Gottlieb 2013, 1).

Did the South Carolina state courts understand the spirit and meaning of ICWA in the *Baby Girl* case? Were ICWA placement preferences considered? Did the guardian ad litem (GAL) for the baby girl understand ICWA? (A guardian ad litem is a legal term meaning a person appointed by the court as a guardian of an infant, child, or adult person to act on the individual's behalf in court proceedings.) From the court records the answer has to be no!

The GAL for "Baby Girl," within the federal court records, does not address tribal involvement, and it appears that the GAL almost assumes that tribal authorities would rule in favor of the biological father without any involvement of the tribal court being entered on the record. The tribe recognized the father's right to be considered, but they were not given input to assess the issue of the "best interests" of the child. The GAL did not even explore cultural or tribal issues or definitions of family. The purpose of the law is to work for the "best interests of the child" and the "best interests of the tribe." The goal is to preserve Indian children, families, and tribes. The *Baby Girl* decision was narrowly decided based upon the legal, strict concept of whether there was a "family" to be protected.

Even though the U.S. Supreme Court considered ICWA in considerable detail, it applied a very narrow legal concept in their decision. That narrow concept was that there was no "Indian family" to protect, since the father had disavowed the child prior to birth and had not assisted or taken part in either the mother's life or the life of the child prior to the legal challenge, which arose many months after the father learned that the biological mother was allowing the child to be adopted. There has been extensive research and litigation at the state and federal levels related to this case; however, a critical review of the many proceedings has left me with the assessment that little or no regard was given to the issues of culture, tribes, or tribal sovereignty.

A review of the various state and federal court proceedings reflects U.S. Supreme Court rulings that key from this very narrow legal definition of family that requires little or no consideration or respect for the spirit of the ICWA, the tribe, Native American culture, or respect for tribal sovereignty.

IMPACTS OF THE FAILURE TO FOLLOW ICWA REQUIREMENTS

When I interviewed adult Native Americans who were removed from their Indian homes and placed in non-Indian homes to be reared, they often stated that in their later teens and young adult years they looked into the mirror and saw an Indian, but did not understand what that meant. This chapter is not designed to address the high rate of teen suicide among Native American youth, the overrepresentation of Native American youth in our dominant culture justice system, nor the failures to respect tribal sovereignty and ICWA. Interviews with traditional elders of the reservations and with parents of children involved in the system have articulated a universal sense that youth removed from the tribes and their families are also removed from the knowledge and access to their Native traditions and the ability to understand who they are. This lack of knowledge and understanding has created more than one lost generation of Native American youth.

The failure of state courts to understand the principles of the legislation that created the federal and state ICWA laws has led to state courts viewing either the motion to intervene or the motion to transfer as interference with the customary functioning of the state court. Such a position reflects what Jeanne Louise Carriere identified back in 1994 as "inherent biases and cultural hostility of state courts" (Carriere 1994, 585).

Observations in state court proceedings have demonstrated little or no understanding on the part of state social service workers, county attorneys, or judges as to the fact that the ICWA laws are designed to protect the interests of the Indian child and family but also to protect the rights and the stability of the tribe. ICWA allows the tribe to intervene in a case to prevent the removal of its children from their rightful and natural cultural heritage as members of the tribe. These legal issues provide the context in which the state of Nebraska began its program to provide training for elders through the Department of Health and Human Services and NICWC to appear as expert witnesses in state court proceedings.

EXPERT WITNESSES IN ICWA CASES

The minimum federal standards for the removal of Indian children from the parental home by state courts include the necessity of expert testimony, the provision of rehabilitative services, and the enhanced burden of proof (Pommersheim 2009, 244). Federal guidelines suggest the following persons are most likely to meet the requirements for qualified expert witnesses: (1) a member of the child's tribe who is recognized by the tribal community as knowledgeable in tribal customs as they pertain to family organization and child rearing practice, (2) a lay expert witness having substantial experience in the delivery of child and family services to Indians and extensive knowledge of prevailing social and cultural standards and child rearing practices within the Indian child's tribe, and (3) a professional person having substantial education and experience in the area of his or her specialty. These federal guidelines should be considered by courts in determining whether a witness is a qualified expert witness. Congress intended "qualified expert witnesses" to refer to experts with particular and significant knowledge of sensitivity to Indian culture and knowledge of social and cultural aspects of Indian life. The phrase "qualified expert witness" in Indian Child Welfare Act cases is meant to apply to expertise beyond the normal social worker qualifications (Snyder 1995, 835). The Iowa ICWA law provides example guidelines of the order of preference, as follows:

a. A member of the child's Indian tribe who is recognized by the child's tribal community as knowledgeable regarding tribal customs as they pertain to family organization or child-rearing practices.

b. A member of another tribe who is formally recognized by the Indian child's tribe as having the knowledge to be a qualified expert witness.

c. A layperson having substantial experience in the delivery of child and family services to Indians, and substantial knowledge of the prevailing social and cultural standards and child-rearing practices within the Indian child's tribe.

d. A professional person having substantial education and experience in the person's professional specialty and substantial knowledge of the prevailing social and cultural standards and child-rearing practices within the Indian child's tribe.

e. A professional person having substantial education and experience in the person's professional specialty and having extensive knowledge of the customs, traditions, and values of the Indian child's tribe as the customs, traditions, and values pertain to family organization and child-rearing practices.

Before accepting testimony of the least preferred type of expert, the court must make and document efforts to procure an expert higher in the preferential order, including, but not limited to, contacting the tribe's governing body, the ICWA office, and the social service agency.

In addition to the disconnect between the prescriptions of law and the practice in the courts, many professionals do not understand the guidelines such as these related to the federal and state ICWA laws for the utilization of expert witnesses. For example, in April 2010 the state of California identified that many people working in California ICWA proceedings did not understand the purpose of ICWA expert witnesses or how they were to be used, and clarification was needed. As a result, the California governor issued a directive that affirms that no Indian child shall be removed from the custody of his or her parents, and no placement in out-of-home care may be ordered in the absence of a determination supported by "clear and convincing evidence, including the testimony of a qualified expert witness" (California Department of Social Services 2010). This action by the governor of California affirms the lack of knowledge and understanding related to Native people and ICWA.

The Native American Rights Fund (NARF) has generated guidelines to address the issues related to ICWA indicating that the use of an expert witness is required whenever a state court places an Indian child in foster care or is taking an action to terminate parental rights (Native American Rights Fund 2007). NARF guidelines also affirm the requirement of an expert witness in efforts to deviate from the placement preferences that are lain out in ICWA. As well, the Bureau of Indian Affairs has generated guidelines for the qualification of expert witnesses in ICWA cases.

The law in Nebraska states, "It shall be the policy of the state to cooperate fully with Indian tribes in Nebraska in order to ensure that the intent and provisions of the federal Indian Child Welfare Act are enforced" (Nebraska Revised Statutes 1986, 966), and further reflecting the federal guidelines, "The State of Nebraska shall give full faith and credit to the public acts, records, and judicial proceedings of any Indian tribe applicable to Indian child custody proceedings to the same extent that the state gives full faith and credit to the public acts, records, and judicial proceedings of any other entity" (Nebraska Revised Statutes 1986, 43–1504[5]). Also, in any case when federal law applicable to child custody proceedings provides a higher standard of protection to the rights of the parent or Indian custodian of an Indian child than the rights provided under the Nebraska Indian Child Welfare Act, the state court shall apply the federal standard (Nebraska Revised Statutes 1986, 43–151).

A review of the Nebraska Department of Health and Human Services found that "state workers did not utilize a lay person with substantial education and knowledge of the social and cultural standards of child rearing practices of the child's tribe in ninety percent of the cases reviewed. They also do not utilize a professional person who has knowledge of the social standards and child rearing practices in the Indian community in ninety-five percent of the cases" (Morrison 1999, 2).

Nebraska passed the Nebraska Indian Child Welfare Act in 1986, yet in 2007 Nebraska ranked as the second highest state in terms of disproportionality of Indian children in foster care (National Indian Child Welfare Association 2007, 2). There is a major disconnect between the prescriptions of state law and the functioning of social services and the court system. Conversations among those working on ICWA issues in Nebraska led to a consensus that there are probably no more than a handful of attorneys and judges outside of the tribal courts who have any knowledge or understanding of Indian culture or ICWA.

As a result of this issue, the state of Nebraska undertook an effort to train elders from the reservations to become the recognized expert witnesses for cases related to their specific tribes. The Nebraska Indian Child Welfare Coalition (NICWC) and Sherri Eveleth, the ICWA specialist for the Nebraska Department of Health and Human Services, led the initiative. NICWC describes itself as offering "customized trainings and presentations, . . . cultural consultation, and conven[ing] the right people. We're experts at trauma-informed, culturally integrated approaches." It provides a wide range of culturally relevant, ICWA-related trainings, including developing and training foster parents and relative caregivers, trauma informed care training, and historical trauma and ICWA training (http://nicwc.org/our-services/).

QUALIFIED EXPERT WITNESS PROGRAM

Training dynamics of this program, also called the elders program, include preparations to help the elders feel at ease in the courtroom and to familiarize them with the parties and procedures in child welfare cases. The participants are given a brief overview of ICWA. Sherri Eveleth indicated that some of the elders are uncomfortable with or intimidated by the term "expert." Eveleth tries to convey the message that they are the experts in their cultures: they know their culture—and what is appropriate or not appropriate in families—better than anyone else in the courtroom. She also lets them know that they do not need to be experts in the state and federal ICWAs or child welfare laws (Eveleth 2010–12).

The participants are provided an overview that includes the types of cases to which ICWA applies—including cases of sexual abuse or physical abuse of a child to the point of serious physical injury. An area that the participants are advised that they do not have to testify to are child custody cases between biological parents. The training includes a summary of Nebraska ICWA case law defining what the court means by the term "qualified expert witnesses." The training is designed to help elders become aware of issues that attorneys may bring up in court, such as the determination of whether active efforts have been provided, and that the testimony of a qualified expert witness is designed to assist the court in areas of knowledge and expertise that go beyond common knowledge and the court's expertise. In the experience of the trainers, most attorneys do not object to a qualified expert witness providing an opinion about whether active efforts have been provided.

In one training, an impromptu mock trial provided a qualified expert witness to testify. The training was held in the Winnebago Tribal Court, and Jerry Denney, a Santee Sioux elder and their ICWA specialist, "testified." Eveleth played the role of county attorney and testimony was elicited to establish his credentials. Danielle Smith and Roz Koob, attorneys for the Winnebago Tribe, assisted with cross-examination. The examination questioned the witnesses' lack of formal education and that they had been living off the reservation. There was an opportunity to rehabilitate the witness, or reestablish his credibility after the cross-examination. The tribal attorneys questioned the witness about his residence off-reservation during his childhood years. Rehabilitation on cross-examination showed that he stayed connected to his tribe and has spent most of his more than seventy years living on the reservation. After having this "court-in-action" mock hearing, participants expressed an appreciation for being able to see a case in action. The training effort is designing further activities to replicate various situations for a full mock trial.

The effort to prepare tribal members to function as expert witnesses will continue with the premise that tribal members should be utilized as qualified expert witnesses. Considerations in the utilization of tribal elders as expert witnesses include:

1. Many courts expect to have the testimony of Qualified Expert Witness (QEW) within forty-eight hours of a child's removal;
2. Locating tribal elders from geographically distant tribes who possess evidence of recognition as an expert by the tribal community is difficult if not impossible;
3. For tribes that do not recognize termination of parental rights, tribal members will not testify to support a Termination of Parental Rights (TPR). For such cases, it is strongly encouraged that a guardianship be established or that the tribe be worked with to develop an alternate permanency plan that does not include TPR; and
4. In some cases, particularly when the child is related to a tribal council member or other person of authority, tribal members are not willing to testify. Tribal elders may also hesitate to testify because of their precise understanding of the extended family, and issues of respect.

CONCLUSION

It is hoped that such a large pool of qualified expert witnesses will emerge from the elders' training program that there is never a need to call a "professional person" who is not a tribal member. Until that time, in those cases in which a tribal member is not available, work will continue to facilitate qualified expert witness testimony from professional persons who have knowledge and expertise of tribal cultures, the historical basis of Indian child welfare, and an understanding of the needs of an Indian child.

In addition to tribal elders as expert witnesses, the key to the effective application of the federal and state Indian Child Welfare Act legislation is increased understanding and awareness on the part of governmental agencies, human service agencies, and members of the court of the intent and philosophy of the law, the various Indian nations, the cultures and values of those nations, and tribal sovereignty. It is a hopeful sign that in 2016 the Nebraska Department of Health and Human Services implemented an ICWA advocate position within each service region. In 2017 there was at least one Indian Child Welfare Act specialist in each Nebraska Department of Health and Human Services district. These positions, along with the tribal expert witnesses, could promote greater understanding and recognition of tribal sovereignty. It remains to be seen, however, if the state courts understand and will honor the plain language standards of the ICWA and tribal sovereignty.

NOTE

1.   25 U.S.C. 1901 (5) (2000): See 1974 Hearings, supra note 56; American Indian Policy Review Commission, Report on Federal, State, and Tribal Jurisdiction 79–80 (Comm. Print 1976) ("1976 Report"). The formal findings included in the act itself provide that "the States, exercising their recognized jurisdiction over Indian child custody proceedings through administrative and judicial bodies, have often failed to recognize the essential tribal relations of Indian people and the cultural and social standards prevailing in Indian communities and families." 25 U.S.C. 1901 (5) (2000).

REFERENCES

Atwood, Barbara Ann. 2002. "Flashpoints Under the Indian Child Welfare Act: Toward a New Understanding of State Court Resistance." *Emory Law Journal* 51:587–676.

———. 2008. "Achieving Permanency for American Indian and Alaska Native Children: Lessons from Tribal Traditions." *Capital University Law Review* 37:239–92.

Black's Law Dictionary. 1979. 5th ed. Saint Paul, MN: West Publishing.

Byler, William. 1974. Statement. U.S. Senate Rep., 93rd Cong. (2d. Sess. 1974). Documented in 1978 U.S. Code Cong.

California Department of Social Services. 2010. Information Notice No. 1-40-10 (April).

Carriere, Jeanne Louise. 1994. "Representing the Native American: Culture, Jurisdiction, and the Indian Child Welfare Act." *Iowa Law Review* 79:585–652.

Eveleth, Sherri. 2010–12. Various conversations and correspondence.

Gottlieb, Mike. 2013. *Details: Adoptive Couple v. Baby Girl*. SCOTUSblog (June 25, 2013, 10:53 a.m.). http://www.scotusblog.com/2013/06/details-adpotive-couple-v-baby-girl/.

Hay, Cedric Ian. 2001. "The Indian Child Welfare Act: An Acknowledgement of Sovereignty in the Best Interest of the Child." Boulder, CO: Native American Rights Fund.

McEwen, Robert. 2008. "ICWA Enforcement: Is It Losing Its Teeth in Nebraska?" Presentation at legal conference. University of Nebraska School of Law.

Metteer, Christine. 1998. "Hard Cases Making Bad Law: The Need for Revision of the Indian Child Welfare Act." *Santa Clara Law Review* 38:419–72.

Morrison, Belva. 1999. "Indian Child Welfare Act Compliance Review." Lincoln: Nebraska Department of Health and Human Services.

National Indian Child Welfare Association. 2007. *Time for Reform: A Matter of Justice for American Indian and Alaskan Native Children*. Oklahoma City: National Indian Child Welfare Association.

Native American Rights Fund. 2007. "A Practical Guide to the Indian Child Welfare Act. Sect. 14: Expert Witnesses." Boulder: CO: Native American Rights Fund.

Painter-Thorne, Suzanne D. 2008–09. "One Step Forward, Two Giant Steps Back: How the Existing Indian Family Exception (Re) Imposes Anglo American Legal Values on American Indian Tribes to the Detriment of Cultural Autonomy." *American Indian Law Review* 33:329–84.

Pommersheim, Frank. 2009. *Broken Landscape: Indians, Indian Tribes, and the Constitution*. New York: Oxford University Press.

Snyder, Michael. 1995. "An Overview of the Indian Child Welfare Act." *St. Thomas Law Review* 7:815–43.

LEGAL RESOURCES

Adoptive Couple v. Baby Girl, 133 S. Ct. 2552; 186 L. Ed. 2d 729; 2013 U.S. LEXIS 4916; 81 (2013)

Adoptive Couple v. Baby Girl, Opinion No. 27148, Supreme Court of South Carolina, 398 S.C. 625; 731 S.E.2d 550; 2012 S.C. LEXIS 212, April 17, 2012, Heard, July 26, 2012, Filed, Rehearing denied by Adoptive Couple v. Baby Girl, 2012 S.C. LEXIS 176 (S.C., Aug. 22, 2012). US Supreme Court certiorari granted by, Motion granted by Adoptive Couple v. Baby Girl, 133 S. Ct. 831, 184 L. Ed. 2d 646, 2013 U.S. LEXIS 11 (U.S., 2013) Reversed by, Remanded by Adoptive Couple v. Baby Girl, 2013 U.S. LEXIS 4916 (U.S., June 25, 2013)

Indian Child Welfare Act § 1901 (1978)

In re Adoption of Baby Boy L, 231 Kan 199, 643 P.2d 168 (1982)

In re Adoption of Halloway, 732 P. 2d 962 (Utah 1986)

In re M.F., 290 Kan. 142, 225 P.3d 1177; 1187–88 (2010)

In re S.M.H., 33 Kan. App. 2d 424, 103 P.3d 976 (2005)

Iowa Code 232B (3)(e)

Mississippi Band of Choctaw Indians v. Holyfield, 490 U.S. 30 (1989)

Nebraska Indian Child Welfare Act (Neb. Rev. Stat. Section 1986, 1501 [1986])

Nebraska Revised Statutes. Sec. 42–1504 (4), 43–1502, 1513; Sec. 1501 et seq. (1986)

5

PROTECTING NATIVE AMERICAN WOMEN

Grassroots Efforts to Address Domestic Violence
and VAWA 2013

MARY JO TIPPECONNIC FOX

VIOLENCE AGAINST Native women is a serious issue in Indian Country; its impact extends beyond the victim, often destroying families and affecting all Native people directly or indirectly. The violence can be physical, psychological, emotional, and/or economic, with many Native women and their families suffering in silence because of fear, shame, or the lack of appropriate responses from law enforcement and the judicial system. Though not perfect, the Violence Against Women Act (VAWA) of 2013 provided hope for these women and their families with provisions that allow tribes to better protect them. Unfortunately, as of early September 2019, VAWA has not yet been reauthorized by Congress.

Domestic violence is physical assault, willful intimidation, and other abusive behavior perpetrated by one intimate partner against another. It is directed at both genders though it is experienced at a higher rate by Native women. Far too many Native American families and communities are affected by domestic violence, including this author's family. Our family's life changed forever when my sister was a victim of domestic violence that occurred at a time when VAWA did not exist, the issue was not talked about openly, and the justice system treated it like a family issue. It was not until the 1980s that domestic violence became a national topic, and Congress passed the first VAWA in 1994 to address this problem (Ballard 2014). In 2007 Amnesty International reported that sexual violence against Native American women in the United States constituted a human rights violation because of its high rates caused by erosion of culture, jurisdictional issues, policing, sentencing, and lack of support for survivors.

Decades before the passage of VAWA, however, American Indian and Alaska Native (AI/AN) women in many tribal communities began grassroots efforts to address domestic violence and protect local women and their children. Grassroots activism by Native women began in the 1970s and grew in subsequent years to directly influence the original passage of VAWA in 1994 and its reauthorizations in 2000, 2005, and 2013. This chapter examines domestic violence against American Indian and Alaska Native women in Indian Country, discusses grassroots efforts to protect Native women and children, evaluates the impact of VAWA 2013, and concludes with a look at next steps.

DOMESTIC VIOLENCE IN TRIBAL COMMUNITIES

Existing data on violence against Native women has a number of limitations, yet existing statistics are disturbing and unacceptable, especially considering that statisticians have chronically undersampled Indian Country and higher rates of domestic violence are therefore probable. More than 1.5 million American Indian and Alaska Native women experience violence in their lifetimes, according to a 2016 National Institute of Justice study (Rosay 2016) which draws data from the 2010 National Intimate Partner and Sexual Violence Survey (NISVS). The 2010 study included a nationally representative sample of 2,473 adult women and 1,505 adult men self-identified as American Indian or Alaska Native alone or with another group; 83 percent of women and 79 percent of men were affiliated or enrolled with a tribe or village. Of these, 54 percent of women and men lived within reservation boundaries or in an Alaska Native village in the past year. This study is the most thorough assessment to date on the extent of violence against American Indians and Alaska Natives. The results show high rates of violence against American Indian and Alaska Native women. More than four in five AI/AN women experience violence in their lifetime, which includes sexual violence (56.1 percent), violence by intimate partners (55.5 percent), stalking (48.8 percent), rape (34.1 percent), and psychological aggression by an intimate partner (66.4 percent). The murder rate of AI/AN women is almost three times that of non-Hispanic white women (Rosay 2016; NCAI 2018a). The lifetime violence against AI/AN female victims experienced at the hands of non-Native perpetrators is estimated at 97 percent and at the hands of American Indian and Alaska Native perpetrators is 35 percent. These statistics provide support for tribes' sovereign right to prosecute non-Native offenders (Rosay 2016). Limitations to these studies include the number of self-identified American Indian or Alaska Native women, the percentage of the sample living on reservations or villages, and the accuracy of intra-racial and interracial attacks on women on tribal lands. In addition, the statistics on existing data do not delineate how many of these attacks occurred on tribal lands or in particular communities, or how many fall under tribal or state jurisdictions. In future studies, there is a need for better data to clarify these questions. The Indian Law and Order Commission (2013) recommends that crime data include information about the location at which a crime occurred as well as the victim's and offender's Indian status. It requires the U.S. Department of Justice (DOJ) to provide reservation-level victimization data in its annual reports to Congress on Indian Country crime, and Congress to ensure data and data reports required by the Tribal Law and Order Act 2010.

Tribal jurisdictional issues involve complex interrelationships between the tribes and federal and state governments that undermine a tribe's ability to effectively respond to sexual assaults (Amnesty International 2007). In Indian Country, as a result of the 1978 U.S. Supreme Court decision in *Oliphant v. Suquamish* and other federal laws, the authority to prosecute crimes is fractured and based upon the identity of the offender, the identity of victim, and the nature of the crime (Tatum 2014). The federal government has the primary responsibility to investigate and prosecute all general federal interracial and major crimes on reservations, but federal case law has created some uncertainty regarding the authority of tribal courts to enter domestic violence protection orders. States have the authority for crimes committed by non-Indians against other non-Indians, and tribes for crimes committed by Indians. For some tribes, Public Law 280 and settlement acts devolved federal authority to state authority, including in the states of Alaska, California, Minnesota, Nebraska, Oregon, and Wisconsin (NCAI 2013b; Tatum 2014).

The high rates of violence experienced by American Indian/Alaska Native women in the United States must be examined in the historical context of colonization, which often leads to internalized oppression and normalization of violence (Futures Without Violence 2017), and federal law and policies that altered tribal societies and eroded the respect and status of Native women (Agtuca and Sahneyah 2014). Prior to European contact, rape, sexual assault, and other violence against Native women were uncommon occurrences in most tribal societies. When violence occurred, systems were in place to deal with such transgressions by tribal members based upon their traditions, philosophies, and standards (Fox 2009). Colonization destroyed many of these tribal systems and traditions that protected Native women. During the colonization and reservation periods, tribal women were often raped or sexually assaulted by European or Euro-American men, and stereotyped as prostitutes, squaws, or drunks who were considered "dirty" and thus "rape-able." Furthermore, European and Euro-American's introduction of alcohol to tribes was devastating because of the link between drinking and violent crimes (Smith 2005).

Colonialism resulted in shifts in the worldview and ideology of Native nations that impacted the social structures and socialization processes of tribes, particularly gender roles. The introduction of Christianity changed gender roles because of European patrilineal ideologies and policies, as well as because of epidemics and warfare (Chenault 2011). During the Indian wars, women and children were often targeted for extermination by troops. To save themselves and their children, Native women were forced to assimilate and give up their traditional roles (Agtuca and Sahneyah 2014).

Beginning in the late nineteenth century, U.S. federal policies also reshaped traditional Native gender roles. The federal government used education as a major strategy to influence and change Native gender roles, especially during the boarding school era of the 1880s to 1950s, which promoted the Protestant ideal of "true womanhood." Native girls were indoctrinated into white Protestant gender and domestic ideals of being pious, pure, obedient, selfless, meek, and clean (Paxton 2006). Without regard to traditional tribal gender roles, the schools' curriculum taught Native girls domestic skills while boys were trained to be farmers and heads of households. Assimilation was the federal policy and goal of education. The removal of children from their parents especially impacted the roles of mothers who were often responsible for passing on the cultural traditions. Many girls in boarding schools were also subject to physical and sexual abuse by school officials. This often led to future generations of Native Americans not speaking their heritage languages, not practicing cultural ways, and experiencing intergenerational trauma. U.S. allotment policy (1887–1934) was also damaging to Native women, as not all of them received land. In the 1970s the U.S. Department of Health and Human Services, and primarily the Indian Health Service, implemented a devastating forced sterilization program that impacted approximately 3,406 Native women without their consent (Agtuca and Sahneyah 2014).

NATIVE WOMEN'S GRASSROOTS ACTIVISM AND VAWA

Native American women's grassroots activism to combat domestic violence was a significant factor behind the U.S. Congress's passage of VAWA in 1994 and its later reauthorizations. Beginning in the late 1970s Native American women concerned about the safety of their peers organized responses to domestic violence. Their actions were motivated by the number of women experiencing violence in their communities, the complex jurisdictional maze, lack of prosecution of non-Indians, and a commitment to maintaining traditional values and roles. These Native women understood the historical root causes of violence against AI/AN women, and the importance of decolonization in the healing process. Two leaders of this movement were Matilda "Tillie" Black Bear (Sicangu Lakota) and Nugange (Lenora "Lynn" Hootch) (Yup'ik), both of whom advocated for safety and justice for tribal women in the lower forty-eight states and Alaska. These women and their allies built a strong national movement that is more than forty years old and informs Congress on policies and laws to end violence against Native women (Agtuca and Sahneyah 2014). They are representative of the many Indigenous women who have provided leadership in addressing social justice issues for all AI/AN peoples.

In response to the severity of violence against women of all backgrounds and the need for a national strategic effort to address the situation, Congress passed VAWA in 1994 to improve criminal justice and community-based responses to domestic violence, dating violence, sexual assault, and stalking. The reauthorizations in 2000 and 2005 were by unanimous consent, reflecting Congress's recognition of the need to enhance the safety of Native women (NCAI 2013b) and "strengthen the capacity of Indian tribes to exercise their sovereign authority to respond to violent crimes committed against women" (Agtuca and Sahneyah 2014, 14–15). These were followed by the passage by Congress of the Tribal Law and Order Act (TLOA) of 2010 and finally, VAWA reauthorization in 2013 (Agtuca and Sahneyah 2014). Congress reauthorized VAWA in part to address the problem of sexual and domestic violence committed by non-Indians against Native women. The law restored to tribes the ability to prosecute non-Indians who commit domestic violence in Indian country, which it referred to as Special Domestic Violence Criminal Jurisdiction (SDVCJ), and set out a series of requirements tribes must satisfy if they want to exercise this restored authority. VAWA 2013 established a two-year time frame for a pilot project and declared its provisions would take effect two years after the date of enactment; accordingly the act became fully effective in March 2015. Alaska Native women were initially exempt from VAWA 2013, but the exemption was repealed in 2014 after protest by Native peoples, and a report by the Indian Law and Order Commission (Langlois 2014).

Native women's grassroots efforts to combat domestic violence in their communities began with opening their homes to women and children in need of a safe place and eventually establishing shelters in their communities. It did not stop there as Native women began to advocate and lobby for laws and policies to protect their peers. The White Buffalo Calf Women's Society (WBCWS) established the first Native women's shelter on an Indian reservation in 1977 on the Rosebud Sioux Reservation. This American Indian and Alaska Native organization for the safety of women is based upon the belief that tribal women are respected, their roles valued, and that colonization and European beliefs about women significantly impacted and continue to impact the treatment of Native women (Agtuca and Sahneyah 2014).

Tillie Black Bear, the founding mother of the White Buffalo Calf Women's Society Shelter, was the leader of this effort both nationally and on the Rosebud reservation. She was known as the "Grandmother of the Battered Women's Movement" for her dedication to the safety of Native women and tribal sovereignty for forty years (NIWRC 2014). The women of Rosebud invited the National Coalition Against Domestic

Violence steering committee to the reservation. Native women, and Tillie especially, took part in the activities of the coalition including going to Capitol Hill to make sure Native women were not forgotten. Tillie's leadership and vision led to the establishment of organizations such as the National Coalition Against Domestic Violence, the South Dakota Coalition Against Domestic Violence, and the National Indigenous Women's Resource Center (NIWRC). Following the passage of VAWA in 1994 and 2000, she stated, "By doing VAWA these many years, we wanted it to become something that would always be there for women" (Tillie Black Bear, August 24, 2004, as quoted in Agtuca and Sahneyah 2014, 5). Tillie was the recipient of many awards, including President George H. W. Bush's "Point of Light" in 1988 and 1999, and she was recognized as one of the founders of the domestic violence movement in the United States. She resigned as executive director of the White Buffalo Calf Women's Society in August 2010 ("Tillie Black Bear . . ." 2010). On July 19, 2014, Tillie Black Bear passed away (NIWRC 2014), but her contributions to the safety of Native women are her living legacy.

Another influential Native woman is Nugange, the founding mother of the Emmonak Women's Shelter in Alaska in 1979, the second oldest Native women's shelter in the United States. She has dedicated more than thirty-five years to ending violence against Native women. Nugange has encountered numerous Native women dealing with domestic violence, often with nowhere to go for safety. This is especially relevant in the remote villages of Alaska where there are no roads and the only transportation is by river (Agtuca and Sahneyah 2014).

Native women, along with the National Congress of American Indians (NCAI) and other allies, were active in advocating for the reauthorizations of VAWA. The inclusion of Title IX, Safety for Indian Women, in the VAWA Act of 2005 was the result of their advocacy at the national level for American Indian/Alaska Native women. Before the 2013 reauthorization vote, NCAI provided tribal nations and peoples with a toolkit of resources to use when meeting with members of Congress. The toolkit, "Speak Out & Act Now!," included a fact sheet, talking points, tips for meeting with policymakers, sample letters and scripts, social media ideas, and a VAWA Policy Insight Brief (NCAI 2013b, 2013a).

When the legislation for VAWA's reauthorization stalled in Congress, it was Native American women like Tillie and Nugange who drew additional attention to the high rates of interracial violence in tribal communities, which had also been noted by the media and some organizations. A turning point occurred in 2012 at a press conference in Washington, DC, with Senator Patty Murray of Washington State, when Deborah Parker, then vice-chairwoman of the Tulalip Tribes, spoke out in favor of tribal provisions in the act and her personal experiences as a survivor of childhood sexual abuse. Her remarks were broadcast and uploaded on YouTube. Capitol Hill opponents and pro-VAWA forces ramped up, with the most opposition coming from Republicans concerned about non-Indian defendants in tribal courts; however, it was Representative Tom Cole, a Republican from Oklahoma and a Chickasaw Nation member, who played a significant role in persuading his colleagues that Native nations had a right to protect their people (Deer 2015).

As a result, due in large part to Tillie and Nugange's efforts, in March 2013 President Obama signed VAWA 2013, which included increased protections against violence for Native American women. He stated, "Tribal governments have an inherent right to protect their people, and all women deserve the right to live free from fear. And that is what today is all about" (White House 2013). The VAWA 2013 and the 2010 TLOA enhanced sentencing by tribal courts are tools to help curb the violence against Native American women.

In 2018 American Indian/Alaska Native women continued their advocacy for protecting their peers from violence, including participation in women's marches focusing on missing and murdered Native women, sex trafficking, man camps, and environmental concerns, among other issues. Native women and organizations at the local, state, and national levels in the United States and Canada lead the Missing and Murdered Indigenous Women (MMIW) movement. The data on the number of missing and murdered Indigenous women is incomplete, with an estimate of 5,712 reported cases in the United States as of 2016 ("Sen. Heitkamp . . ." 2017).

THE IMPACT OF TLOA 2010 AND VAWA 2013

TLOA and VAWA are shifts in federal policy that would not exist without the efforts of Native women (Deer 2015). VAWA 2013 reinstates tribal criminal jurisdiction and TLOA restores tribal sentencing authority; tribes can choose to comply with either, neither, or both. These laws create mechanisms for tribes to resume exercising sovereign powers that were previously limited by the federal government, but both VAWA 2013 and TLOA require compliance with a complicated and expensive set of prerequisites. Operating a criminal justice system is costly and some tribes do not have the funds to do so. Yet it might be worth the expense considering the issues facing tribal communities (Tatum 2016).

TLOA is a comprehensive statute focused on all aspects of investigating and prosecuting crime in Indian Country. One aspect of TLOA is the enhanced sentencing procedures by which tribes comply with statutory prerequisites.[1] Tribes cannot impose a sentence of more than three years in prison and/or a \$15,000 fine for any one offense, and the total for any criminal proceeding can be no more than nine years of imprisonment.

VAWA 2013 allowed tribes to prosecute non-Indians for three categories of crimes—domestic violence, dating violence, and violations of protection orders—provided the tribe satisfies the prerequisites.[2] The statute also required that at least one of the parties in the case must be Indian and that the defendant must have some connection to the tribe. Section 904 of VAWA 2013 addressed the legal loopholes that contributed to violence against Native American women by expanding tribal court jurisdiction so that tribes can prosecute non-Indians accused of domestic and dating violence (Harvard Law Review 2014). Tribes had not been able to prosecute non-Indians for any crimes since 1978 when the Supreme Court in *Oliphant v. Suquamish Tribe* ruled that tribes had no jurisdiction over non-Indians. The restoration of this authority was a major victory for tribes (Ballard 2014); however, VAWA 2013 has a major shortcoming: it only applied to cases of domestic violence or dating violence by non-Native Americans who live on tribal lands, are employed within tribal boundaries, or are married to or in a relationship with a partner who is a tribal member. It did not cover those who are strangers to the victims (Ballard 2014).

In February 2014 the U.S. attorney general approved three tribes (Pascua Yaqui, Umatilla, and Tulalip) for a pilot project (although the jurisdiction provision of VAWA 2013 was not effective until March 7, 2015), and three additional tribes (the Assiniboine and Sioux Tribes of

Fort Peck Reservation, and the Sisseton Wahpeton Oyate of the Lake Traverse Reservation) in March 2015. The six tribes worked with forty other tribes in an Inter-tribal Technical Assistance Working Group to answer questions on the implementation of Special Domestic Violence Criminal Jurisdiction (SDVCJ) and develop best practices (NCAI 2015). For a tribe to exercise jurisdiction over a non-Indian offender, the victim must be Indian, the non-Indian defendant must have ties to the Indian tribe (the crime must take place in the Indian country of the participating tribe), and as mentioned earlier, the defendant must reside in the Indian country of the participating tribe, be employed in the Indian country of the participating tribe or be a current or former spouse, intimate partner, or dating partner of a member of the participating tribe, or an Indian who resides in the Indian country of the participating tribe (NCAI 2015). VAWA 2013 required tribes exercising SDVCJ to provide certain due process protections to defendants, and any SDVCJ cases where a term of imprisonment occurs may have additional rights such as those required of tribes to exercise felony jurisdiction under the TLOA (NCAI 2015).

The pilot project's success allowed the participating tribes to prosecute offenders, many of whom were long-time repeat offenders. It also revealed some inherent limitations of Special Domestic Violence Criminal Jurisdiction and obstacles to its implementation. The SDVCJ Pilot Project Report identified nine lessons (NCAI 2015, 30) outlined in table 5.1.

TABLE 5.1 Lessons from the SDVCJ Pilot Project Report

---

1. Non-Indian domestic violence is a significant problem in tribal communities.
2. Most special domestic violence criminal jurisdiction defendants have significant ties to the tribal community.
3. Children are impacted by non-Indian domestic violence at high rates.
4. Training is critical for success.
5. Federal partners have an important role.
6. Peer-to-peer learning is important.
7. Special Domestic Violence Criminal Jurisdiction is too narrow.
8. There is confusion about the statutory definition of "domestic violence."
9. Tribes need resources for SDVCJ implementation.

Source: NCAI 2015.

The five pilot project tribes continue to be leaders in the number of prosecutions, assist other tribes, and send representatives to meetings of the SDVCJ. They also work closely with tribes considering implementation and seeking guidance. The codes developed by the pilot tribes, reviewed by the DOJ, are often used as models for other tribes (NCAI 2018b).

Congress passed the VAWA 2013 to address the high rates of domestic violence against American Indian/Alaska Native women by non-Indian men. The law "recognized and affirmed the inherent sovereign authority of tribal governments to exercise criminal jurisdiction over certain non-Indians who violate qualifying protection orders or commit domestic or dating violence against Indian victims on tribal lands" (NCAI 2018b, 1). The act created a framework for tribal courts to prosecute non-Indians, which had not happened since the *Oliphant v. Suquamish Tribe* decision by the U.S. Supreme Court. This limited reaffirmation of inherent tribal criminal jurisdiction over non-Indians is known as SDVCJ (as mentioned earlier), and the eighteen tribes now exercising this jurisdiction are referred to as implementing tribes. NCAI published a report, *VAWA 2013's Special Domestic Violence Criminal Jurisdiction (SDVCJ) Five-Year Report*, on March 20, 2018. The report summaries the implementation of VAWA 2013 and analyzes its impact in the five years since its enactment, which suggests the landmark legislation has been a success (NCAI 2018b). The eighteen implementing tribes reported 143 arrests of 128 non-Indian abusers, leading to 74 convictions, 5 acquittals, and 24 pending cases. Positive outcomes from the implementation of SDVCJ include community conversations about domestic violence, more comprehensive updated tribal criminal codes, increased collaboration among tribal, state, and federal governments, and increased safety and justice for victims; however, it has revealed places where federal administrative policies and practices need to be strengthened to enhance justice and where the jurisdictional framework continues to leave victims, including children and law enforcement, vulnerable. Also, additional resources are needed so that the act can be reauthorized and the benefits of the law can be expanded to more reservations. The four key findings from the NCAI report (2018b, 2) are presented in table 5.2.

TABLE 5.2 Key Findings from VAWA 2013's SDVCJ Five-Year Report

1. Tribes use SDVCJ to combat domestic violence by prosecuting offenders harming their communities:
   - Non-Indian perpetrated domestic violence is a real problem.
   - Many defendants have numerous prior contacts with tribal police, demonstrating SDVCJ can end impunity.
   - Many SDVCJ defendants have criminal records or outstanding warrants.
   - A diverse array of tribes has successfully implemented SDVCJ.
2. Tribal courts uphold the rights of defendants and are committed to their rehabilitation:
   - SDVCJ case outcomes demonstrate fairness.
   - Tribes are invested in helping defendants get the help they need.
3. Implementation revealed serious limitations in the law:
   - The statute prevents tribes from prosecuting crimes against children.
   - The statute prevents tribes from prosecuting alcohol and drug crimes.
   - The statute prevents tribes from prosecuting crimes that occur within the criminal justice system, thereby endangering law enforcement and undermining the integrity of the system.
   - There was initial confusion concerning the scope of the federal statutory definition of "domestic violence."
   - SDVCJ is prohibitively expensive for some tribes.
   - Detention issues and costs create implementation challenges.
   - SDVCJ is jurisdictionally complex.
4. SDVCJ implementation promotes positive changes:
   - SDVCJ promotes positive tribal reforms.
   - Intertribal collaboration creates successes beyond SDVCJ.
   - SDVCJ promotes better relationships with other jurisdictions.

Source: NCAI 2018a.

NEXT STEPS

The long-lasting effects on Native societies of colonization and federal laws and policies have led to intergenerational trauma and the victimization of AI/AN women. These factors continue to manifest in contemporary Native lives (Hamby 2009), as seen in the high rates of violence against American Indian/Alaska Native women and the lack of respect given to Native women by men (Mihesuah 2003). The outcome for Native American women is a change in roles, decline in status, and increased racism, sexism, classism, marginalization, oppression, stereotypes, and violence.

VAWA legislation is a positive step toward change for Native American women, but it is unlikely to be a solution for the high rates of rape, assault, and domestic violence in tribal communities. Former U.S. Attorney General Holder said what many people feel about the 2013 law, "What we have done, I think, has been game-changing, but there are still attitudes that have to be changed. There are still resources that have to be directed at the problem. There's training that still needs to go on. We're really only at the beginning stages of reversing what is a horrible situation" (quoted in Horwitz 2013, 8). VAWA 2013 and TLOA were and are positive steps toward protecting Native women against violence but the statutes are not perfect and there is more to be done to revise and strengthen tribes' ability to protect their communities.

Major organizations dedicated to ending violence against Native women include the National Indigenous Women's Resource Center (NIWRC), the Indian Law Resource Center, and the National Congress of American Indians. For example, NIWRC initiated the Strong Hearts Native Helpline in 2017 to provide a culturally relevant, safe, and confidential resource for Native American survivors of domestic and dating violence. The hotline is dedicated to serving tribal communities in Kansas, Oklahoma, and Nebraska, and is the first of its kind for Native people (NIWRC 2017). These organizations are supported by efforts of women and men in local Indian communities who are committed to the protection of Native women by advocating for the reauthorization and expansion of VAWA provisions at the national level.

One thing is certain: the commitment and advocacy of Native women will be at the forefront at the local, state, and national levels. Their voices and actions will continue the movement started in the 1970s by courageous Native American women like Tillie, Nugange, and many others across Indian Country. As Tillie stated, "As tribal women, as indigenous women, we are helping to create a safer, more humane world" (Agtuca and Sahneyah 2014, 11).

NOTES

1.   "TLOA requirements provide defendant with attorney who satisfies licensing standards and provides effective assistance of counsel; presiding judge has sufficient legal training and is licensed; make publicly available (including interpretive documents) criminal laws, rules of evidence, rules of criminal procedure and Judicial recusal standards and procedures, and record proceedings" (Tatum 2016, slide 7).

2.   VAWA 2013 required that tribes wishing to exercise the restored authority must provide the defendant with: (1) All the rights guaranteed by the statute [the Indian Civil Rights Act]. (2) Including (if the defendant is sentenced to jail time) all rights listed in 1302(c) [TLOA]. (3) The right to a trial by an impartial jury that is drawn from sources that (a) reflect a fair cross-section of the community; and (b) do not systematically exclude any distinctive group in the community, including non-Indians. (4) "All other rights whose protection is necessary under the Constitution of the United States in order for Congress to recognize and affirm the inherent power of the participating tribe to exercise special domestic violence criminal Jurisdiction over the defendant" (Tatum 2014, slide 30).

REFERENCES

Agtuca, Jacqueline, and Dorma Sahneyah, eds. 2014. *Safety for Native Women: VAWA and American Indian Tribes.* Lame Deer, MT: National Indigenous Women's Resource Center.

Amnesty International. 2007. *Maze of Injustice: The Failure to Protect Indigenous Women from Sexual Violence in the USA.* New York: Amnesty International.

Ballard, Amanda. 2014. "UA Alums Involved in Effort to Legally Prosecute Non-Indians on Pascua Yaqui Tribe." *UA NEWS,* University of Arizona, April 21, 2014. http//uanews.arizona.edu.

Chenault, Venida S. 2011. *Weaving Strength, Weaving Power, Violence and Abuse Against Indigenous Women.* Durham, NC: Carolina Academic Press.

Deer, Sarah. 2015. *The Beginning and End of Rape: Confronting Sexual Violence in Native America*. Minneapolis: University of Minnesota Press.

Fox, Mary Jo Tippeconnic. 2009. "Criminal Justice Challenges for Native American Women." In *Criminal Justice in Native America*, edited by Marianne O. Nielsen and Robert Silverman, 46–60. Tucson: University of Arizona Press.

Futures Without Violence. 2017. https://www.futureswithoutviolence.org/the -facts-on-violence-against-native-americanalaska-native-women/.

Hamby, Sherry. 2009. "Finding Their Way: Challenges and Resources of American Indian Victims of Sexual Assault." In *Criminal Justice in Native America*, edited by Marianne O. Nielsen and Robert Silverman, 61–76. Tucson: University of Arizona Press.

Harvard Law Review. 2014. "The Violence Against Women Reauthorization Act of 2013: Congress Recognizes and Affirms Tribal Courts' Special Domestic Violence Jurisdiction over Non-Indian Defendants." *Harvard Law Review* 127 (5): 1509–18.

Horwitz, Sari. 2013. "New Law Offers Protection to Abused Native American Women." *Washington Post*, February 8, 2013. http://www.Washingtonpost.com/ world/national-security/new-law-offers-a-sliver-of-protection-to-abused -native-american-women.

Indian Law and Order Commission. 2013. *A Roadmap for Making Native America Safer, Report to the President and Congress of the United States*, November 2013. https://www.aisc.ucla.edu/iloc/report/files/A_Roadmap_For_Making_Native _America_Safer-Full.pdf.

Langlois, Krista. 2014. "New Law Protects Alaska Native Women." *High Country News*, December 24, 2014. http://www.hcn.org/articles/new-law-protects -alaska-native-women.

Mihesuah, Devon Abbott. 2003. *Indigenous American Women: Decolonization, Empowerment, Activism*. Lincoln: University of Nebraska Press.

National Congress of American Indians (NCAI). 2013a. "Policy Insights Brief: Statistics on Violence Against Native Women." Washington, DC: NCAI Policy Research Center.

———. 2013b. "Speak Out & Act Now: Advocating for the Reauthorization of the Violence Against Women Act; A Toolkit for Tribal Nations." Washington, DC: NCAI.

———. 2015. "Special Domestic Violence Criminal Jurisdiction Pilot Project Report." http://www.ncai.org/tribal-vawa/pilot-project itwg/Pascua Yaqui _VAWA_Pilot_Project_Summary_2015.pdf.

———. 2018a. "Research Policy Update: Violence Against American Indian and Alaska Native Women." NCAI Policy Research Center. http://www.ncai.org/ policy-research-center/research-data/prc-publications/VAWA_Data_Brief _FINAL_2_1_2018.pdf.

————. 2018b. "VAWA 2013's Special Domestic Violence Criminal Jurisdiction (SDVCI) Five-Year Report," March 20, 2018. http://www.ncai.org/resources/ncai-publications/SDVCJ_5_Year_Report.pdf.

National Indigenous Women's Resource Center (NIWRC). 2014. *National Resource Center to Enhance Safety of Native Women and Their Children.* "Lenora ('Lynn') Hootch, Yupik Eskimo Board Member." http://www.niwrc.org/content/lenora-%E2%80%9Clynn%E2%80%9D-hootch.

————. 2017. "StrongHearts Native Helpline Launches as a Critical Resource for Domestic Violence and Dating Violence in Tribal Communities." http://www.niwrc.org/news/stronghearts-native-helpline-launches-critical-resource-domestic-violence-and-dating-violence.

Paxton, Katrina A. 2006. "Learning Gender: Female Students at the Sherman Institute, 1907–1925." In *Boarding School Blues, Revisiting American Indian Educational Experiences,* edited by Clifford E. Trafzer, Jean A. Keller, and Lorene Sisquoc, 174–86. Lincoln: University of Nebraska Press.

Rosay, Andre B. 2016. "Violence Against American Indian and Alaska Native Women and Men." Washington, DC: U.S. Department of Justice, Office of Justice Programs, National Institute of Justice. https://www.ncjrs.gov/pdffiles1/nij/249736.pdf.

"Sen. Heitkamp Introduces Bill to Address 'Epidemic' of Missing and Murdered Native Women." 2017. IndianZ.com (October 5, 2017). https://www.indianz.com/News/2017/10/05/sen-heitkamp-pushes-bill-to-address-cris.asp.

Smith, Andrea. 2005. *Conquest, Sexual Violence and American Indian Genocide.* Cambridge, MA: South End Press.

Tatum, Melissa. 2014. "VAWA 2013: Making a Difference." Power Point presentation at Lunch in Indian Country CLE Series (a partnership of the State Bar of Arizona and Indigenous Peoples Law and Policy Program) (May). Tucson: University of Arizona.

————. 2016. "Continuing Development of Tribal Criminal Jurisdiction: Setting the Stage: Statues, Requirements, and Issues." Power Point presentation at the meeting of the Federal Bar Association (April). Scottsdale, AZ.

"Tillie Black Bear Resigns from WBCWC." 2010. *Lakota County Times,* August 18, 2010. www.lakotacountytimes.com/news/2010–08 18/Headlines/Tille_Black_Bear_ Resigns_from_WBCWC.html.

White House. 2013. "President Signs 2013 VAWA-Empowering Tribes to Protect Native Women." White House blog, March 7, 2013. https://obamawhitehouse.archives.gov/blog/2013/03/07/president-signs-2013-vawa-empowering-tribes-protect-native-women.

LEGAL RESOURCES

Oliphant v. Suquamish Indian Tribe 435 U.S. 191 (1978)

Public Law 280 18 U.S.C. § 1162, 28 U.S.C. § 1360, and 25 U.S.C. §§ 1321–1326 (1953)

Tribal Law and Order Act 25 U.S.C. 2801 (2010)

Violence Against Women Act 42 U.S.C. 13701 (1994, 2000, 2005, 2013)

PART III

INTERNATIONAL LAW

INTRODUCTION BY MARIANNE O. NIELSEN
AND KAREN JARRATT-SNIDER

Colonialism is a global phenomenon. It has been occurring for thousands of years on many continents, but it is the wave of European colonialism beginning in the 1600s that most affects Indigenous Peoples of the Americas. Indigenous Peoples have many cultural, historical, social, and other differences, but because of colonialism, they also share some common traits, such as depopulation through disease and violence; political, economic, and social marginalization; and the deprivation of human rights (Coates 2004). Other things they share are resistance and resilience. With very few exceptions, Indigenous individuals, as collective Peoples, survived European colonialism of North America; they are still here, even though their lives have been changed forever. They continue to resist though a wide variety of means, including social movements, maintaining and using traditional ecological knowledge, maintaining and rediscovering traditional culture and language, maintaining spiritual practices, remaining collectivities aimed at the public good, and building international networks of organizations (Hall and Fenelon 2009). The use of international law to pressure settler-colonist governments into recognizing Indigenous rights is also an important tool.

After World War II, many diverse groups formed social movements and became vocal about their civil rights. National and international meetings of Indigenous Peoples beginning in the 1930s led to collaboration and sharing of strategies to increase sovereignty and overcome the terrible impacts of colonization (Cowger 1999, as described by Alvarado). International conventions that developed after World War II, such as the UN Declaration of Human Rights (1948) and the Convention on the Prevention and Punishment of the Crime of Genocide (1948) gave Indigenous Peoples impetus and a foundation on which to make their claims (Nakata 2001).

The human and civil rights of Indigenous Peoples and individuals were deliberately destroyed as part of colonization; colonialism's focus on resource acquisition and control meant that colonial governments developed law, justice, and educational processes to end Indigenous family structures, leadership institutions, economies, law, and cultures. Indigenous Peoples had no rights, not even those of the average citizen. They certainly did not have the rights that had been guaranteed in the international treaties that they had signed on a nation-to-nation basis with the settler-colonial governments during the early years of colonialism. Every one of these treaties was broken almost immediately by the settler-colonists and colonial governments (Nielsen and Robyn 2019). As a result, Indigenous Peoples were the victims of global-scale crimes of theft and violence.

With the emergence of civil rights movements in the early twentieth century, Indigenous individuals were seen as members of ethnic minorities even though their Indigenous nations were political entities. In the accompanying cultural revitalization movements, Indigenous people acted collectively as peoples to use the tools at their disposal. Individual civil rights, however, were not and are not the collective rights defined by Indigenous Peoples as inherently part of Indigenous sovereignty. As was seen in the first section of the book, some Indigenous nations use customary law as a way of exerting sovereignty. In the second section of this book the authors point out that some national laws (in this case, some of those of the United States) might seem well-intentioned, but on the whole they encroach on Indigenous human rights, especially self-determination. Some laws, such as the Indian Gaming Regulatory Act (1988) used by American Indian nations to enable economic development, have met with tremendous resistance by state governments and competing non-Indigenous corporations (see, for example, Harvey 2000).

While some Indigenous groups, such as the National Congress of American Indians and their allies, continue lobbying at the national level, there is a growing focus on the international level. The UN Declaration on the Rights of Indigenous Peoples (2007) has a long history and there are still some nations that have not ratified it, but it stands as a symbol of hope for Indigenous Peoples worldwide, even during the long process of its negotiation (Ewen 1994). The United Nations plays a leading role in providing a voice for Indigenous Peoples and developing tools to put pressure on States to preserve the rights of Indigenous Peoples. For example, in 2001 at the regional meeting of Indigenous Peoples of the World Conference Against Racism, Racial Discrimination, Xenophobia, and Related Intolerance, a satellite meeting of the UN Commission on Human Rights, four recommendations were made about law reform, including: "The World Conference calls on States to undertake processes for constitutional arrangements, treaties, agreements, judicial, legislative and other mechanisms relating to protection of Indigenous Peoples' right in order to entrench, promote and secure such rights, with a view to achieving co-existence on the basis of mutual respect and full recognition of Indigenous rights and status" (quoted in Nakata 2001, 226). The increased recognition of Indigenous rights comes at a time when many countries are stepping up efforts to curtail Indigenous sovereignty. It can only be hoped that more settler-colonist governments will fulfill their international commitments to protect the rights of Indigenous Peoples, in the face of pressure from corporate and political entities to do the opposite.

In his chapter Alvarado describes how some governments, particularly in Latin America, have tried to use international conventions to recognize and protect their Indigenous citizens, primarily by incorporating customary laws into their domestic legislation. Nielsen provides examples of how Indigenous organizations, in this case justice service organizations, are operationalizing these international rights so they exist "on the street" in local communities and not just in law books. In fact, even though only some of these organizations are a division of an Indigenous government, they are practicing de facto sovereignty in response to the failures of national law and justice systems to effectively serve Indigenous communities. As Nielsen describes, by capacity-building they also contribute to the building of communities and nations. Her chapter shows how international, national, and traditional law can intersect in everyday Indigenous life.

REFERENCES

Coates, Ken S. 2004. *A Global History of Indigenous Peoples: Struggle and Survival*. New York: Palgrave Macmillan.

Cowger, Thomas W. 1999. *The National Congress of American Indians: The Founding Years*. Lincoln: University of Nebraska Press.

Ewen, Alexander. 1994. *Voice of Indigenous Peoples: Native People Address the United Nations*. Santa Fe, NM: Clear Light.

Hall, Thomas D., and James V. Fenelon. 2009. *Indigenous People and Globalization: Resistance and Revitalization*. Boulder, CO: Paradigm.

Harvey, Sioux. 2000. "Winning the Sovereignty Jackpot: The Indian Gaming Regulatory Act and the Struggle for Sovereignty." In *Indian Gaming: Who Wins?*, edited by Angela Mullis and David Kamper, 14–34. Los Angeles: UCLA American Indian Studies Center.

Nakata, Martin, ed. 2001. *Indigenous Peoples, Racism and the United Nations*. Sydney, AU: Common Ground Publishing.

Nielsen, Marianne O., and Linda Robyn. 2019. *Colonialism Is Crime*. New Brunswick, NJ: Rutgers University Press.

LEGAL RESOURCES

Indian Gaming Regulatory Act Pub. L. 100–497, 25 U.S.C. § 2701 et seq. (1988)

UN Convention on the Prevention and Punishment of the Crime of Genocide (1948)

UN Declaration of Human Rights (1948)

UN Declaration on the Rights of Indigenous Peoples (2007)

6

INTERNATIONAL AND COMPARATIVE PERSPECTIVES ON THE RECOGNITION AND PROMOTION OF INDIGENOUS JUSTICE

LEONARDO J. ALVARADO

I N THE international legal arena, Indigenous Peoples have sought the recognition of their systems of justice and law, particularly in the context of the development of international human rights instruments within international bodies like the United Nations (UN) and the Organization of American States (OAS). Indigenous juridical customs, laws, and institutions are recognized in the main international instruments on Indigenous Peoples' rights, which helps cement the notion that these are fundamental human rights of Indigenous Peoples. The incorporation of such fundamental human rights into domestic constitutions and legislations, particularly in the Latin American region, demonstrates the extent of the importance of these international legal developments and how Indigenous systems of justice are legally and politically recognized and conceptualized outside of North America; however, certain limitations can be gleaned from how the recognition of Indigenous justice in these international legal sources is understood and applied, which might indicate areas of further work and legal conceptual development by international bodies, academic scholars, Indigenous Peoples, and justice operators in other areas of the world.

By looking at developments that have taken place in Latin America, this chapter will seek to demonstrate the strengths, limitations, and gaps present in the current international normative framework on this specific aspect of Indigenous Peoples' rights law. The chapter will first discuss international standards on Indigenous justice and legal systems. Secondly, some examples of domestic recognition in Latin America will be presented. Thirdly, the chapter addresses the main issues and challenges of implementing international standards on Indigenous justice. The chapter concludes with a discussion of areas where further attention is needed both at the domestic and international levels.

INTERNATIONAL STANDARDS ON INDIGENOUS JUSTICE

In the area of international human rights law for Indigenous Peoples, a series of international treaties, declarations, resolutions, and jurisprudence by international institutions within the universal (UN) and regional (OAS) levels—including treaty supervisory bodies, commissions, and tribunals—represent the main sources of law or legal standards. Three international instruments need to be highlighted in this respect: the Indigenous and Tribal Peoples Convention, Convention No. 169, of the International Labour Organization (ILO 169); the UN Declaration on the Rights of Indigenous Peoples (UN Declaration); and the American Declaration on the Rights of Indigenous Peoples (American Declaration).

The application of these instruments and the resolutions and jurisprudence of international bodies concerning Indigenous Peoples' rights have been more salient on issues related to land, territory, and natural resource rights, as well as on the rights to consultation and free, prior, and informed consent in the context of extractive industry and other development projects that affect Indigenous Peoples. Mention is made in general terms of Indigenous customs, juridical systems, and institutions.

ILO 169

ILO 169 is the only international treaty specific to Indigenous Peoples and is legally binding on all State governments that have ratified it. The International Labour Organization (ILO), an agency affiliated with the UN that examines labor rights issues and related social protections, adopted ILO 169 in 1989 as an effort to update the previous Convention No. 107 (1957) on Indigenous Peoples which advocated for the assimilation of Indigenous Peoples. Twenty-two countries have ratified ILO 169, the vast majority in Latin America, but these also include countries in other regions like Norway, Nepal, Fiji, and the Central African Republic (ILO 2017, 1).

Article 8 of ILO 169 recognizes the rights of Indigenous Peoples to their customs, customary laws, and institutions, adding that these are not to be "incompatible with fundamental rights defined by the national legal system and with internationally recognized human rights." It further adds, under Article 9(1), that "to the extent compatible with the national legal system and internationally recognized human rights, the methods primarily practiced by the Peoples concerned for dealing with offences committed by their members shall be respected." Indigenous Peoples' customs "in regard to penal matters shall be taken into consideration by the authorities and courts dealing with such cases," according to Article 9(2). Under Article 8(2), "procedures shall be established . . . to resolve conflicts which may arise in the application of [their right to their indigenous customs, customary laws, and institutions]."

UN DECLARATION

The UN Declaration on the Rights of Indigenous Peoples is not a treaty but rather a resolution adopted by the UN General Assembly in 2007. It is the product of more than two decades of debates and negotiations at the UN level between Indigenous Peoples and State governments. This provides it with great legitimacy in terms of the procedure leading up to its adoption and its substantive content that coherently articulates Indigenous Peoples' fundamental rights under international law (Charters 2009, 280–303). Since the vast majority of the member States of the UN voted in favor of the declaration, it represents the highest degree of acknowledgment at the global level of the rights of Indigenous Peoples in areas such as lands, natural resources, language, cultural preservation, traditional knowledge, and spiritual practices (Alvarado 2015, 70).

Significantly, Article 3 of the UN declaration affirms Indigenous Peoples' rights to self-determination, by which they can freely determine their political status and pursue their own economic, social, and cultural development. This is in line with the right of self-determination of all peoples under standard general human rights instruments—for example, common Article 1 of the International Covenant on Civil and Political Rights and the International Covenant on Economic, Social and Cultural Rights.

The UN Declaration on the Rights of Indigenous Peoples states under Article 4 that "Indigenous Peoples, in exercising their right to self-determination, have the right to autonomy or self-government in matters relating to their internal and local affairs, as well as ways and means for financing their autonomous functions." Article 5 of the UN declaration recognizes Indigenous Peoples' rights "to maintain and strengthen their distinct political, legal, economic, social and cultural institutions." Under Article 34, they have the right to promote, develop, and maintain their institutional structures, which includes their juridical systems or customs, in accordance with international human rights standards. As can be seen from this declaration, the recognition of Indigenous Peoples' legal institutions, juridical systems, and customs is an integral component to exercising the right to self-determination and self-governance.

AMERICAN DECLARATION

Similar to the development of the UN declaration, Indigenous Peoples from the Americas also participated in negotiations with State members of the OAS for almost three decades regarding the development of a declaration on Indigenous Peoples. In June 2016 the OAS General Assembly adopted the American Declaration on the Rights of Indigenous Peoples. Like the UN declaration, it is a resolution affirming the commitment of OAS member States toward Indigenous Peoples. It reaffirms many of the rights and principles contained in the UN declaration in the areas of cultural identity, language, spirituality, land, territorial and natural resource rights, self-determination, education, health, and other rights.

Under the heading of Indigenous Law and Jurisdiction, Article XXII (1) of the declaration recognizes Indigenous Peoples' right to promote, develop, and maintain their institutional structures, distinctive customs, procedures, practices, and juridical systems or customs. "Indigenous law and legal systems shall be recognized and respected by national, regional and international legal systems," according to Article XXII (2). In cases where Indigenous individuals are before national jurisdictions, they are "entitled without discrimination, to equal protection and benefit of the law, including the use of linguistic and cultural interpreters" (Article XXII [3]). Further, it adds that "States shall take effective measures in conjunction with indigenous peoples to ensure implementation of this article [on Indigenous law and jurisdiction]" (Article XXII [4]).

The adoption of the American declaration is significant within the regional inter-American human rights system of the OAS, as it forms part of the authoritative legal sources used by the two regional human rights monitoring bodies which examine specific cases regarding human rights violations: the Inter-American Commission on Human Rights and the Inter-American Court of Human Rights.

INTER-AMERICAN JURISPRUDENCE

The Inter-American Commission and Court have both contributed to the further development of the field of international Indigenous Peoples' law through a significant body of jurisprudence on Indigenous Peoples. This jurisprudence has centered on land and natural resource rights, consultation and consent, and extractive industries (Inter-American Commission on Human Rights 2009, 2015).

Specific issues on Indigenous law and jurisdiction and potential conflicts with national legal systems have not been adjudicated by these and other similar international bodies. Within the inter-American system, Indigenous Peoples' customary law, values, and customs are addressed as elements that State governments must take into account in providing remedies for violations of land rights, for example in devising legislation for demarcating Indigenous lands (see, for example, Inter-American Court of Human Rights 2001, 82), or in assessing nonmonetary reparations for Indigenous victims of mass killings and family and community members (see, for example, Inter-American Court of Human Rights 2004, 81–83).

Indigenous customary law, values, and customs are also addressed with regard to the right of access to justice. According to the Inter-American Court of Human Rights, the right to judicial protection under the

American Convention on Human Rights, as applicable to Indigenous Peoples, entails consideration of their "specificities, their economic and social characteristics, as well as their situation of special vulnerability, their customary law, values and customs" (Inter-American Court of Human Rights 2005, 58).

COMMENTS BY OTHER INTERNATIONAL BODIES

At the level of the United Nations, the Expert Mechanism on the Rights of Indigenous Peoples (EMRIP)—a body composed of independent experts that provides advice on Indigenous rights issues to the UN Human Rights Council through thematic studies—conducted a study on access to justice, which includes a discussion on Indigenous juridical systems. As the EMRIP study notes, Indigenous juridical systems play a crucial role in facilitating Indigenous Peoples' and individuals' access to justice. This is because it is more suitable in terms of cultural, linguistic, geographic, and economic accessibility, and this is particularly true "where State justice systems are plagued by inefficiency and corruption" (EMRIP 2014, 7).

As the EMRIP study notes, UN bodies like the Committee on the Elimination of Racial Discrimination and the UN Special Rapporteur on the Rights of Indigenous Peoples have issued specific recommendations to countries regarding the need to recognize Indigenous legal systems and traditional dispute resolutions, in general terms (EMRIP 2014, 7).

DOMESTIC RECOGNITION OF INDIGENOUS JUSTICE SYSTEMS AND JURISDICTION

As mentioned earlier, important legal and constitutional developments in the area of Indigenous Peoples' rights have occurred in Latin America that have in many ways been prompted by international human rights legal instruments. Due to its widespread ratification by countries in the region, after 1989 ILO 169 played a major role in that regard and has served as the basis for framing many of the provisions in domestic constitutions and laws on Indigenous Peoples, as well as for jurisprudence by domestic courts in the region. This has been facilitated by the fact that under most of the constitutions in the region, ratified international human rights treaties have a constitutional status equal to national constitutions or have a hierarchical status superior to regular laws (ILO 2009a, 6–14).

The openness and deference, at least on paper, to international human rights treaties took place within a regional context where, following the end of dictatorships in the late 1980s and 1990s, countries wanted to demonstrate the establishment of more democratic legal and political structures through widespread ratification of international human rights treaties. Indigenous Peoples and representative organizations took advantage of this regional trend, particularly after the ILO's adoption in 1989 of its Convention 169, to push for legal recognition of Indigenous Peoples' rights, thus reverting centuries of exclusion and "invisibilization" within the dominant legal systems that were based on notions of one homogenous culture, language, religion, and legal system. In that way, a "multicultural regional model" of constitutionalism emerged in the region that, as Van Cott explained, included among other features the recognition of Indigenous languages, the right to bilingual education, and the protection of collective land rights and customary Indigenous law (Van Cott 2007, 132). The recognition of "legal pluralism" in these countries was part of the multicultural constitutional developments that recognized multiple forms of law and justice, and thus became an important barometer for measuring the actual degree of respect of multiculturalism in the case of Indigenous Peoples (Van Cott 2000, 208).

In general, Indigenous justice systems in the Latin American region have operated in a de facto manner despite centuries of nonrecognition, because Indigenous communities are mostly located in remote areas where State institutions are largely absent. Indigenous legal systems do not necessarily always follow a precolonial model, as the colonial and current republican eras in those countries brought changes to Indigenous legal, political, and other social structures. Many forms of traditional Indigenous justice continually adopt new practices and concepts, or new legal structures in some cases may be created. Therefore, "the authenticity of these new structures and norms comes not from their age but, rather, from their autonomous adoption in the absence of effective access to state justice" (Van Cott 2000, 212).

Indigenous legal norms and institutions are as diverse as the many distinct Indigenous Peoples, communities, or nationalities that exist in the region. In general, as in other parts of the globe, Indigenous justice systems generally seek restoration of harmony in community, clan, or family relations, the rehabilitation of offenders, and sanctions and forms of punishment other than incarceration. Procedurally, Indigenous justice systems are less formal, less expensive, and less adversarial than national Western-based justice systems (for further reference, see EMRIP 2014, 4–5; Tobin 2014, 29–31).

The constitutional and legislative provisions in many of the countries that have explicitly recognized Indigenous justice share certain characteristics with regard to content, scope, limits, and jurisdictional reach. These include the applicability of Indigenous justice systems to the respective territory of the community or people concerned, that the Indigenous justice systems must not be contrary to fundamental rights in domestic or international law, and in various cases, that subsequent legislation would establish the ways of coordination or interface between Indigenous and national "ordinary" jurisdictions. The most advanced legal developments in this area can be seen in the Andean countries in South America where the influences of ILO 169 (1989) and the UNDRIP (2007) are evident.

Colombia's 1991 constitution states that Indigenous authorities may exercise jurisdictional functions within their territories according to their laws and procedures, provided they are not contrary to the constitution and national law. It states that subsequent legislation would establish the forms of coordination between Indigenous special jurisdiction and the national justice system (Article 246). As the latter legislation has not yet been adopted, the Colombian constitutional court has developed a significant body of jurisprudence on Indigenous justice, as will be seen further below. In interpreting Article 246, the constitutional court has held that Indigenous Peoples have the capacity to establish their own authorities, to preserve or articulate their own norms and procedures, and for Indigenous members to be judged by their own authorities according to their own norms and procedures, as opposed to the ordinary justice system (Constitutional Court of Colombia 2010).

In Ecuador, the 2008 constitution guarantees the right of Indigenous authorities to exercise jurisdictional functions in accordance with their ancestral traditions and systems of law, within their own territories, and with the participation and decision-making capacity of women. Indigenous authorities can apply their own norms and procedures for the settlement of internal disputes as long as they are not contrary to the constitution and international human rights. The decisions of Indigenous jurisdictional authorities are to be respected by State institutions and authorities and can be subject to constitutional review. It also states that legislation would establish mechanisms for coordination and cooperation between Indigenous and ordinary jurisdictions (Article 171).

The 2009 constitution of the Plurinational State of Bolivia recognizes the rights of Indigenous Peoples to exercise jurisdictional functions through their own authorities and cultural values, norms, and procedures. Regarding personal, material, and territorial jurisdiction, it provides that it is applicable to members of Indigenous Peoples, whether as complainants, defendants, appellants, or respondents. It states that a jurisdictional demarcation law would specify the matters Indigenous authorities would decide. In addition, all public officials and persons are to comply with the decisions of Indigenous jurisdiction authorities, and to that end Indigenous authorities can request the assistance of State institutions.

Aside from the Andean region, there have been efforts in countries like Guatemala to improve coordination between Indigenous and State justice authorities and recognize Indigenous conflict resolution mechanisms (EMRIP 2014, 6). Since 1985 Guatemala's constitution has essentially recognized the multiethnic, multilingual, and multicultural character of the country (Articles 58 and 66); however, a recent movement to amend the Guatemalan constitution in order to specifically recognize jurisdictional functions of Indigenous authorities (as part of a general set of reforms on justice administration) was suspended after Indigenous leaders desisted in their efforts due to hostility by powerful political sectors of the country (Gonzalez 2017).

Following reforms in 2001, Mexico's federal constitution recognized Indigenous Peoples' rights to apply their own normative and internal conflict resolution systems, subject to the constitution, human rights, and respecting the dignity and integrity of women (Article 2[11]). The same provision, however, states that validation of these justice systems by judges and tribunals would be established under legislation. This has created a situation in which the recognition by different federal, state, and local authorities of decisions made by Indigenous justice authorities has been inconsistent and, in many cases, has undermined the full exercise of these rights (OHCHR-Mexico 2007, 99–101). In addition, due to the deficiencies in justice administration at the federal and state levels, Indigenous Peoples in Mexico have proactively readapted or created new autonomous governance structures and justice systems, such as Indigenous municipal courts, "good governance councils," community police, and "autonomous councils for territorial defense," present in states such as Guerrero and Chiapas, and that exist alongside or outside of state-created institutions (see, for example, Sierra 2005; UN Special Rapporteur on the Rights of Indigenous Peoples 2018, 10–12). For additional examples and discussions on the types of legal recognition of Indigenous justice systems and jurisdiction in these regions and others, see EMRIP (2014, 5–6) and Tobin (2014, 57–73).

ISSUES AND CHALLENGES FACING INDIGENOUS JUSTICE SYSTEMS

Despite the recognition of Indigenous justice systems at the international level and the domestic recognition of Indigenous justice and jurisdictions in some countries of the region, Indigenous Peoples still face challenges in the effective enjoyment of these rights. Indigenous Peoples still face prejudicial attitudes and stereotypes by local, regional, and national authorities. Problems also arise in devising effective methods of coordination and interface between Indigenous and national State authorities and defining Indigenous jurisdictional competencies. Judicial review and concerns over the observance of fundamental human rights by Indigenous authorities is another concern expressed, particularly regarding Indigenous individuals and vulnerable sectors, including women, children, and disabled persons.

ONGOING PREJUDICIAL ATTITUDES AND STEREOTYPES

In various Latin American countries, incidents of vigilante justice or lynchings have occurred in areas inhabited by Indigenous Peoples and other rural populations. Unfortunately, these have been portrayed as being representative of Indigenous justice systems, and thus utilized as a pretext to thwart efforts to officially recognize Indigenous justice systems. It must be noted, however, that such incidents are not expressions of Indigenous justice. They tend to occur in areas where there is frustration at the general level of impunity enjoyed by criminal offenders because the State justice system is not present or is inefficient and corrupt (Van Cott 2003, 9).

In a well-known case in the Indigenous community of La Cocha in Ecuador, the application of Indigenous justice was subject to legal challenges. A climate of polarization and stigmatization ensued after media coverage and statements by public officials perpetuated negative stereotypes of Indigenous justice systems. In response to this climate, in 2010 the UN Special Rapporteur on the Rights of Indigenous Peoples issued a public statement urging Ecuadorian authorities and society "to recognize the effective and peaceful application of ancestral justice systems in the vast majority of cases, but also not to confuse cases of vigilante and riotous violence with the genuine expression of indigenous justice" (UN Special Rapporteur on the Rights of Indigenous Peoples 2010a).

During a country mission to Ecuador, the Special Rapporteur on Extrajudicial, Summary or Arbitrary Executions also expressed concern over mischaracterizations of the causes of lynchings and how it reinforces negative stereotypes about Indigenous Peoples. According to the Special Rapporteur, when he asked government officials and others about specific cases of death sentences handed down by Indigenous authorities, only one case was mentioned and it was actually not applied. As correctly noted, "In contrast to calls to minimize, restrict or abolish Indigenous justice, it might actually be appropriate to strengthen it in situations in which lynching is caused by the absence of the State" (UN Special Rapporteur on Extrajudicial, Summary or Arbitrary Executions 2011, 15–16).

In the Ecuadorian case, it was also suspected that the negative rhetoric against Indigenous justice was aimed at discrediting Indigenous movements who opposed government positions on mining and water issues (UN Special Rapporteur on Extrajudicial, Summary or Arbitrary Executions 2011, 16). As noted by the ILO, the level of acceptance of legal pluralism and Indigenous customary law in some cases may be conditioned on how customary rights over lands, territories and resources affect economic interests of the state or third parties (ILO 2009b, 82–83). This is another factor prompting negative stereotypes and attitudes against Indigenous justice systems.

INDIGENOUS JURISDICTIONAL COMPETENCIES AND METHODS OF COORDINATION

The definition of jurisdictional competencies also presents challenges to efforts to develop legislation in the areas of interlegal coordination between Indigenous and State justice authorities. A particular problem that arises in efforts to legislate in the area of interlegal coordination is whether specific competencies and limits to Indigenous jurisdictional functions need to be established or codified beforehand through legisla-.tion, regulations, or other similar mechanisms.

In Bolivia, constitutional recognition of Indigenous jurisdiction was followed by the enactment in 2010 of the Law of Jurisdictional Demarcation. The law affirms that only members of the respective Indigenous Peoples or nation are subject to Indigenous jurisdiction, which would apply to events occurring or whose effects take place within the jurisdiction of the Indigenous Peoples. Decisions by Indigenous authorities are legally binding and are not reviewable by the ordinary jurisdiction (Articles 8, 9, 11, and 12).

Article 10 states that Indigenous authorities can decide on matters or conflicts that they have historically and traditionally decided through their laws, procedures, and knowledge systems. It then proceeds to list specific areas where Indigenous authorities have no material jurisdiction. Regarding criminal matters, these include crimes against humanity, international law, and State security; terrorism, drug, and human trafficking; crimes against the physical integrity of children and adolescents; rape; and homicide. In civil matters, Indigenous jurisdiction would not apply in any matter where the State is a party or an interested third party. It also excludes cases related to labor law, social security, tax law, mining, forestry and hydrocarbons, and agrarian matters except issues dealing with internal distribution of lands owned by Indigenous communities.

While this law is part of the advanced efforts undertaken in Bolivia to promote Indigenous Peoples' rights, there have been concerns that the scope of Indigenous jurisdiction has been significantly restricted due to the codification of the range and limits of Indigenous jurisdictional powers. Indigenous organizations have criticized the law because they deem Indigenous jurisdiction to be subordinated to the ordinary justice through the codification of where and in what domains Indigenous justice can be applied (EMRIP 2014, 9).

In evaluating issues of jurisdictional limits, the Colombian constitutional court applies a principle of seeking the "maximization of autonomy" of the Indigenous Peoples concerned, in which only the restrictions that are necessary to safeguard constitutionally higher interests or that are the least burdensome are permissible. This is part of a balancing of interests between constitutionally recognized rights to Indigenous cultural integrity and autonomy and constitutional rights of individuals (Indigenous or non-Indigenous). It has stated that Indigenous jurisdiction is composed of personal, territorial, institutional, and objective elements that take into account an Indigenous person's cultural background and his/her community's norms if before State ordinary authorities; whether the Indigenous community or Peoples concerned has a higher juridical interest or concern in the matter in question; and an assessment of an Indigenous People's existing institutions and procedures to provide access to justice (Constitutional Court of Colombia 2010).

In various cases decided by that court, lower courts asserted jurisdiction over cases involving statutory rape or rights of children even if the events occurred in an Indigenous territory and involved Indigenous parties. The court has had to decide if the particular rights and concerns of individual Indigenous victims would be better served by the Indigenous or the ordinary jurisdiction. In one particular case, consideration was given to the institutional capacity of the Indigenous community in question to deliver justice to the victims, as well as personal and territorial elements. The court deemed that in that case there was no real certainty that the victim's right to access to justice would actually be violated if the Indigenous community authorities adjudicated the matter, while it was clearly certain that Indigenous autonomy and jurisdictional rights would be restricted if the case was settled exclusively by the ordinary jurisdiction (Constitutional Court of Colombia 2010).

The Colombian constitutional court's approach does not appear to preliminarily determine specific criminal or civil matters that Indigenous authorities could adjudicate or not with regard to their members. It has explained that while most of the cases it has adjudicated concerned Indigenous jurisdiction in the area of criminal jurisdiction, Indigenous authority transcends all areas of social regulation. As noted by the court, Indigenous jurisdiction has decided matters that under the ordinary jurisdiction would fall under civil, labor, criminal, political, and administrative law (Constitutional Court of Colombia 2010).

Important issues that require attention are cases or offenses committed by non-Indigenous members within an Indigenous territory and matters that may arise outside an Indigenous territory but are of concern to an Indigenous community or people. Effective cooperation mechanisms could be devised wherein the initial investigation, interrogation, and detention of non-Indigenous offenders are done by Indigenous justice authorities. Subsequent actions could involve, if deemed necessary by the Indigenous people concerned, the transfer of that person to ordinary justice authorities where sanctions are imposed based on the investigations and information obtained by the Indigenous justice authorities. An example of that was a well-documented case in the Indigenous community of Santa Cruz del Quiché, Guatemala (Flores 2012).

JUDICIAL REVIEW AND OBSERVANCE OF HUMAN RIGHTS

As previously noted, both domestic and international legal instruments provide that Indigenous Peoples' rights to apply their customary justice practices are subject to the limitation that they respect fundamental human rights. In several cases, as in the Ecuadorean constitution, these decisions can be subject to constitutional review.

This becomes a sensitive issue, especially when sectors skeptical of Indigenous justice systems point to problems or deficiencies in the operation of justice. Just like ordinary justice systems, Indigenous justice authorities may run the risk of being susceptible to practices of political or familial favoritism, and disadvantaged sectors such as women, children, youth, and disabled persons could face barriers to justice. Concerns may exist regarding customary sanctions that may involve some forms of corporal punishment.

The Colombian constitutional court has addressed cases involving challenges to the decisions and penalties imposed by Indigenous justice authorities. It has used cultural expert testimonies as a way of ascertaining an Indigenous Peoples' views on justice and the penalties and sanctions in their justice systems. Throughout its jurisprudence, it has determined that on the basis of an "intercultural consensus," Indigenous authorities are to observe a "hard core" of fundamental human rights consisting of the rights to life, personal integrity, freedom from torture and slavery, and due process. The evaluation of possible violations to personal integrity and due process are to be made in light of the specific culture, laws, norms, and procedures of the Indigenous community concerned (Constitutional Court of Colombia 1997; 1998).

Similar to its analysis on jurisdiction, the court has evaluated individual and collective rights based on the principle of maximization of autonomy. In that sense, the restriction of Indigenous autonomy would only be constitutionally valid if there are reasoned and well-founded arguments that the impacts on other human rights would be particularly grave and certain, and the impact on the Indigenous Peoples would be minimal (Constitutional Court of Colombia 2010). In one case, it commented that in reviewing whether decisions by Indigenous authorities comply with human rights, consideration must be taken of how intervention by outside institutions could be detrimental to Indigenous autonomy rights. It recognized that a more prudent approach would be to promote internal dialogue within a community so conflicts related to competing human rights and interests can be resolved within their cultural worldview (Constitutional Court of Colombia 2010).

AREAS FOR FURTHER ATTENTION

Indigenous Peoples' systems of justice and law are recognized as human rights; this recognition has prompted domestic legal reforms in regions like Latin America. This important international normative recognition, however, is understandably limited as it is framed in general terms. How these international standards translate domestically will necessarily depend on the particular legal, policy, and institutional framework of the States and Indigenous Peoples concerned. As discussed in this chapter, certain challenges tend to present themselves in the domestic application of international human rights on Indigenous justice. These include addressing issues of jurisdictional competencies and coordination between Indigenous and State ordinary jurisdictions and addressing expectations that Indigenous justice systems are to respect fundamental human rights. All these are particularly daunting where prejudices and resistance against Indigenous justice systems still exist.

There must be concerted efforts by State governments, national media, international institutions, and academia to prevent the propagation of negative stereotypes, prejudicial attitudes, and incorrect information about Indigenous Peoples and their systems of justice. This includes promoting an understanding of the value and contributions of Indigenous justice systems to the administration of justice in many States, since they provide access to justice for members of Indigenous Peoples and help address impunity in Indigenous-inhabited regions where State justice authorities are not present or effective.

Lawmaking and policy-making on justice administration and access to justice in Indigenous territories or regions should not be conceptually limited to relatively minor matters or offenses between Indigenous community members, or that occur only on Indigenous territories. State justice operators, lawmakers, and policymakers need to be mindful and aware of cases where Indigenous justice and jurisdictional competencies should apply in cases concerning major offenses, especially if the Indigenous Peoples concerned have the willingness and capacity to adjudicate these matters. As was also discussed in this chapter, the resolution of these jurisdictional issues should not be limited to strict codification.

The last two UN Special Rapporteurs on Indigenous Peoples made general observations on this matter when addressing efforts to coordinate Indigenous and ordinary justice systems. They emphasized the need for flexibility in determining spheres of competency as opposed to strict codification of Indigenous jurisdictional functions. This includes official recognition of the jurisdictional powers Indigenous authorities have exercised de facto and in their day-to-day decisions. Flexibility also entails considering scenarios where Indigenous jurisdiction is not restricted to cases involving members of the same community or people or that take place on a particular Indigenous Peoples' territory (see UN Special Rapporteur on the Rights of Indigenous Peoples 2016, 4–5). This is particularly necessary where the absence, inefficiency, or indifference of State authorities would result in impunity in cases where offenses are committed by non-Indigenous persons.

An important point made by the Special Rapporteurs is that Indigenous Peoples need a space to speak with State authorities about matters Indigenous justice authorities consider they should adjudicate and how those could be recognized and accommodated. As pointed out by the Special Rapporteur, a possible criterion for cases involving people outside the community or cases arising outside Indigenous territories is the degree to which the issue or matter would "have a significant effect on the cultures, traditional institutions, economic livelihood, social cohesion or physical security of an indigenous community or people" (UN Special Rapporteur on the Rights of Indigenous Peoples 2016, 5).

In that sense, Indigenous and ordinary justice authorities need to engage in a process of intercultural dialogue, capacity-building, and exchange of information about each other's legal systems (UN Special Rapporteur on the Rights of Indigenous Peoples 2010b, 6). This would be an important way to first address prejudicial attitudes that State authorities might have about Indigenous cultures, customs, laws, and procedures and also address issues related to interlegal coordination and judicial review of decisions by Indigenous authorities.

Discussions on the issue of judicial review should avoid situations where decisions by Indigenous authorities are examined through dominant or Western perceptions of fundamental human rights. There needs to be an intercultural understanding about the diverse manifestations of human rights (UN Special Rapporteur on the Rights of Indigenous Peoples 2010b, 6). The use of cultural expert testimonies in Colombia and other countries has been an important avenue for the understanding of fundamental rights such as due process from the perspective of Indigenous Peoples. Consideration could also be given to intercultural review bodies composed of Indigenous and ordinary justice authorities where there are legitimate questions about issues of jurisdiction and observance of international human rights within decisions made by Indigenous authorities. In any case, any method of review should be based on the respect for Indigenous self-determination and should constructively aid in strengthening Indigenous justice systems (UN Special Rapporteur on the Rights of Indigenous Peoples 2010b, 8). This would be similar to the principle of maximization of autonomy applied by the Colombian constitutional court.

Despite conceivable scenarios that may arise where the application of Indigenous justice may offend contemporary notions of human rights, this must not be used to obstruct the legitimate efforts by Indigenous Peoples to promote and maintain their systems of justice and self-governance, also recognized under international human rights law. Indigenous Peoples must be provided a space to internally debate, in an autonomous manner, the appropriateness of those norms and practices and any possible need to reform or modify them. This would be preferable to external interventions that may undermine Indigenous Peoples' social, cultural, and political fabric and cohesion and which may also be perceived as perpetuating actions and attitudes reminiscent of colonialist eras and related historically oppressive connotations.

With the above consideration in mind, Indigenous Peoples could also address possible disadvantages that women, children, youth, disabled persons, and other population sectors could face within their respective Indigenous societies and justice systems. In this regard, the Expert Mechanism on the Rights of Indigenous Peoples has recommended that States establish working relationships with Indigenous Peoples to promote human rights education as a means of empowerment of these particular population sectors and their participation in ordinary and Indigenous justice systems (EMRIP 2014, 22–23).

Another important matter that international instruments like the UN declaration and some previously mentioned domestic constitutions is that States should provide assistance to Indigenous Peoples in developing and maintaining their justice systems. The UN declaration provides that Indigenous Peoples have the right to technical and financial assistance from States and international cooperation for the enjoyment of their rights (Article 39), which also includes assistance to finance their autonomous functions (Article 4). The Expert Mechanism has also emphasized that the "United Nations and its bodies and specialized agencies have an essential role in the promotion and protection of indigenous peoples' human rights, including their right to promote, develop and maintain their juridical systems" (EMRIP 2014, 23). In regions such as Latin America, international organizations like the UN and donor agencies would need to play a greater role along with governments and Indigenous Peoples to help strengthen and promote Indigenous justice systems.

CONCLUSION

The above discussion on international and comparative experiences in the recognition and promotion of Indigenous justice and law could help identify areas of further work and conceptual development to address the challenges that arise in the domestic application of these rights. The international and domestic normative instruments mentioned, as well as the criteria and principles used by domestic tribunals like the Colombian constitutional court and the mandate of the UN Special Rapporteur, provide some useful reference in that regard. These would also be relevant in specific cases that international bodies and tribunals would possibly examine regarding the domestic application of international standards on Indigenous justice and law.

State authorities, ordinary and Indigenous justice operators, academic scholars, and international bodies would need to keep in mind how the effective exercise of Indigenous justice and law is essential for the internationally recognized rights of Indigenous Peoples to self-determination, self-governance, and the maintenance of their culture and social, political, and legal institutions. It is also an essential component in shared interests and efforts in strengthening the administration of justice and fighting impunity. Indigenous justice and Indigenous justice operators and authorities are important partners in that regard.

REFERENCES

Alvarado, Leonardo J. 2015. "Advances and Ongoing Challenges in the Protection of Indigenous Peoples' Rights Within the Inter-American System and the United National Special Procedures System." In *Closing the Rights Gap: From Human Rights to Social Transformation*, edited by LaDawn Haglund and Robin Stryker, 69–84. Oakland: University of California Press.

Charters, Claire. 2009. "The Legitimacy of the UN Declaration on the Rights of Indigenous Peoples." In *Making the Declaration Work: The United Nations*

Declaration on the Rights of Indigenous Peoples, edited by Claire Charters and Rodolfo Stavenhagen, 280–303. Copenhagen, DK: IWGIA.

Expert Mechanism on the Rights of Indigenous Peoples (EMRIP). 2014. *Study on Access to Justice in the Promotion and Protection of the Rights of Indigenous Peoples: Restorative Justice, Indigenous Juridical Systems and Access to Justice for Indigenous Women, Children and Youth, and Persons with Disabilities*, A/HRC/27/65, August 7. http://www.un.org/ga/search/view_doc.asp?symbol=A/HRC/27/65.

Flores, Carlos Y. 2012. "Two Justices: The Challenges of Interlegal Coordination." https://vimeo.com/51473674.

Gonzalez, Luis. 2017. "Totonicapán se aleja de movimiento que impulsaba cambio al artículo 203." *República*, March 8, 2017. http://republica.gt/2017/03/08/totonicapan-se-aleja-de-movimiento-que-impulsaba-cambio-al-articulo-203/.

Inter-American Commission on Human Rights. 2009. "Indigenous and Tribal Peoples' Rights over Their Ancestral Lands and Natural Resources: Norms and Jurisprudence of the Inter-American Human Rights System," OEA/Ser. L/V/II. Doc. 58, December 30. http://www.oas.org/en/iachr/indigenous/docs/pdf/AncestralLands.pdf.

———. 2015. "Indigenous Peoples, Afro-Descendent Communities, and Natural Resources: Human Rights Protection in the Context of Extraction, Exploitation, and Development Activities," OEA/Ser.L/V/II.Doc.47/15, December 2015. http://www.oas.org/en/iachr/reports/pdfs/ExtractiveIndustries2016.pdf.

International Labour Organization (ILO). 2009a. *Application of Convention No. 169 by Domestic and International Courts in Latin America: A Casebook*. http://www.ilo.org/wcmsp5/groups/public/---ed_norm/---normes/documents/publication/wcms_123946.pdf.

———. 2009b. *Indigenous and Tribal Peoples' Convention in Practice: A Guide to ILO Convention No. 169*. International Labour Office. http://www.ilo.org/wcmsp5/groups/public/@ed_norm/@normes/documents/publication/wcms_106474.pdf.

———. 2017. *Ratifications of C169—Indigenous and Tribal Peoples Convention, 1989 (No. 169)*, NORMLEX (Information System on International Labour Standards). http://www.ilo.org/dyn/normlex/en/f?p=NORMLEXPUB:11300:0::NO:11300:P11300_INSTRUMENT_ID:312314:NO.

Office in Mexico of the United Nations High Commissioner for Human Rights (OHCHR-Mexico). 2007. *El reconocimiento legal y vigencia de los sistemas normativos indígenas en México*. OHCHR-Mexico. https://www.hchr.org.mx/images/doc_pub/sistnorm.pdf.

Sierra, María Teresa. 2005. "The Revival of Indigenous Justice in Mexico: Challenges for Human Rights and the State." *Political and Legal Anthropology Review* 28 (1): 52–72.

Tobin, Brendan. 2014. *Indigenous Peoples, Customary Law and Human Rights— Why Living Law Matters.* London: Routledge.

UN Special Rapporteur on Extrajudicial, Summary or Arbitrary Executions, Philip Alston. 2011. "Report: Mission to Ecuador." A/HRC/17/28/Add.2. May 9. https://documents-dds-ny.un.org/doc/UNDOC/GEN/G11/131/05/PDF/G1113105.pdf?OpenElement.

UN Special Rapporteur on the Rights of Indigenous Peoples, James Anaya. 2010a. "Ordinary and Indigenous Justice in Ecuador: 'The Key Lies in Dialogue' Says UN Expert." Press Release, June 8. http://unsr.jamesanaya.org/statements/ordinary-and-indigenous-justice-in-ecuador-the-key-lies-in-dialogue-says-un-expert.

———. 2010b. "Report: Addendum: Observations on the Progress Made and Challenges Faced in the Implementation of the Constitutional Guarantees of the Rights of Indigenous Peoples in Ecuador." A/HRC/15/37/Add.7. September 13. http://unsr.vtaulicorpuz.org/site/images/docs/special/2010-special-a-hrc-15-37-add-7-ecuador-constitutional-en.pdf.

UN Special Rapporteur on the Rights of Indigenous Peoples, Victoria Tauli-Corpuz. 2016. "Human Rights, Indigenous Jurisdiction and Access to Justice: Towards Intercultural Dialogue and Respect." Presentation at the International Seminar on Investigative Techniques and Indigenous Issues, Bogotá, Colombia (February 2016). "UNSR Presentation—Indigenous jurisdiction." http://unsr.vtaulicorpuz.org/site/index.php/en/statements/116-indigenous-jurisdiction.

———. 2018. "Report of the Special Rapporteur on the Rights of Indigenous Peoples on Her Visit to Mexico." A/HRC/39/17/Add.2. June 28. http://unsr.vtaulicorpuz.org/site/images/docs/country/2018-mexico-a-hrc-39-17-add2-en.pdf.

Van Cott, Donna Lee. 2000. "A Political Analysis of Legal Pluralism in Bolivia and Colombia." *Journal of Latin American Studies* 32:207–34.

———. 2003. "Legal Pluralism and Informal Community Justice Administration in Latin America." Paper presented at *Informal Institutions and Latin American Politics*, University of Notre Dame, April 24–25.

———. 2007. "Latin America's Indigenous Peoples." *Journal of Democracy* 18 (4): 127–42.

LEGAL RESOURCES

American Declaration on the Rights of Indigenous Peoples (2016)

Bolivia Law on Jurisdictional Demarcation (2010)

Constitutional Court of Colombia, Sentencia SU-510 (1998)

——. Sentencia T-523 (1997)

——. Sentencia T-617 (2010)

Constitution of Colombia (1991)

Constitution of Ecuador (2008)

Constitution of Guatemala (1985)

Constitution of the Plurinational State of Bolivia (2009)

Federal Constitution of Mexico (2001)

Inter-American Court of Human Rights. 2001. *Case of the Mayagna (Sumo) Awas Tingni Community v. Nicaragua.* Merits, Reparations and Costs, Judgment of August 31, 2001, Series C No. 79.

——. 2004. *Case of the Plan de Sánchez Massacre v. Guatemala.* Reparations. Judgment of November 19, 2004, Series C No. 116.

——. 2005. *Case of the Yakye Axa Indigenous Community v. Paraguay.* Merits, Reparations and Costs, Judgment of June 17, 2005, Series C No. 125.

International Labour Organization Indigenous and Tribal Peoples Convention, Convention 169 (1989)

United Nations Declaration on the Rights of Indigenous Peoples (2007)

United Nations International Covenant on Civil and Political Rights (1966)

United Nations International Covenant on Economic, Social and Cultural Rights (1966)

7

HOW INDIGENOUS JUSTICE PROGRAMS CONTRIBUTE TO INDIGENOUS COMMUNITY CAPACITY-BUILDING AND ACHIEVING HUMAN RIGHTS

MARIANNE O. NIELSEN

INDIGENOUS PEOPLES worldwide supported the development of the UN Declaration on the Rights of Indigenous People (UNDRIP) (2007), an international legal covenant that was ratified reluctantly by the governments of some colonized countries, especially Australia, Canada, and the United States. The principles and the intentions of that document promote human rights touchstones for Indigenous Peoples and, in turn, their communities, trying to overcome the economic, political, social, and legal marginalizations that result from living in colonized countries. This long overdue UN document provides broad guidelines concerning the human rights of Indigenous Peoples but provides little guidance about how to operationalize these rights on a day-to-day basis. How can Indigenous Peoples and their Indigenous communities live within a European-based colonial system, meet the demands of that system, and at the same time ensure their human rights, including the right to nondiscrimination under the law? How can they get access to local, inexpensive, effective, culturally based services that protect their human rights, while at the same time contend with the colonially caused, criminogenic marginalizations under which they live, such as poverty, poor health, poor self-esteem, discrimination, and lack of legal and political power? More specifically how can they decrease the disadvantages that they face in colonially based criminal justice systems that are often unfair, from discriminatory laws to ineffective and biased courts, corrections, and community correctional programs?

Indigenous-run justice organizations try to provide the answers to these questions.[1] They offer a wide range of direct services to overcome the impacts of structural and institutional discrimination remaining in colonially based national laws (see the book's introduction), that Indigenous individuals, communities, and nations face daily. But this chapter's focus is not on these direct services—legal advocacy, legal assistance in courts, dispute resolution, correctional healing programs, alternative sentencing, and crime prevention—since they are described elsewhere (Nielsen 2004; and see also table 7.1). The focus of this chapter is on the Indigenous-run agencies' long-term efforts to assist Indigenous Peoples and their communities to overcome the marginalizations rooted in colonialism that affect every aspect of Indigenous life.

These agencies have holistic philosophies based in Indigenous cultures, which means that Indigenous traditional law informs their operations and missions as much as possible. They aspire to the equality and fairness found in traditional law and reflected in the UNDRIP. These organizations bring together the best aspects of all three levels of law—traditional, national, and international—and operationalize them "on the street" for the benefit of Indigenous individuals, communities, and nations.

Some of these organizations are operated by Indigenous governments of land-based, self-governing communities such as reserves and reservations, or "Nations." Others are nonprofit Indigenous organizations serving Indigenous populations living in Indigenous communities within urban, semi-urban and rural, non-land-based, non-self-governing areas, often intermixed with non-Indigenous populations. Some organizations provide services to both populations. Indigenous nations exist in both Canada and the United States, although both countries also have many mixed communities that have Indigenous individuals as a significant part of their population. Indigenous communities in Australia and New Zealand do not have the same type of legal recognition, although they do have some legal standing due to land claim settlements. Communities of Indigenous individuals living within settler cities, towns, and rural areas can be defined as communities because they have "social attributes and interests . . . shared by inhabitants and commonly used to designate

TABLE 7.1 Key Features of the Case Study Organizations*

ORGANIZATION	HISTORY	MISSION	STRUCTURE/ STAFF	LOCATION(S)	CLIENTS	PROGRAMS	FUNDING
Australian Legal Rights Movement, Inc, of South Australia [ALRM]; Established 1971; Incorporated 1973; www.alrm.org.au	Grassroots mobilization by Aboriginal and non-Aboriginal leaders; Responding to large numbers of Aboriginals appearing in the justice system without legal representation; Support from other Aboriginal organizations	Promote legal, cultural, economic, political, and social rights of Aboriginals through the provision of legal services and associated activities	Aboriginal board of directors; 75 full and part time staff; 32 percent of staff were of Aboriginal descent	Head office in the state capital, and two regional offices in areas of high Indigenous population density	Aboriginal and Torres Strait Islander adults, youth, and children	Legal Services in criminal, family, and civil jurisdictions, Native Title Unit (1994–2008), Community legal education, financial counseling; Host: Aboriginal Prison Visitor Scheme	Legal services funded via federal govt. contract
Native Counseling Services of Alberta [NCSA]; Established 1970; www .ncsa.ca	Aboriginal grassroots initiative; Responding to the overrepresentation of Aboriginals in prisons and the cultural and linguistic disadvantages they experienced in courts	Promote the fair and equitable treatment of Aboriginal people; Contribute to the holistic development of Aboriginal individuals, families, and communities	Aboriginal board of directors; 190 full-time and contract staff; 85 percent of staff are of Aboriginal descent	Head office in the provincial capital, 22 branch offices in areas of high Indigenous population density; ceremonial site in Edmonton	Primarily men, women, youth, and children of Aboriginal descent, however, some programs also assist non-Aboriginal clients	Native court-workers; Family, youth, children, and community wellness; employment; housing; healing and health; men and women's healing lodges; legal education, research, and training; residential school recovery	Primarily funded by federal and provincial govt. depts.; Some funds from municipal govt. and private foundations

TABLE 7.1 *continued*

ORGANIZATION	HISTORY	MISSION	STRUCTURE/ STAFF	LOCATION(S)	CLIENTS	PROGRAMS	FUNDING
Stan Daniels Healing Centre [SDHC]; Established 1988; Renamed SDHC 1999; www.nsca .ca/programs/ corrections	NCSA contracted to operate this federal correctional facility for conditionally released prisoners; Responding to high rates of Aboriginal incarceration and recidivism	Provide programs addressing residents' social, educational, spiritual and physical needs and to develop prosocial behaviors; Enable residents' participation in goal formulation	Legislatively mandated to provide Aboriginal-specific programs and promote Aboriginal autonomy; Aboriginal board of directors (NCSA); 40 staff, 65 percent of Aboriginal descent	SDHC is located in the provincial capital	Almost all residents of the Centre are males of Aboriginal descent (72 beds)	Institutional services for conditionally released prisoners, or with inmate status; Skills development, treatment, relationahsip, cultural programs (Elder counseling and ceremonies)	Funded by Corrections Service Canada
Youth Justice Committee Program of Alberta [YJC]; Established 1990; www.solgps.alberta .ca/programs	Initiative of one remote Indigenous community with the assistance of a local judge; Responding to the large numbers of Native youths incarcerated away from their local community; Rapid expansion to other areas	Increase community involvement in sentencing; Promote community harmony, promote healing of offenders, victims, and communities; Reduce recidivism	Alberta Justice oversight and "designation" on showing local CJS support; 6–60 volunteers per YJC comprised of respected individuals ethnically representative of the local community	YJCs (about 130) operate in both Aboriginal and non-Aboriginal communities; About 30 are Aboriginal	Primarily young offenders involved in the CJS; Some YJCs informally assist adults or youths not involved in the CJS	Community-based sentencing advice to youth courts after a YJC hearing involving offenders and persons affected by their behavior; Non-judicial alternative measures	Unfunded by law but the provincial govt. provides small grants for ancillary expenses

| Hamilton Abuse Intervention Project [HAIP]; Established 1991; www.terunanga.org.nz/haip.html | Govt.-initiated trial of coordinated justice and social service responses to family violence. Responding to a perceived lack of govt. and societal concern for the female victims of family violence and to address the high rates of Māori men incarcerated for family violence offenses | To support, advocate, and work to empower families affected by family violence | 50/50 Māori/Pakeha; Charitable trust; 11 full-time, and 12 part-time, 4 contract staff; 50 percent of staff are Māori | Hamilton, an area heavily populated by Māori, on the north island of New Zealand | Māori and non-Māori victims and perpetrators of family violence | Interagency coordination and monitoring, women's court and advocacy, men's and women's education and support offered in Māori and non-Māori formats, youth protection | Govt. funding withdrawn after three-year pilot; Presently funded through municipal and Lotteries Board grants, private foundations, and corporations |
| Native Americans for Community Action of Flagstaff, AZ [NACA]; Established 1968; Incorporated 1971; www.nacainc.org | Grassroots initiative of Native American community and Native and non-Native lawyers responding to lack of access to Indian health clinics and police treatment of Native Americans | Provide community wellness strategies, empower and advocate for Native peoples and others in need to create a healthy community based on harmony, respect, and Indigenous values | Mainly Native American board of directors; Non-profit organization, 30 staff, of whom 65 percent are of Indigenous descent | Flagstaff, Arizona | Anyone (in practice, primarily Indigenous individuals); Geographical limit of service delivery to Flagstaff and surrounding county | Family medical center, substance abuse and mental health counseling, youth crime prevention programs, health promotions, wellness center, community forums, suicide prevention | Varying amounts of funding provided by tribal, state, and federal govts.; Private foundations and some fees for services |

(continued)

TABLE 7.1 continued

ORGANIZATION	HISTORY	MISSION	STRUCTURE/STAFF	LOCATION(S)	CLIENTS	PROGRAMS	FUNDING
Peacemakers of the Navajo Nation [PM]; Established 1982; Formal reorganization 1991; www.navajocourts.org/indexpeacemaking.html	Initiative of the Navajo Nation Judiciary Responding to judicial dissatisfaction with the adversarial court process and its limited ability to address the justice needs of nation members	No official mission statement, however, the principles and objectives of peacemaking have been adopted by the Navajo judiciary and peacemakers are mandated under the Navajo Nation code	Peacemaker liaisons are located in each of the 12 judicial districts of the nation; At least one active peacemaker per district	Coordinated from Window Rock, Arizona, peacemakers practice throughout the 110 semiautonomous communities that comprise the Navajo Nation	Primarily adult members of the Navajo Nation	Peacemaking for civil, family, and criminal matters via Navajo courts, police, or self-referral; Use Navajo spiritual narratives to help parties reach a harmonious settlement of disputes and restitution (nályééh)	Funded by the Navajo Nation and a small fee from participants

*These data were derived from a wide variety of organizational documents and scholarly writings by and about the case study organizations. Organizational documents included annual reports, minutes of board and staff meetings, pamphlets, websites, audit reports, organizational charts, training manuals, and policy manuals. This chart is an updated version of a chart in Nielsen and Brown (2012). The information is current as of 2018 where possible, but organizations are living entities whose characteristics change constantly, therefore their website addresses are provided. Information on staff numbers, their Indigenous status, and programs are very likely out of date but give an indication of staff composition and services.

(continued)

them as a collective identity, regardless of geographic proximity," though in the case of non-legally recognized Indigenous groups aspiring to be legally recognized as nations, they may also be a community of "people living within a geographic area that is recognizable by a set of attributes tied to its physical location or appearance, such a natural boundaries, a recognized history, [and] demographic patterns" (Chaskin et al. 2001, 8).

The findings in this chapter are based on longitudinal case-study research done between 1988 and 2008 with seven justice service organizations in four countries—Australia, Canada, New Zealand, and the United States.

INDIGENOUS MARGINALIZATION

One symptom of colonization and the resulting marginalizations of Indigenous Peoples and their communities is a consistent pattern of overrepresentation of Indigenous offenders in the criminal justice system of colonized countries. Criminogenic conditions result from colonialism, as Indigenous Peoples, their communities, and individual members are marginalized economically, politically, legally, and socially, and certain behaviors are criminalized by law. Government task forces and scholarly reports point to Indigenous individuals being overrepresented in the statistics on poverty, unemployment, low educational achievement, substance abuse, loss of culture and language, and post-traumatic distress from generations of oppression. Discrimination as a remnant of colonial ideologies of superiority and inferiority also has an impact, both societally through national legislation and in how Indigenous individuals are treated by criminal justice personnel and institutions enforcing these laws. Decisions influenced by prejudice and stereotypes may inform the arrest, sentencing, length of time served, and availability of community correctional services for Indigenous people, and how they are treated as victims of crime. These scholarly and government reports have concluded that there is indeed a relationship among colonialism, marginalization, and criminal justice system overinvolvement. Few authors go so far as to call these issues human rights abuses but some patterns and incidents in the criminal justice systems of these countries fit the profile (see, for example: Fixico 2013; Nielsen and Silverman 2009; Duran 2006; Sarre

2000; National Inquiry 1997; Royal Commission 1993, 1996; Hamilton and Sinclair 1991; Walker 1990; Project Waitangi 1989).

Incarceration statistics, despite the many problems in their collection and interpretation, are the most comparable and accurate statistics across countries for illustrating the impact of marginalizations as these contribute to the overrepresentation of Indigenous individuals as offenders. In Australia, for example, Indigenous Australians are 27 percent of the adult incarcerated population despite being less than 3 percent of the Australian population (Australian Bureau of Statistics 2015). In Canada, 28 percent of those sentenced to custody are Aboriginal, yet Aboriginal Peoples constitute about 4 percent of the population (Perreault 2014). In New Zealand, Māori are more than 50 percent of the prison population and about 15 percent of the general New Zealand population (United Nations 2014). In the United States the picture is more difficult to determine since not all states collect data on American Indian/Alaskan Native status.[2] American Indians and Alaska Natives make up about 2 percent of the total population but have much higher overrepresentation in some states (U.S. Department of Health 2018). In states that collect American Indian/Alaskan Native/Native Hawaiian status for prisoners, the most dramatic overrepresentations are in Hawaii (39 percent of incarcerated, 10 percent of total), Alaska (38 percent of incarcerated, 15 percent of total), North Dakota (29 percent of incarcerated, 5 percent of total), South Dakota (29 percent of incarcerated, 9 percent of total) and Montana (22 percent of incarcerated, 6 percent of total) (Sakala 2014).

These statistics suggest that the human rights of Indigenous Peoples and individuals are not being sufficiently protected by the laws and governments of their home countries and that societal and institutional conditions are such that Indigenous individuals are either committing more crimes than non-Indigenous citizens, are being unfairly treated once they are accused of crimes, or both. Their own traditional justice systems are still recovering from the damage caused by colonialism and the imposed replacements. Despite the creation and adoption of the UN Declaration on the Rights of Indigenous Peoples, it has been neither completely accepted nor internalized by the Euro-based justice systems of their countries, including the national laws.

INDIGENOUS HUMAN RIGHTS

Indigenous individuals are ostensibly protected and guaranteed fair and equal treatment by the laws of the country in which they live but there is a great deal of evidence, as reported in the reports and studies cited above, that this does not happen on a consistent basis, individually or institutionally. In many colonized countries, one way that Indigenous communities and Indigenous nations have decided to improve, protect, and maintain their human rights, including rights to fairness in the justice system, is to set up Indigenous justice service programs. These are separate from and sometimes alternatives to Euro-based criminal justice system organizations but work cooperatively with them for the benefit of their Indigenous clients.

These programs play important roles in counteracting discrimination in the Euro-based justice system by ensuring effective and culturally sensitive access to justice services at the local and regional levels, thereby fulfilling Article 2 of the United Nations Declaration on the Rights of Indigenous Peoples, "the right to be free from any kind of discrimination" (UN General Assembly 2007, 4). These programs provide many essential justice services but also do much, much more. The programs are the concrete manifestations of Article 3, the right to self-determination (UN General Assembly 2007, 4). The programs have been designed by and for Indigenous individuals, communities, and nations using Indigenous "distinctive customs, . . . traditions, procedures and practices" (UN General Assembly 2007, 10). By their structures, processes, and missions, they not only contribute to counteracting discrimination, they contribute to Article 5, "the right to maintain and strengthen their distinct political, legal, economic, social and cultural institutions" (UN General Assembly 2007, 4). As they assist Indigenous communities and nations to accomplish these three UN principles, they are involved in Indigenous community and nation capacity-building by modifying and reinventing traditional justice practices and values not found in the dominant justice systems, and assisting Indigenous communities and nations to self-determine their justice practices. They do this by not only providing "juridical systems or customs," as described in Article 34 (UN General Assembly 2007, 10) but by providing specific resources within Indigenous communities and nations. In addition to their direct legal and other justice services, these resources include building skills in community members, the legitimization of Indigenous service provision in general, and a number of other pragmatic assets to be described later in this chapter.

INDIGENOUS JUSTICE ORGANIZATIONS

In the last two hundred years the law, police, courts, and prisons of most colonized countries have had serious impacts on the lives of Indigenous peoples. In the past, the various branches of the criminal justice system wrote, passed, and enforced discriminatory laws of many kinds—laws that stole Indigenous land and resources; that defined Indigenous people as inferior beings; that forbid ceremonies, marriages, voting, and off-reservation jobs; that forbid Indigenous nations from protecting their own people; and much more. The police arrested and occasionally killed Indigenous resisters and protesters. To this day, the dominant criminal justice systems of all four countries continue to have problematic relationships with Indigenous communities, including: under- and overpolicing, uneven application of laws, jurisdictional legal mazes, unfair sentencing, unfair correctional practices, and discriminatory behavior from police, judges, and correctional officers (for example, see Long et al. 2008). Impacts of the justice systems may be less overt and extreme than they were in early colonial days, but serious impacts still happen as seen in the previous incarceration statistics and also the scholarly and government reports previously cited.

Governments in these four colonized countries eventually implemented services, mostly based on European models, to assist Indigenous individuals involved in the criminal justice system as victims or offenders; however, on the whole with a few exceptions, these are generic, ineffective, based in colonial ideology, culturally insensitive, biased toward punishment rather than restitution, and overly punitive compared to the same application in non-Indigenous communities. The dominant justice systems provide few crime prevention, legal education, and rehabilitation services that are effective for Indigenous people. The programs do not lower recidivism rates or fulfill the culturally based needs of the Indigenous offenders and victims, they do not get Indigenous offenders fairer treatment in terms of equal sentencing and release, and most especially, they do not attempt to tackle the underlying problems that lead to criminal offending and victimization (Fixico 2013; Nielsen and Silverman 2009; Duran 2006; Sarre 2000; National Inquiry 1997; Royal Commission 1993, 1996; Hamilton and Sinclair 1991; Walker 1990; Project Waitangi 1989).

As a result of the issues with the imposed systems of justice services, Indigenous justice organizations began to offer parallel and innovative justice services based in Indigenous values and practices where these were allowed by law and organizational resources. New tribal government programs, new Indigenous organizations, or already existing Indigenous organizations such as Indian centers began to develop programs to supplement dominant government services. These programs were funded by a variety of sources—state/provincial and federal governments, tribal governments, private foundations, and a few by client fees. Many of these funding sources had "strings attached" that put limits on how "Indigenous" these organizations could be (Nielsen and Brown 2012). Nevertheless, the organizations had and continue to have some very specific Indigenous characteristics: they hire Indigenous people, have boards of directors that are wholly or partly Indigenous, offer services that are holistic and interconnected in nature, use Indigenous values and practices where possible and practical, and recognize the impact of colonization on Indigenous lives. For an analysis of what else makes these Indigenous justice service organizations distinctly "Indigenous," see Nielsen and Brown (2012). Many of these programs became active in the early 1970s as part of the wave of worldwide Indigenous human rights movements, political mobilizations, and cultural resurgence efforts.

The seven organizations participating in this research project provided an extensive array of justice programs as well as other services aimed at counteracting underlying problems of marginalization: (1) Aboriginal Legal Rights Movement, Inc. (ALRM), based in Adelaide, South Australia; (2) Native Counselling Services of Alberta (NCSA), located province-wide in Alberta, Canada; (3) Stan Daniels Healing Centre (SDHC), located in Edmonton, Alberta; (4) Youth Justice Committees (YJC) found in multiple locations in Alberta, Canada; (5) Native Americans for Community Action, Inc. (NACA), located in Flagstaff, Arizona; (5) Navajo Nation Peacemaking, located throughout the Navajo Nation, USA; and (7) the Hamilton Abuse Intervention Project (HAIP), located in Hamilton, New Zealand. See figure 7.1 for a summary of their major characteristics. As will be seen in the next section, these organizations not only provide local and regional Indigenous people with access to justice and other services but help to develop resources in Indigenous communities and nations, and thereby promote human rights through community capacity-building, and nation-rebuilding.

HUMAN RIGHTS, COMMUNITY CAPACITY-BUILDING, AND NATION-REBUILDING

All of the organizations were the results of Indigenous self-determination—they were designed, run by, and continue to serve Indigenous Peoples and individuals. While the organizations had to meet government mandates and national, state, and tribal laws where applicable, their structures, processes, and values were based in Indigenous cultures as much as possible. As the organizations provided these services, they also improved the resources of Indigenous communities and nations so that they could challenge the economic, political, legal, and social marginalizations resulting from colonization. In Indigenous communities, ALRM, SDHC, HAIP, and NACA assist to develop community capacities in a wide variety of skill and knowledge areas, to be discussed shortly. The YJC and NCSA do the same in both communities and nations. The peacemakers serve only the Navajo nation. Community capacity-building and nation-rebuilding are intricately linked—when (or if) individuals with tribal and band membership work on or return to their nation, the skills they have or bring back contribute to nation-building or -rebuilding, with nation-building referring to "the processes by which a Native Nation enhances its own foundational capacity for effective self-governance and for self-determined community and economic development" (Jorgensen 2007, xii). Indigenous communities face most of the same marginalization issues as nations, but nations also face issues of regaining self-governance or sovereignty and in turn of providing all of the essential services (i.e., public safety, educational, and social services) that non-Native nation governments provide to their citizens.

Various colonial processes ensured that Indigenous social institutions were severely harmed and that Indigenous Peoples and their communities

did not have the time to judiciously adapt their own institutions to changing societies (hence Article 5 of the UN Declaration). Indigenous communities and nations are in the process of developing or redeveloping
Indigenous-based social institutions such as education, health, law, and
justice.

Presently the majority of Indigenous individuals live outside of their
culturally traditional or geographically imposed communities, though
some live close by (Nielsen and Robyn 2003; Pettit et al. 2014). Some
of these Indigenous individuals are not directly affiliated with a specific
land-based group due to factors such intermarriage, enfranchisement,
adoption, disenrollment, not having state or federal legal recognition,
and/or discriminatory laws. As well, Indigenous individuals were and
continue to be pushed out of nations by poverty and a lack of jobs and
other opportunities. They were also pulled away by government promises
(for example, "relocation" in the United States) and self-perceived opportunities to get more education, jobs, and/or an improved existence (see
also Fixico 2000; Walker 1990).

For Indigenous nations to keep their members and their skills at home,
and possibly to have the migrants return, they need to ensure that their
members' human rights are protected and that the nations "possess the
collective rights which are indispensable for their existence, well-being
and integral development as peoples" (United Nations General Assembly
2007, 4). In day-to-day terms this means that Indigenous peoples need to
have effective, safe, sustainable communities with good jobs, good schools,
skilled workers, functional infrastructures, and opportunities to learn or
relearn and to practice cultural heritage, language, and lifeways. These
essential conditions serve to reinforce the need for functioning justice
services.

CAPACITY-BUILDING AND NATION-BUILDING

In order to rebuild a nation, the self-sufficiency of its citizens must be
increased. Research by the Harvard Project found that for Indigenous
nations to be effective they need to assert decision-making power, or
what Jarratt-Snider and Nielsen (2018, 191) describe as "de facto self-
determination" and Cornell and Kalt (2007, 18) call "practical sovereignty

or self-rule." They also need to have effective governing institutions and government institutions that are appropriate for their culture, use strategic decision-making, and have leaders who are "nation-builders and mobilizers" (Cornell and Kalt 2007, 18). Indigenous justice service organizations are one set of players in improving or building these capacities, along with other kinds of organizations and individual and organizational networks as Chaskin et al. (2001) discovered in their research on non-Indigenous communities. Chaskin and his colleagues (2001, 7) define community capacity as "the interaction of human capital, organizational resources, and social capital existing within a given community that can be leveraged to solve collective problems and improve or maintain the well-being of the community. It may operate through informal social processes and/or organized efforts by individuals, organizations, and social networks that exist among them and between them and the larger systems of which the community is a part."

Community capacity-building is an essential part of Indigenous communities and nations overcoming marginalizations by establishing new programs and services, but for Indigenous nations capacity-building also contributes to building self-governance. As Chaskin et al. (2001, 2) point out, "Each constituency comes to the task of community building in a somewhat different way, with distinct interests and roles in building and sustaining capacity." In Indigenous communities and nations, the distinct interests shared are increasing their human rights through increased self-determination and incorporating Indigenous culturally based characteristics in their initiatives.

For many Indigenous communities and nations, providing access to justice services to lower overrepresentation in the criminal justice system is just one issue among many. As a result, many Indigenous justice service organizations become innovative and holistic in the way they tackle criminal justice services. The organizations identify needs in the communities and nations that underlie criminal behavior and that lead to contact with the criminal justice system, and they develop additional programs (if laws, funding, and resources allow) or modify old ones to meet those needs or as many needs as they can handle. These needs may include lack of community resources such as dispute resolution or crime prevention programs, or other programs to counteract poor parenting skills resulting from boarding schools, or substance abuse due to internalized violence (that is, violence aimed at the self due to internalized oppression), and family violence (that is, externalized violence from the same source) (Duran 2006). While the organizations build these programs, they also build a range of capacities in their staff, their leaders, their clients, and their communities and/or nations.

CAPACITY-BUILDING BY INDIGENOUS JUSTICE PROGRAMS

Chino and DeBruyn (2006) look at capacity-building activities by organizations from an Indigenous perspective of community contributions by people as they go through life's stages. This framework honors Indigenous Native American ways of knowing and points out that "mainstream models, programs, and funding agencies too often assume that tribal community members and practitioners can immediately begin to resolve an issue; they pay little attention to the social, cultural, historical, and political environment and the time needed to build effective working relationships" (Chino and DeBruyn 2006, 597). Their model consists of four steps: (1) building relationships, which focuses on open communication and identifying common ground and common goals; (2) building skills, in which participants develop new interpersonal and practical skills; (3) working together, in which the tradition of community is integrated with solving problems together; and (4) promoting commitment, where participants give back by teaching and advocating for future generations.

Native Americans for Community Action (NACA) is an urban-based health and crime prevention organization that exemplifies how the participating organizations contribute to capacity-building within their staff and nearby Native American communities and American Indian nations. Its mission is "to provide preventive wellness strategies, empower, and advocate for Native people and others in need to create a healthy community based on Harmony, Respect, and Indigenous Values" (nacainc.org). It considers crime prevention programs such as its substance abuse counseling, mental health counseling, and youth recreation ("Pathways") programs as part of healthy communities. Per Chino and DeBruyn's (2006) framework, the agency has excellent relationships and communications with a variety of other organizations as exemplified by the Native and non-Native members of its board of directors who represent tribal community members and local medical, legal, social service, and educational providers (among others). Some of its staff members belong to community and regional child crisis networks and to boards and committees in the child welfare arena. As part of these networks, staff members disseminate information about their organization, Indigenous issues, and ideas for many kinds of reform. They work with other organizations to develop needed programs such as the suicide prevention program NACA now operates. The agency hosts cultural events like the Sacred Mountain Prayer Run that educates both Indigenous and non-Indigenous individuals and communities about services and issues in Native American communities.

The agency helps its clients build new skills to improve physical and mental health, but it also provides its staff members with on-the-job training in organizational and job-specific skills, as well as additional training for a variety of skills, such as substance abuse counseling certification. Once staff members are trained at the organization, they are seen as desirable employees by other Indigenous and non-Indigenous service, political, legal, and business organizations, and the agency often loses good staff because other organizations can pay them more.

As part of their commitment to future generations, staff members speak in schools, either as part of their jobs or on their own time. Their presentations are on a variety of topics, but their very presence as American Indian professionals is also important. Some staff bring their children or foster children to organizational events so that the children become familiar with their parent's work and see Indigenous individuals who are successful and respected service providers. One staff member commented that she thought clients seeing Native Americans with good jobs and helping people would be an incentive for them to finish their education and get good jobs.

An alternative model of capacity-building for nations (and communities) was proposed by Stephen Cornell, Miriam Jorgensen, Joseph P. Kalt, and Katherine S. Contreras (2007); it also focuses on process but from a different though related Indigenous perspective. Cornell and his colleagues examine the role of community leaders in "changing the story" through four practical steps that move an Indigenous nation along the path of nation-building: (1) changing the situation, which means building up a nation's expertise in how to negotiate successfully

with external environmental players, as well as developing the management capabilities of its personnel, investing in media and public
relations to transform outsiders' views, and changing insiders' views of
the nations' leaders as true governors as well as being service-deliverers
and problem-solvers; (2) building on culture, which means using the
nation's shared culture for nation-building so that it incorporates
the knowledge of what people value and believe concerning "power,
authority and consent" as part of decision-making, and how things
operate (Cornell et al. 2007, 316); (3) acquiring knowledge in order to
rebuild, because nations need knowledge in a great many areas from
management to law to economic development and onward, remem-
bering that learning from others "is part of a long native tradition of
exchange" (Cornell et al. 2007, 317); and (4) exercising leadership in
that the nations' leaders need to take on many roles depending on the
culture of the nation. They can be "educators, decision makers, strate-
gists, managers, consensus builders, inspirers" (Cornell et al. 2007, 318),
and have to be able to help the nation dwell not on the past but on
building a new story of "what happens now," as well as having to be
doers by making that story a reality (Cornell et al. 2007, 318). This
nation-building model can be modified with little alteration to apply
to Indigenous community capacity-building.

The emphasis of Cornell's model on the role of the leaders in the
community can be seen in the example of Native Counselling Services
of Alberta (NCSA). It is a community-based organization that has contributed to Indigenous capacity-building in the urban and semi-urban
communities in which it provides court worker and other services (see
figure 7.1), as well as making enormous contributions in its nearly fifty
years to capacity-building in First Nations. Before a meeting with First
Nations community leaders attended by the author and the director of the
agency, the director pointed to a photo of the chief and council on the wall
and explained that over the years, 80 percent of the council's members
(including the chief) had worked for and been trained by NCSA. They
had gone through job-related training, such as court worker training, but
also cultural awareness training, writing skills development, leadership
training, and others, and consequently had developed the confidence and
networks to assist them in their careers as First Nation leaders. This had
helped to change the story for this nation.

In particular, NCSA worked with this and other nations and communities over several years to develop Youth Justice Committees because all concerned had the common goal of preventing Native youth from entering the criminal justice system. At one point NCSA assigned a staff member as a development officer to work with local court workers to help the community and nation leaders and members to develop the necessary skills to set up and operate the committees, including how to interact and work with the Euro-based justice system (which was really a two-way street as the justice personnel learned about First Nations' cultures, issues, and resources). The NCSA research department developed a how-to manual, and their media department developed videos on the program in action (in addition to many other educational videos available to communities, such as preventing family violence, youth decision-making, changes in law, and financial management). Community and nation members not only used these materials as part of the development process, but their leaders used them to persuade the dominant justice system members to cooperate with the program. By these actions, NCSA assisted the communities and nations with self-determination in solving an important problem by developing their own versions of Youth Justice Committees. They also assisted the communities and nations to build capacity in their members and to practice nation-rebuilding.

Using either or both of these frameworks, all seven organizations can be analyzed to show how they assisted Indigenous communities and nations to assert their human rights. Given that every Indigenous community and nation is culturally different, has different needs, and has had difference experiences with settler-colonists, a one-size-fits-all, capacity-and/or nation-building framework would be useless. The two previous frameworks contribute different perspectives about how to develop the resources needed by Indigenous communities and nations. The frameworks suggest multiple paths to success.

DISCUSSION

All seven of the justice service organizations operationalized human rights for Indigenous people by assisting with capacity-building and thereby "changing the story." These organizations are evidence that the accomplishment of capacity-building and human rights are closely related to justice service provision, and the Indigenous justice organizations are important players in this process.

There are a number of issues that affect the ability of the organizations to contribute to capacity- and nation-building. The first is that nation-building is a concept usually used only with Indigenous Peoples living on Indigenous land with some degree of self-governance; however, only a relatively small percentage of Indigenous Peoples in these four countries live within the borders of an Indigenous nation. For people living in the non-land-based communities, community capacity-building is the most appropriate approach. These groups exercise self-determination to increase the capacity of their communities. In the United States and Canada, Indigenous communities that are not recognized by federal or state governments may build the capacity of their communities to prove their legitimacy as nations. In any of the four countries, Indigenous individuals of mixed ancestry or who live away from their homelands may work together to create Indigenously sensitive urban organizations (such as NCSA, NACA, HAIP, or ALRM) to provide desperately needed services.

Second, these countries have legal restrictions on how much autonomy and self-governance Indigenous nations may exert. For example, in the United States, the Major Crimes Act (1885) and the *Oliphant* decision (1978) restrict tribal police and courts to handling minor felonies and all misdemeanors committed only by American Indians, and only a few sexual assault-related felonies by non-Native Americans (under the Violence Against Women Act of 2013), and while the Tribal Law and Order Act (2010) increases the amount of time and fines to which tribal courts can sentence offenders, most tribes cannot afford to implement the institutional changes required by these acts.[3] If Indigenous nations wish to develop justice services they need to successfully lobby for changes in Euro-based law (with all the difficulty that entails) and/or develop more resources to provide their own services.

Third, the capacity-building literature contains warnings about capacity-building imposed from above by well-meaning but culturally insensitive non-Indigenous decision makers. Very importantly, it also warns about top-down capacity-building being a cover for not dealing with the serious marginalizations and other human rights abuses faced daily by Indigenous Peoples and their communities (Howitt et al. 2014;

Morrissey 2006). The need for specific human rights is best understood by the victims, as are the strategies for ensuring that these needs are met. Effective Indigenous capacity-building starts from the bottom up.

CONCLUSION

These Indigenous justice service organizations are success stories such as Cornell et al. (2007) write about. Such success stories are important because as they are told they increase the amount of knowledge available to Indigenous communities and nations about what is possible in terms of increasing their human rights in pragmatic, everyday ways and how to accomplish this (Cornell et al. 2007). As Cornell et al. (2007, 311) explain,

> Citizens' experiences in arenas such as the private sector job market, the military, or college may provide them with transferable knowledge about what's required to change things, as well as more of a can-do attitude toward the tasks at hand. . . . The more such people there are in the community, the more likely the population as a whole will be inclined to be proactive in dealing with problems, to imagine that *they can change things*, that the Nation itself can fix what needs to be fixed, and to know *what needs to be done*. (Italics in the original)

According to Begay et al. (2007, 282), "North America's Indigenous peoples are generating more and more such stories every day, stories of Native nations taking hold of their future, reclaiming control of their own affairs, and meeting difficult challenges with innovative, homegrown solutions." They are following the guidelines outlined in the UN declaration and doing it in ways best suited to them. The contributions of Indigenous justice organizations to changing the story are evident. On the whole, their efforts are not meant to be political or aimed specifically at nation-building, as reflected in the mandates and missions of the organizations; nevertheless, their actions *are* political and they *do* contribute to nation-building in that these efforts have political effects: new and effective leaders are developed; more workers are trained with skills needed in service, political, legal, and economic development organizations and government programs; non-Indigenous political decision makers are better informed about Indigenous needs; the communities and nations have more resources with which to wage the fight; and the communities and nations have models of successful Indigenous-operated institutions. The organizations' capacity-building roles have contributed greatly to developing the communities and nations in ways that have supported them in becoming more economically self-sufficient, politically powerful, legally knowledgeable, and effective overall in a wide range of areas.

These organizations are leaders in envisioning the accomplishment of human rights through Indigenous self-determination. They develop programs to meet the needs of Indigenous communities and nations because other programs are nonexistent or ineffective. They present a story of where Indigenous Peoples and their communities could be and what they could accomplish. By telling their stories of success and innovation, they are educating others about how to succeed in practical ways. As Cornell et al. (2007, 309) state, "Knowledge of what is necessary and what works tells a Nation *what needs to be done*, focusing the effort to change things on what's most likely to be effective. The primary source of that knowledge is experience—the Nation's own experience or someone else's" (italics in the original). These organizations are lending their experiences as well as their resources to assist in community capacity-building and nation-rebuilding. These success stories are further examples of Indigenous resilience and are critical to Indigenous resurgence.

NOTES

1. Because of the continuing theoretical development of these concepts, there is overlap with Nielsen (2004) and Nielsen and Brown (2012). Many thanks are extended to the directors and staff of the participating organizations who shared their knowledge and expertise with patience, humor, and enthusiasm. This is a revised version of a paper presented at a 2014 conference on "Human Rights and Legal Pluralism in Theory and Practice" in Oslo, Norway.

2. Federal incarceration statistics are not included because of their problematic nature resulting from missing, inconsistent, and inadequate data (see Long et al. 2008).

3. "VAWA 2013 requires that tribes wishing to exercise the restored authority must provide the defendant with: '1) All the rights guaranteed by the statute [the Indian Civil Rights Act]. 2) Including (if the defendant is sentenced to jail time) all rights listed in 1302(c) [TLOA]. 3) The right to a trial by an impartial jury that is drawn from sources that (A) Reflect a fair cross section

of the community; and (B) Do not systematically exclude any distinctive group in the community, including non-Indians. 4) All other rights whose protection is necessary under the Constitution of The United States in order for Congress to recognize and affirm the inherent power of the participating tribe to exercise special domestic violence criminal Jurisdiction over the defendant'" (Urbina and Tatum 2014, 7).

REFERENCES

Australian Bureau of Statistics. 2015. "Summary of Findings: Persons in Corrective Services." http://www.abs.gov.au/AUSSTATS/abs@.nsf/allprimarymainfeatures/6A57BD9A3CF02618CA257F0F00115C28.

Begay, Manley A., Jr., Stephen Cornell, Miriam Jorgensen, and Nathan Pryor. 2007. "Rebuilding Native Nations: What Do Leaders Do?" In *Rebuilding Native Nations: Strategies for Governance and Development*, edited by Miriam Jorgensen, 275–95. Tucson: University of Arizona Press.

Chaskin, Robert J., Prudence Brown, Sudhir Venkatesh, and Avis Vidal. 2001. *Building Community Capacity*. New York: Aldine de Gruyter.

Chino, Michelle, and Lemyra DeBruyn. 2006. "Building True Capacity: Indigenous Models for Indigenous Communities." *American Journal of Public Health* 96 (4): 596–99.

Cornell, Stephen, Miriam Jorgensen, Joseph P. Kalt, and Katherine S. Contreras. 2007. "Seizing the Future: Why Some Native Nations Do and Others Don't." In *Rebuilding Native Nations: Strategies for Governance and Development*, edited by Miriam Jorgensen, 296–323. Tucson: University of Arizona Press.

Cornell, Stephen, and Joseph P. Kalt. 2007. "Two Approaches to the Development of Native Nations: One Works, the Other Doesn't." In *Rebuilding Native Nations: Strategies for Governance and Development*, edited by Miriam Jorgensen, 3–33. Tucson: University of Arizona Press.

Duran, Eduardo. 2006. *Healing the Soul Wound: Counseling with American Indians and Other Native Peoples*. New York: Columbia University.

Fixico, Donald L. 2000. *The Urban Indian Experience in America*. Albuquerque: University of New Mexico Press.

———. 2013. *Indian Resilience and Rebuilding*. Tucson: University of Arizona Press.

Hamilton, A. C., and C. M. Sinclair. 1991. *Report of the Aboriginal Justice Inquiry of Manitoba: The Justice System and Aboriginal People*. Volume 1. Winnipeg: Province of Manitoba, Canada.

Howitt, Richard, Claire Colyer, Mitchell R. Hammer, Olga Havnen, Karen Huchendorf, and Carol Hubert. 2014. "Organizational Capacity for Engaging with Indigenous Australians." *Geographical Research* 52 (3): 250–62.

Jarratt-Snider, Karen, and Marianne O. Nielsen. 2018. "Conclusion." In *Crime and Social Justice in Indian Country*, edited by Marianne O. Nielsen and Karen Jarratt-Snider, 185–95. Tucson: University of Arizona Press.

Jorgensen, Miriam. 2007. "Editor's Introduction." In *Rebuilding Native Nations: Strategies for Governance and Development*, edited by Miriam Jorgensen, xi–xiv. Tucson: University of Arizona Press.

Long, Larry, Rich Braunstein, Brenda Manning, and William D. Anderson. 2008. "Understanding Contextual Differences in American Indian Criminal Justice." *American Indian Culture and Research Journal* 32 (4): 41–65.

Morrissey, Michael. 2006. "Community, Social Capital and Indigenous Health in the Northern Territory." *Ethnicity and Health* 11 (3): 229–46.

National Inquiry into the Separation of Aboriginal and Torres Strait Islander Children from Their Families (Australia). 1997. *Bringing Them Home: National Inquiry into the Separation of Aboriginal and Torres Strait Islander Children from Their Families*. Sydney, NSW: Human Rights and Equal Opportunity Commission.

Nielsen, Marianne O. 2004. "A Comparison of the Community Roles of Indigenous-Operated Criminal Justice Organizations in Canada, the United States, and Australia." *American Indian Culture and Research Journal* 28 (3): 57–75.

Nielsen, Marianne O., and Samantha Brown. 2012. "Beyond Justice: What Makes an Indigenous Justice Organization?" *American Indian Culture and Research Journal* 36 (2): 47–73.

Nielsen, Marianne O., and Linda Robyn. 2003. "Colonialism and Criminal Justice for Indigenous Peoples in Australia, Canada, New Zealand, and the United States." *Indigenous Nations Studies Journal* 4 (1): 29–45.

Nielsen, Marianne O., and Robert A. Silverman. 2009. *Criminal Justice in Native America*. Tucson: University of Arizona Press.

Perreault, Samuel. 2014. *Admissions to Adult Correctional Services in Canada, 2011/2012*. Ottawa, ON: Statistics Canada. www.statcan.gc.ca/pub.

Pettit, Kathryn L. S., G. Thomas Kingsley, Jennifer Biess, Kassie Bertumen, Nancy Pindus, Chris Narducci, and Amos Budde. 2014. *Continuity and Change: Demographic, Socioeconomic, and Housing Conditions of American Indians and Alaska Natives*. Washington, DC: U.S. Department of Housing and Urban Development. https://www.huduser.gov/portal//publications/pdf/housing_conditions.pdf.

Project Waitangi. 1989. *A Summary Produced by Project Waitangi of Moana Jackson's Report: The Maori and Criminal Justice System, He Whaipaanga Hou—A New Perspective*. Wellington, NZ: Project Waitangi.

Royal Commission on Aboriginal Peoples. 1993. *Aboriginal Peoples and the Justice System*. Ottawa, ON: Supply and Services Canada.

————. 1996. *Bridging the Cultural Divide*. Ottawa, ON: Supply and Services Canada.

Sakala, Leah. 2014. "Breaking Down Mass Incarceration in the 2010 Census: State-by-State Incarceration Rates by Race/Ethnicity." Northampton, MA: Prison Policy Initiative. www.prisonpolicy.org/reports/rates.html.

Sarre, Rick. 2000. "Indigenous Australians and the Administration of Criminal Justice." In *Considering Crime and Justice: Realities and Responses*, edited by Rick Sarre and John Tomaino, 211–41. Adelaide, SA: Crawford House.

United Nations. 2014. "High Rate of Maori in Prison Among Concerns as UN Experts Wrap Up New Zealand Visit." https://news.un.org/en/story/2014/04/465682-high-rate-maori-prison-among-concerns-un-experts-wrap-new-zealand-visit.

United Nations General Assembly. 2007. "United Nations Declaration on the Rights of Indigenous Peoples." United Nations (07–58681-Match 2008–4,000). www.un.org/esa/socdev/unpfii/documents/DRIPS_en.pdf.

Urbina, Alfred, and Melissa Tatum. 2014. "Considerations in Implementing VAWA's Special Domestic Violence Criminal Jurisdiction and TLOA's Enhanced Sentencing Authority: A Look at the Experience of the Pascua Yaqui Tribe." Tucson, AZ: Pascua Yaqui Tribe. http://www.ncai.org/tribal-vawa/getting-started/Practical_Guide_to_Implementing_VAWA_TLOA_letter_revision_3.pdf.

U.S. Department of Health and Human Services. 2018. "Profile: American Indian/Alaska Native." https://minorityhealth.hhs.gov/omh/browse.aspx?lvl=3&lvlid=62.

Walker, Ranguini. 1990. *Ka Whawhai Tonu Matou: Struggle Without End*. Auckland, NZ: Penguin.

LEGAL RESOURCES

Major Crimes Act 18 U.S.C. § 1153 (1850)

Oliphant v. Suquamish Indian Tribe 435 U.S. 191 (1978)

Tribal Law and Order Act 25 U.S.C. 2801 (2010)

Violence Against Women Act 42 U.S.C. 13701 (2013)

CONCLUSION

KAREN JARRATT-SNIDER AND
MARIANNE O. NIELSEN

T
HIS CONCLUSION speculates about the future of community
responses to laws by and for Indigenous Peoples, primarily the
reawakening of Indigenous traditional law and the use of international law by Indigenous Peoples to battle the multifaceted, tragic,
often continuing impacts of colonialism. Today, traditional, national
(also "federal" or "domestic"), and international laws are interlinked and
interdependent. International law, for example, often focuses on the
need for national laws to recognize customary laws, making national
law an important touchstone for Indigenous Peoples for resolutions to
Indigenous issues. Because of the damage done to Indigenous Peoples
by settler-colonial national law over time, national law is central to the
need for law reform in the United States and other colonized countries.
It is also the most resistant. This chapter builds on specific examples of
Indigenous community and nation responses given by the contributors
in their chapters.

NATIONAL LAW

Not only has non-Indigenous domestic law been used to exploit and control Indigenous Peoples and individuals as discussed in many books and
documents (see, for example, Echo-Hawk 2010, the introduction chapter

by Nielsen and Jarratt-Snider, and almost any history book written from an Indigenous point of view), it has been remarkably successful in doing so, as the vast tracts of land including sacred sites lost by Indigenous Peoples in all colonized countries exemplify. Colonial law was used deliberately, and deliberately misunderstood, to advance the colonial project in each country over hundreds of years, as described by Zion and Yazzie. Today domestic law continues in many cases to disadvantage Indigenous Peoples economically, politically, socially, and legally. This includes both civil and criminal law. The colonially based assumptions that domestic laws make about Indigenous Peoples ensure that these laws are discriminatory.

In the United States, incarceration statistics are just one example of the continuing disadvantages faced by Indigenous Peoples. Non-Indigenous criminal justice systems have proven themselves singularly ineffective in preventing Indigenous individuals from offending and reoffending. In the United States the statistics on Indigenous incarceration are difficult to find. American Indians, who make up about 2 percent of the total population (U.S. Department of Health 2018), are overrepresented as prisoners in most states with a significant Indigenous population. The most serious overrepresentations are in Hawaii (39 percent of incarcerated, 10 percent of state population), Alaska (38 percent of incarcerated, 15 percent of state), North Dakota (29 percent of incarcerated, 5 percent of state), South Dakota (29 percent of incarcerated, 9 percent of state), and Montana (22 percent of incarcerated, 6 percent of state) (Sakala 2014). Indications are that Native American women and juveniles are also overrepresented in prisons (Ross 1998; Martin 2014).

The current political climate in the United States is not one that presents a great deal of hope for American Indians lobbying for changes in domestic criminal and other laws despite the successful efforts of Indigenous communities in the past, as described by Fox, for example. Fortunately, this cannot be said for the efforts of Indigenous Peoples in every colonized country. For example, legislation has been introduced in Canada by Indigenous national politicians to change the Indian Act (1876, last amended 1985) to make it less sexist, in response to a Quebec Superior Court ruling that the act violated the Canadian Charter of Rights and Freedoms of 1982 (Kirkup 2017; Galloway 2017). On the other hand, in the United States non-Indigenous men can still enter reservations and rape Indigenous women with legal impunity (see the chapter by Fox) despite the best efforts of community activists. The United States should be embarrassed by this contrast.

There are ways, however, that Indigenous individuals can use traditional law as it is found in everyday life to creatively bend or circumvent existing national laws in order to successfully resolve serious problems in their communities, as Siedschlaw, Jocks, Austin, and Nielsen describe in their chapters. Indigenous Peoples are not waiting for national or state governments to provide solutions, a wise decision considering the disastrous consequences of such interference in the past. They are developing and implementing solutions themselves, often based in traditional law, which is an aspect of what Tsosie (2002) and Wilkins (2003) refer to as cultural sovereignty. Cultural sovereignty is integral to real sovereignty, as Nalwood (2009, 39) writes, "Native American perceptions of sovereignty are based on culture, religion, and the laws of nature that are beyond the U.S. government's perception, a perception that is based on legal concepts."

But the fact remains that Indigenous communities should not have to maneuver around the discriminatory national laws. They should not have to practice de facto sovereignty, no matter how useful and creative a solution it is, as exemplified in the chapters by Austin and Nielsen. National governments should respect the inherent sovereignty of Indigenous nations to do what is best for themselves, their children, and their communities. This is another way of saying that legal common sense and original inherent sovereignty should be returned to national laws affecting Indigenous communities and nations. In many instances, that will mean reestablishing Indigenous nation and community institutions based in customary law. That right is guaranteed in international law and therefore should be enshrined in national law.

TRADITIONAL LAW

In Indigenous communities worldwide, community leaders and scholars point out the persistence of traditional law and encourage its use as an alternative to the non-Indigenous justice system. Rather than concentrating on punishment, traditional law focuses on healing the underlying issues and returning the community to harmony. It is more responsive to the needs of the individual, their families, and the community. It is more centered on the restoration of positive relations, as Austin describes in his chapter. It works toward the prevention of wrongdoing and healing the parties involved. This focus allows it to be more creative in interpreting law and finding resolutions, such as Austin describes in his chapter on peacemaking.

Customary law was nearly destroyed or seriously fragmented among many Indigenous Peoples partly as a result of depopulation but also as a deliberate attempt by the settler-colonists to extinguish Indigenous cultures, as Zion and Yazzie describe. Methods included using national law to force Indigenous children to go to boarding schools, ban Indigenous spirituality and ceremonies, and destroy Indigenous families, economic structures, and leadership, as mentioned previously. Many tribal communities marginalized their own traditional law because their legal decision makers became too assimilated into non-Indigenous culture, or because of pressures to conform or lose federal funding for critical programs, or because they believed traditional law to be lost. These colonial marginalization efforts have led to the need for Indigenous communities to rediscover their own customary laws. Indigenous communities, whether land-based or urban, have resources in their culture, language, ceremonies, narratives, and spirituality that are ignored or devalued by decision and policy makers. Indigenous communities and nations need to focus on community resilience and strength rather than focus on community deficits. The many obstacles to operationalizing traditional law, however, cannot be ignored. These include gaining legitimacy, finding funding, providing training for traditional practitioners, and negotiating the boundaries between customary and national law. As Alvarado points out, more domestic recognition of Indigenous customary law is needed and the ability of Indigenous Peoples to use it needs to be improved. It is less costly, more informal, and so far seems to be more effective when it is incorporated into tribal justice systems (see, for example, Nielsen and Zion 2005).

Customary law is also very diverse. Like every non-Indigenous nation, every Indigenous cultural group has its own version of customary law and justice processes. For example, some groups traditionally relied on counseling of wrongdoers by elders, others on the chief and his council. Traditional justice was and continues to be adaptive and changes to suit the times and needs of the community. The codification of customary laws, for example, to benefit younger generations as Zion and Yazzie suggest needs to be done in such a way as to maintain their flexibility and ability to deal with the unique features of each community or nation. Otherwise it will limit the jurisdiction and powers of Indigenous justice systems. The nations also need to maintain a balance between Indigenous legal interests and the human rights of all participants (see the chapter by Alvarado).

Indigenous nations probably cannot completely replace their current tribal justice systems, which are modeled on the European-based justice system, with customary law and the processes that use it; the world has changed a great deal. Interpersonal violence such as family violence and sexual assault were rare in traditional times, as were post-traumatic stress and anger management issues. Incarceration of some offenders may still be necessary, and the involvement of medical personnel to help some offenders (e.g., sex offenders) may be necessary. Legal pluralism already exists within some colonial countries such as Canada where Quebec law is based on the French Napoleonic Code, and the same with Louisiana in the United States. Alvarado also gives several examples from Latin America. The point is that the development of Indigenous justice systems with full authority to practice traditional law is simple legal pluralism, for which there are precedents.

Customary law is a field where a great deal of research is needed, preferably by Indigenous community-based scholars. Customary law's potential for dealing effectively and appropriately with Indigenous wrongdoing needs to be fully explored. Academically, customary law has been marginalized; there are few comparative legal studies between Indigenous and European laws, for example, as Zion and Yazzie point out. There are resources, however, for rediscovering these laws. In addition to the growing number of Indigenous scholars, anthropologists, as reviled as they have been over the years in some quarters, have collected and recorded information. Cousin cultures may have stories and ceremonies that can be adapted.

Traditional knowledge holders in the community are key if such knowledge is still in tribal oral history, language, ceremonies, stories, and creation narratives. Elders can act as cultural experts in developing laws, as Alvarado points out in his chapter. But they can also take active roles in providing justice, for example, as "expert witnesses" in the non-Indigenous system, as Siedschlaw describes, or members of boards of directors for Indigenous service organizations, as Nielsen mentions. Today customary law is being used in some courts and justice programs across Indian Country, as the chapter by Austin describes for the Navajo Nation.

INTERNATIONAL LAW

International law is the primary reference point for Indigenous Peoples in achieving their human rights. Indigenous Peoples have been working for decades to develop such laws and covenants, as with the working group on the draft Declaration on the Rights of Indigenous People (https:// www.ohchr.org/EN/Issues/IPeoples/Pages/WGDraftDeclaration.aspx). In his chapter Alvarado provides an overview of the most important pieces of international legislation, including the United Nations Declaration on the Rights of Indigenous Peoples (UNDRIP) (2007), which the major settler-colonial powers—the United States, Canada, Australia, and New Zealand—resisted signing for many years. Zion and Yazzie also see UNDRIP as providing hope for the future of Indigenous law. In theory, international conventions inform the domestic laws of the signatories concerning the Indigenous Peoples that inhabit those lands. For example, according to these conventions settler-colonist governments must provide Indigenous nations with political and economic support in promoting, developing, and maintaining their juridical systems (see the chapter by Alvarado). As a result, international law can serve as a guiding light for Indigenous activists, as Zion and Yazzie describe.

Even though Indigenous Peoples have the human right to use their own law and justice institutions according to these international conventions, domestic legal reform is made difficult by the resistance of settler-colonial governments. In the United States, these rights are still under attack as is evident in the recent discussions of the federal Subcommittee on Indian, Insular, and Alaska Native Affairs, which wants to limit the development of Indian trust land, despite its legality under federal law (Ditmer 2017). It would be interesting to analyze current American laws (and the laws of other colonized countries) to discover just how many of them follow not only the letter of these conventions but the spirit. The Major Crimes Act (1885), which is still in effect in the United States, is an obvious example of a domestic law that contravenes the UN Declaration on the Rights of Indigenous People. The reform of such discriminatory law is a worthwhile project for Indigenous nations and the increasing number of federally elected Indigenous politicians.

As Alvarado describes in his chapter, some countries have recognized in their constitutions the right of Indigenous Peoples to their own law and justice systems. This may be a radical suggestion for the United States in our conservative political times, but it would be a way to fulfill the mandates of the international declarations and conventions.

More exchange of information, dialogue, and capacity-building are needed between Indigenous and non-Indigenous lawmakers and justice personnel in all colonized countries. Indigenous and non-Indigenous justice systems need to interact, coordinate, and complement each other (see the chapters by Alvarado and Nielsen). In the United States this is particularly important in dealing with the jurisdictional maze and non-Indigenous offenders who fall through the legal cracks.

CONCLUSION

In an ideal world, international law and traditional law would inform the workings of domestic laws. Domestic laws would be used to ameliorate the dreadful harms caused by colonialism and colonial law. Indigenous Peoples would receive the respect and practical and political support guaranteed in international law to overcome the many negative effects of colonialism for individuals and communities alike. They would be able to rebuild their nations. Domestic law would confirm the rights of Indigenous Peoples to exercise their inherent sovereignty as guaranteed in international law. Indigenous communities and nations would rediscover their customary law, modify it as they see fit to work effectively in the modern world, and modify their justice systems to incorporate it. As an additional significant benefit, non-Indigenous societies would learn about justice values and practices that might make non-Indigenous justice systems more humane and effective.

But this is not an ideal world, and the interests of colonial governments and corporate entities still outweigh the interests of Indigenous communities and nations, despite the many allies that support Indigenous

Peoples in their efforts to overcome colonialism. National law still works to the disadvantage of Indigenous Peoples. It still allows exploitation and discrimination, money still trumps morality, and in most cases national law gives Indigenous Peoples very few weapons with which to respond to greed and discrimination. We cannot overstate the importance of Indigenous nations in the United States using intergovernmental relations where opportunities arise to protect and expand sovereignty in national law. They can, as our authors have shown us, assume authority for programs and services that would otherwise rest with states or the federal government. There is also hope in the use of customary law and international law by Indigenous communities and nations if they can overcome the hostility and obstacles built by settler-colonist lawmakers.

REFERENCES

Ditmer, Renae. 2017. "Native Voices Ignored as House Committee Ponders Changes to Indian Trust Land Policy." *Indian Country Today*, July 26, 2017. http://Indiancountrymedianetwork.com/news/politics/native-voices-ignored -house-committee-ponders-changes-Indian-trust-land-policy/.

Echo-Hawk, Walter. 2010. *In the Courts of the Conquerors: The 10 Worst Indian Law Cases Ever Decided*. Golden, CO: Fulcrum.

Galloway, Gloria. 2017. "Senators Amend Legislation Aimed at Removing Sexism from the Indian Act." *The Globe and Mail*, May 24, 2017. https://beta .theglobeandmail.com/new/politics/.

Kirkup, Kristy. 2017. "Liberals Urged to Accept Senate Change to Indian Act Sex Discrimination Bill." CBC News, October 31, 2017. https://www.cbc.ca/news/ politics/s3-indian-act-sex-discrimination-bill-1.4380009.

Martin, Favian Alejandro. 2014. "Native Youth Delinquency." In *American Indians at Risk*, edited by Jeffrey Ian Ross, 135–52. Santa Barbara, CA: Greenwood.

Nalwood, Anna. 2009. "The Meaning of Sovereignty to the Diné: A Study of Urban Phoenix Navajo." PhD diss., Northern Arizona University.

Nielsen, Marianne O., and James W. Zion, eds. 2005. *Navajo Nation Peacemaking: Living Traditional Justice*. Tucson: University of Arizona Press.

Ross, Luana. 1998. *Inventing the Savage*. Austin, TX: University of Austin Press.

Sakala, Leah. 2014. "Breaking Down Mass Incarceration in the 2010 Census: State-by-State Incarceration Rates by Race/Ethnicity." Northampton, MA: Prison Policy Initiative. https://www.prisonpolicy.org/reports/rates.html.

Tsosie, Rebecca A. 2002. "Reclaiming Native Stories: An Essay on Cultural Appropriation and Cultural Rights." *Arizona State Law Journal* 34: 299–359.

U.S. Department of Health and Human Services. 2018. "Profile: American Indian/ Alaska Native." https://minorityhealth.hhs.gov/omh/browse.aspx?lvl=3&lvlid =62.

Wilkins, David E. 2003. *The Navajo Political Experience*. New York: Rowman and Littlefield.

LEGAL RESOURCES

Canadian Charter of Rights and Freedoms (1982)
Indian Act (1985) (Canada)
Major Crimes Act (1885)
United Nations Declaration on the Rights of Indigenous Peoples (2007)

CONTRIBUTORS

Leonardo J. Alvarado (Maya/Lenca) is an international Indigenous human rights law expert and independent legal consultant. He collaborates with the United Nations Special Rapporteur on the Rights of Indigenous Peoples and the Offices of the UN High Commissioner for Human Rights in Honduras and Mexico. Recent publications include book chapters and articles on the domestic implementation of Indigenous human rights and various specialized reports for UN agencies, NGOs, and Indigenous organizations in Latin America. He holds a JD, an LLM, and an MS in American Indian studies from the University of Arizona.

The Honorable **Raymond D. Austin** is a faculty member with the Applied Indigenous Studies Department at Northern Arizona University. Dr. Austin is Diné (Navajo) from the Navajo Nation. He earned a law degree (JD) from the University of New Mexico Law School in 1983 and a PhD from the University of Arizona in 2007. Dr. Austin served as associate justice on the Navajo Nation Supreme Court for sixteen years. He is the author of *Navajo Courts and Navajo Common Law: A Tradition of Tribal Self-Governance* and numerous articles on Navajo law and courts for law journals.

Lomayumtewa K. Ishii (Hopi) is an artist from the village of Sichomovi, First Mesa, on the Hopi Reservation in northern Arizona. He is of the

Rabbit/Tobacco clan and is a Hopi practitioner of religious activities and Hopi dry-farming agriculture. He recently completed an artist fellowship at the School for Advanced Research in Santa Fe, New Mexico.

Mary Jo Tippeconnic Fox is an enrolled member of the Comanche Nation of Oklahoma, a research professor of American Indian Studies, and an affiliate faculty member in Gender and Women's Studies at the University of Arizona, Tucson. Her scholarly activities focus on historical and contemporary Native American women's issues, American Indian/Native Studies, and American Indian education with an emphasis on higher education. Dr. Fox has numerous publications and extensive experience working nationally with American Native communities and organizations.

Karen Jarratt-Snider (Choctaw descent) is an associate professor and chair of the Department of Applied Indigenous Studies at Northern Arizona University. She is the co-editor, with Marianne O. Nielsen, of *Crime and Social Justice in Indian Country*. Her expertise is in the areas of Indigenous environmental justice, management, and policy; federal Indian policy, tribal administration, sustainable economic development, and tribal environmental management—all of which coalesce around the overall topic of Indigenous sovereignty and self-determination. She has more than fifteen years of experience working with tribal nations' projects in applied community-based research.

Chris Jocks (Kahnawà:ke Mohawk) studies, teaches, and writes about the continuous development of post-invasion traditional knowledge and practice in Indigenous territories surrounded by Canada and the United States. He has taught in the Applied Indigenous Studies Department at Northern Arizona University since 2014. Religious freedom conflict, Indigenous understanding of gender, and what is lost in translation between North American and European languages are some of the issues he focuses on. He obtained his PhD in religious studies from the University of California, Santa Barbara, in 1994.

Marianne O. Nielsen is a professor in the Department of Criminology and Criminal Justice at Northern Arizona University. She is co-author with Linda M. Robyn of *Colonialism Is Crime* and co-editor with Robert Silverman of *Aboriginal Peoples and Canadian Criminal Justice, Native Americans, Crime and Criminal Justice*, and *Criminal Justice in Native America*; with James W. Zion of *Navajo Peacemaking: Living Traditional Justice*; and with Karen Jarratt-Snider of *Crime and Social Justice in Indian Country*.

Kurt D. Siedschlaw is a professor in the Criminal Justice Department at the University of Nebraska at Kearney where he has served for twenty-eight years in a variety of capacities. He has addressed various Native American and reservation issues over the past forty years. He has served as ombudsman for the university, was director of the Ethnic Studies Program, and is currently involved in research related to guardian ad litem services for juveniles. Professor Siedschlaw is a licensed attorney in South Dakota and Nebraska and has served the court in Nebraska as an expert witness in Indian Child Welfare Act cases for seventeen years.

The Honorable **Robert Yazzie**, JD, (Diné) is a frequent collaborator with James W. Zion. He turns problem-solving theory into justice from the standpoint of a Navajo jurist, former chief justice, and serves as an important voice in the field of Indigenous law and justice. He holds a juris doctor degree from the University of New Mexico and he was the chief justice of the Navajo Nation from 1992 through 2003. He has global recognition as a representative of traditional Indian justice and Navajo peacemaking, and his leadership on Indigenous issues is widely accepted.

James W. Zion, JD, is a student of applied Indigenous justice, seeking ways of making theory work in practice. He has served as an adjunct professor in the Department of Criminology and Criminal Justice of Northern Arizona University and has published extensively on Indigenous justice, traditional Indian law, and human rights. He is a frequent collaborator with the Honorable Robert Yazzie.

INDEX